AFTER THE MEDIA

This provocative text considers the state of media and cultural studies today after the demolition of the media as a meaningful idea, and engages with the alternative 'ways of seeing' culture.

Media Studies, particularly within schools, has until recently been concerned with mass media and the effects of 'the media' in society and on people. As new media technology has blurred the boundaries between the audience and the media, the value of this area of education is undermined. Whilst some have called for a drastic re-think (Media Studies 2.0), others have called for caution, arguing that the power dynamics of ownership and gatekeeping are left intact.

This book uses cultural and technological change as a context for a more forensic exploration of the traditional dependence on the idea of 'the media' as one homogenous unit. It suggests that it would be liberating for students, teachers and academics to depart from such a model and shift the focus to people and how they create culture in this contemporary 'mediascape'.

The authors work through the classic conceptual framework of media studies considering a wide variety of topics, including:

- genre
- narrative
- audience
- representation
- identity
- ideology
- power.

For each concept, using a rich range of texts and events, this book wrestles with the pressing question of how media education should deal with these areas 'after the media'.

Peter Bennett is Senior Lecturer in Post-Compulsory Education at the University of Wolverhampton, UK. He is co-author and co-editor of a range of Communications, Media and Film textbooks as well as *Framework Media: Channels* (2003). He is co-author and Chief Examiner of the new Communication and Culture A Level and a regular provider of INSET for teachers.

Alex Kendall is Associate Dean for Research in the School of Education, Law and Social Science at Birmingham City University, UK. She is well published in the areas of literacy and professional education and is co-editor of *Insights from Research and Practice* (2005).

Julian McDougall is Reader in Media and Education at Newman University College, Birmingham, UK. He is the editor of the *Media Education Research Journal*, *The Media Teacher's Book* (2010), *Studying Videogames* (2008) and a range of Media Studies textbooks. He is a Principal Examiner for A-Level Media and runs undergraduate, postgraduate and teacher training courses.

AFTER THE MEDIA

Culture and Identity in the 21st Century

*Peter Bennett, Alex Kendall and
Julian McDougall*

Routledge
Taylor & Francis Group

LONDON AND NEW YORK

First published 2011
by Routledge
2 Park Square, Milton Park, Abingdon, Oxon, OX14 4RN

Simultaneously published in the USA and Canada
by Routledge
711 Third Avenue, New York, NY 10017

Routledge is an imprint of the Taylor & Francis Group, an informa business

Typeset in Bembo by Saxon Graphics Ltd, Derby

British Library Cataloguing in Publication Data
A catalogue record for this book is available from the British Library

Library of Congress Cataloging in Publication Data
  Bennett, Peter, 1961–
  After the media : culture and identity in the 21st century / by Peter Bennett, Alex Kendall and
Julian McDougall.
    p. cm.
  Includes bibliographical references and index.
  1. Mass media and culture. 2. Mass media--21st century. 3. Mass media--Study and teaching--
Great Britain. I. Kendall, Alex. II. McDougall, Julian. III. Title.
  P94.6B46 2011
  302.23--dc22
                                    2010044559

ISBN13: 978-0-415-58682-5 (hbk)
ISBN13: 978-0-415-58683-2 (pbk)
ISBN13: 978-0-203-81788-9 (ebk)

Printed and bound in Great Britain by
TJ International Ltd, Padstow, Cornwall

CONTENTS

ACKNOWLEDGEMENTS

After the Media is for Lydia and Ned, Jack, Kate, Molly, Tom and Karon (without whom this would not be possible).

The authors owe thanks for help and support to Jackie Marsh, Matt Hills, Richard Berger, Jon Wardle, Mark Readman, Henry Jenkins, Aileen Storry, Nigel Ward, Jerry Slater, Pete Fraser, Richard Sanders, Dave Trotman, Paul Taylor, David Gauntlet and the 2009/2010 cohort of adult literacy teachers at the University of Wolverhampton.

INTRODUCTION

And what remains when disbelief has gone?

(Philip Larkin, 'Church going')

All of this left me feeling more than a little deflated. Media didn't seem that important to the students.

(Ruddock, 2007: 159)

In this book we offer an extended deconstruction of what we call *subject media* – the institutionalised framing of the study of popular culture – and we argue that new media and technology do not provide in themselves a paradigm shift that necessitates new kinds of pedagogy. Instead we suggest that in fragmenting the idea of 'the media' as a construct, an object of study or an employment sector, these new digital media have simply opened our eyes to the always-already dubious nature of that idea. So we take Gauntlett's (2008) assertion that media studies has been too concerned with 'the media', paying scarce attention to people, and we extend that idea in relation to the broader orthodoxy of media education.

In each chapter we will interrogate a key concept from the discipline, as we see it evolving into a 'vertical discourse' (Bernstein, 1990). Each of these framing ideas – power, genre, representation, ideology, identity, audience and narrative – is deconstructed and in each case, put back together again in such a way as to continue without recourse to the idea of 'the media'.

The major object of our attention is media education – and for the most part this means media studies – in the United Kingdom. However, in the 'schooled' version of media learning it is manifestly the case that the international community has been informed, if not overtly influenced, by practice in the United Kingdom, and this being the case, there is less 'local difference' to reduce the global relevance of our work than we might expect. Equally we are confident that the socio-cultural framing of *subject media* reaches out across sectors and modalities so that any assumptions of exemption – in 'the academy', in cross-curricular or informal variants of media education – are, if not spurious then at least vulnerable to challenge.

While the key assumptions of *subject media* as formulated in the UK context are embedded globally, there are local nuances. New Zealand, Canada and the United States operate with more freedom from the discourse of derision which has stained 'poor old Media Studies' (McDougall, 2009) in the United Kingdom, but the protectionist impulse is more robust in these territories. Lin (2009) accounts for the relationship between the United Kingdom and East Asian media education in two ways – the adoption of UK and, more broadly, Western discourses in new media education programmes in Taiwan, China, Hong Kong, Korea and Singapore, and the modifications to these discourses – a 'glocal' framing of/for *subject media*:

> Sometimes, various discourses are adopted strategically. The citizenship discourse with a negative assumption from the protectionist discourses of media is an example of a hybrid discourse. As late-comers to media education, advocates in Asia are aware of the dangers of solely applying the protectionist discourse. They strategically adopt the negative effect as rationale for promoting media education while adding the flavour of the active 'civic engagement' rhetoric. The hybrid discourse carries contradictions in itself.
>
> *(Lin, 2009: 40)*

As we will argue at length, we observe, even within such hybridity, the preservation of an unhelpful set of precepts for media education which we call *subject media*. These consist of the construction of 'the media' as a 'Big Other' (Zizek, 1999) to be at once looked at 'critically' and desired as a destination (for employment); the sovereign nature of the text – inherited from the socio-cultural framing of English teaching and the confining of empirical engagement with people (in their situated weaving of media activity into their everyday lives and the performance of identities) and the maintenance of a modernist conception of representation that ultimately serves to undermine the 'emancipatory' spirit of the (ideal) subject. The incomplete project we must press on with requires the removal of 'the media' from the equation.

Three authors bring their ideas to this book from different starting points. As such we offer a collection of analyses, symbiotic but happily contesting some key assumptions and sometimes one another's. Between us we have taught in compulsory, further and higher education, from the youngest stage of secondary education to doctoral supervision, and our experience in the United Kingdom spans English, media and cultural studies as well as teacher training, extensive research, the editing of a journal publishing pedagogic research and senior awarding-body roles for media studies, communication and culture. As such much of this work comes from the heart of the subject – it is not an 'attack' from the outside. Rather we attempt an analysis of the *imagined identity* of media studies in the context of techno-cultural affordances. Previously we have published our research in the 'in-between spaces' that concern these environments, but here we bring together our work, framed by a central shared belief – that 'the media' is a problematic idea, that its privileged status in the teaching and study of popular culture shares many of the alienating characteristics of the 'schooled' version of English, and that many of the possibilities of post-structuralist pedagogy are enabled further by changes in technology, culture and literacy at the close of the first decade of the twenty-first century.

The content is a convergence of research outcomes, pedagogic strategies and dialogic work with texts of various kinds. Our agenda is to raise a set of important and challenging questions for everyone concerned with media education and its current and deeply problematic variant – 'media literacy'. Defining precisely whom this will interest, enthuse and deter is as awkward as the notion of a 'target audience' for a 'media text'. Although we are focusing largely on contemporary media studies in schools and colleges in the United Kingdom, we want to resist the idea of a 'target audience' for these discussions. This book will be of interest to reflexive teachers, as an argument to be challenged by. It will provoke a response from academics and researchers in the fields we explore. And it will be, in many cases, 'of use' for both communities to work with their students. As such it is 'in between' a textbook and a purely academic intervention.

At the start of the twentieth century, the media disappeared from the Western world

Foucault's genealogy (1971), here adapted, infamously resists imposing judgement. It only traces discourse, power and knowledge, in this case in relation to the exercising of power by discourses of medical (with regard to leprosy) and mental abnormality and marginalisation. In this book we want to reverse the gesture and actively seek to exile, and in so doing impose a judgement upon, the very idea of 'the media' from the way we study culture. The idea of 'the media' has obscured the study of culture. Thus, just as the postmodern is an element of the modern, so is 'after the media' a necessary and liberating part of media studies, we will argue.

This book develops further an emerging field of 'post-media cultural studies' strategies for students/academics/researchers (and these are not exclusive categories) engaged in cultural analysis in the early stages of the twenty-first century. The central argument is that the hybrid media landscape, in which traditional power is exercised alongside 'prosumer' distribution of culture, allows for an easier 'application' of various critical theories associated with such hybridity and bricolage – post-structuralism, postmodernism and their attendant 'remixing' of feminism and literacy studies. However, our title does not represent the latest instalment in the temporal proclamations of various '2.0' or '3.0' would-be paradigm shifts. (See Chapter 7 for a discussion of the contested term Media 2.0.) Nor does it lend itself to the 'end of everything' discourse or the 'before and after' version of postmodernity. Instead we seek to more productively rework the orthodoxy of media studies and its conceptual framework. Rather than merely replacing the conceptual discourse with new modes – ludology, frivolity, playback, parody – each chapter will engage with the aforementioned 'hybrid zeitgeist'.

Cultural studies in the United Kingdom, so the history goes, entered the academic discourse as a politically motivated strategy for theorising everyday life and mobilising social change. Media studies has been partly imagined in the same way, but its status as a horizontal discourse has undermined any coherent structure, especially since it has been colonised – in schools at least – by English, almost entirely on the terms of the longer-established discipline. In universities, the privileging of textuality is a site of more contest, but the 'cultural studies project' is no better served since the 'disciplinary logic of University based teaching' (Carrington, 2006: 278) has led to the development of medium-specific silos which are now outdated but were always too narrow (Berger and McDougall, 2010). Recently, Gauntlett (2008) has argued that media studies is, bluntly, too interested in the media and not sufficiently concerned with people. While we do not want to further develop here potentially parodic ideas about 'Media 2.0', we do agree with that charge and so, in its simplest explanation, our argument is that media studies will do well to return to the project of theorising everyday life (and the part of our lives that cultural products of various kinds connect with) by 'forgetting the media'.

This project is framed, then, by the argument that the institutionalised practices of teaching about popular culture must be understood as a technology for the naturalisation of specific reading and writing practices, particular ways of making meaning and understanding the world which are far from neutral. This range of practices we call *subject media* (McDougall, 2004; 2006), and we wish to engage with the cultural politics of media studies through this 'way of seeing'. Peim (2000) dealt with the cultural politics of *subject English* and its extraordinarily suspect and self-regarding imposition of the idea of literature, and in so doing set up media studies as its other – a more radical cousin:

> Theories of popular culture and audience-oriented work in Media Studies … propose alternative models of communications theory, and challenge the centrality of literature in educational practices …. From a Media Studies perspective, not only is canonical literature oddly exclusive, limited and indeterminate (nobody knows how to draw its boundaries), but its cultural politics are deeply questionable. From a Media Studies perspective, the general category of literature is extremely restricted. The apparently free category of personal response is, in fact, much more constrained than has been represented … English has incorporated Media Studies into itself entirely on its own terms, without revising its cherished beliefs and practices about text and language according to the alternative perspective that Media Studies powerfully offers.

> *(Peim, 2000: 173)*

Has this potential been realised? We argue that media studies has obscured, that the 'project' of making popular culture a legitimate object of study has – since the misinterpreted encoding/decoding model from the Birmingham Centre for Contemporary Cultural Studies coupled itself to the 'textual' obsessions of English – started from the wrong place, and that the problem has been our belief in the idea of 'the media' and its separation from ourselves, just as the category of literature imposes an alienating model of reading.

> It is doubtful whether those who taught within adult and workers' education colleges during the 1930s, 1940s and 1950s and whose intellectual work was directly connected to political engagement and social change, would recognise what constitutes cultural studies today.
>
> *(Carrington, 2006: 292)*

Carrington's suggestion does not herald any desire for a return to the more explicitly counter-ideological ferment of 'pre-media' cultural studies, with its attendant derision of critical theory, seen as relativist and apolitical in its apparent fetishising of difference and subsequent ignorance of the structural politico-economic, or the 'mass' in communication. However, we can trace, in the genealogy of cultural studies, a reduction of the field of culture, through the prism of ideology, to first communications and then mass media, with an unhelpful tripartite separation of production from textuality and from reception. The theorising of 'everyday life', we will argue, has been undermined not by critical theories of culture but by cultural study of 'the media'.

Writing in the first edition of the *Media Education Research Journal (MERJ)*, Richard Berger (in Berger and McDougall, 2010) condemns the way that 'the academy' has clung to alienating and inward-looking forms of 'media theory', despite the obviously dialogic nature of culture being made more visible by the internet:

> Undergraduates, who had studied Media before gaining a place at university, were perpetually confused by the clash of medium-specific teaching and the silos they were now expected to occupy. Instead, 'Media Theory' as it was now called seemed to be replicating the activities of the academics of Lagada in Gulliver's Travels; instead of trying to extract sunbeams from cucumbers, Media theorists were busy inventing increasingly impenetrable terminology and making vast assumptions about audiences and texts.
>
> *(Berger and McDougall, 2010)*

MERJ states as its objective the bringing together of practitioners and researchers across sectors, and it is certainly true that higher education academics have distanced themselves from the broader project of 'media literacy' and even added their voices to the discourse of derision circulating around media studies, in the United Kingdom at least. And yet the majority of their students are institutionalised by the encounter with *subject media*. The precepts (intended or not) spoken by media education about 'the media' and its assumed audiences form a framing within which discourses reside, and such discourses (ways of speaking and writing about texts in particular) need to be deconstructed and 'denaturalised' in order for us to understand how they are socio-culturally located – in other words how they are not natural, or simply formed through an emancipatory project, but how they are politically and culturally loaded in order to preserve a range of shifting and permeable illusions about legitimate knowledge and the nature of 'media literacy'.

In *Screen Education: From Film Appreciation to Media Studies*, Bolas (2009) offers a forensic history of the struggle to gain legitimate curriculum space for the study of film and later more generally 'the media'. In so doing Bolas never questions the project – whereby 'film and media education began to get general acceptance in education' (2009: 21), describing throughout the institutional and private struggles experienced by teachers earnestly striving to 'find space' with which to teach children 'about film' and 'about the media'. Of course, this history is framed from the outset by the institutional framing of such social practices around literature, and as such the study merely reinforces existing power relations and situates 'media studies' within such a view of history.

Putting Bolas's work in dialogue with the recent debate over the idea of 'Media Studies 2.0' (Merrin, 2008, Gauntlett, 2009), the community of educators and students this book seeks to interest can certainly be generalised as self-regarding (ourselves included very clearly). But the origin of this perennial navel gazing has emerged from the shifting sands of the 'virtual revolution'. In this book we offer an alternative reading to Bolas, to argue that 'the media' as an object of study is a questionable construct and that media educators have been guilty of a 'grand narrative' – the quest to convince themselves of the importance of such an object of study. As many have said before us, what people do with culture, how they interact with identities, how they engage with the public sphere unevenly, increasingly with the use of digital tools for 'being with others' – these are of import to academics and students. The media? We do not suggest that the media have ceased to exist, that by 'after' the media we mean a temporal change – a moment, a wall coming down. Instead we call upon Lyotard's version of the postmodern to frame our suggestions – that 'the media' as an object of study is always-already compromised by the regarding of its own idea.

Memorandum

Media education remains in a state of confusion. The division of academic and 'vocational' approaches is still attacked by long-standing discourses of derision – on the one hand for being at once overly intellectual in proportion to its subject matter and at the same time 'lightweight', or for what Elliot (2000) discusses as the irony of the economy-regarding curriculum – that jobs in the media are preserved for those who take the least vocational route to them. Either way, the idea of the media is reproduced both by courses which seek to prepare students to work there and by those that seek to equip them with the skills to critically 'read' their output. One lesser-spoken origin of the confusion is, however, the subject's closer proximity to Leavis and Hoggart than its 'ideal subject' identity presents. 'The media', as more than a technical grammatical plural, is constructed out of a need to preserve a status outside of them, to maintain them as other, to be looked upon with the pedagogic gaze through judgements which – in the case of *subject media* – are conservative in their preservation of the idea that there exist 'the media' to be critical about. The media exist no more than literature exists. Both are constructions, demarcated for particular forms of pedagogic attention, but neither are read critically by students, in Gee's sense (2003).

'The media', then, still occupy the minds of students, but as a stable object of study the media have always been elusive, and yet for decades a deeply conservative practice has been masquerading as inclusive, progressive education. We mean 'after the media' in precisely the same way as Lyotard (1992) explains the paradox of the postmodern condition – as a state of mind, as an ethics, not as a temporal shift. In other words, when we talk about 'after the media' we do not suggest that the media have ceased to exist or that they have been replaced by the 'prosumer'. But just as Lyotard argues that the conditions of possibility of the later part of the twentieth century facilitated new ways of thinking about politics, identity, history and language, and that these ways of thinking would be other to the assumptions of modernity, so we argue in this book that the conditions of contemporary cultural exchange (including but not restricted to the possibilities of seemingly more democratic exchange of media content) allow us to think about culture and identity in new ways, and to resist the reduction of such thinking to the normative discourse of 'mass media'. Equally the sovereign nature of the insulated text is challenged by this way of thinking of culture 'after the media'.

To what extent is the internet an 'inconvenient truth' for media studies? At the level of the public sphere, insulation is tangible. Gillmor's (2004) 'we the media' claims are set against the idea that being a witness with a camera phone does not make you a journalist in the context of the status of funded journalism in a democracy. The vertical discourse, with its horizontal inflections from Sociology, can hold. But what of the millions of productively meaningless comedic exchanges – pets doing amusing things, for example? Media texts? If not, how can the discipline impose its surveillance? If so, how to mark 'the object' with its concepts? Currently the state of confusion treats such 'memes' as objects of study at the 'macro' – prosumers, participation, frivolity – but is afraid of the 'micro' – what does a singular, meaningless event represent, how can it work with theories of mass communication?

And so we seek to reformulate the study of culture and identity without recourse to any notion of 'the media' as a stable construct. In so doing we challenge the 'key concepts' of *subject media* – the institutional, and we argue deeply conservative, framing of the social practices brought together in the formal study of media in schools, colleges and – in many cases but not all – universities. And we suggest pedagogic strategies for a critical theory of culture and identity after the media that we hope might inform learning, teaching and research. Even the key concepts of our own reformulations are 'under erasure', potentially making way for 'the irruptive emergence of a new "concept", a concept that can no longer be and never could be, included in the previous regime' (Derrida, 1981).

We do not wish to further develop the idea of 'Media Studies 2.0', highly influential though that intervention has been on our thinking. The parodic construction of the debate, between the 'everything is changing' thesis of Media 2.0 and the reactionary responses to it, represent what Lyotard calls a 'differend', an impasse between two language games where there is no possibility of understanding one without recourse to the idioms of the other. The differend between Lyotard's postmodern condition and Habermas's 'ideal speech situation' provides a useful framework for dealing with what Jenkins (2006) describes as 'convergence culture' – people taking media into their own hands, with more or less positive consequences, or 'the competing and contradictory ideas about participation that are shaping this new media culture' (2006: 23). An academic discipline must always be looking at 'competing and contradictory ideas', of course, so the notion of these shifts in participation need not necessitate a paradigm shift in themselves. But we will argue throughout this book that the very idea of 'the media' becomes awkward in the context of all this 'being' in culture.

Cultural theory, when performed (Hills, 2005), 'does things' to what it observes. This performative understanding of theory is often set up as undermining, but as Hill argues, this is a limiting view:

> Performativity is, in fact, not at all the same thing as failed objectivity, whether via jargonizing or losing touch with the real. While constative discourse innocently describes the world, performative discourse tends to be stigmatised for the way in which it performs in the world, sometimes seeming unreal or 'stagey'.
>
> *(Hills, 2005: 174)*

What does cultural theory do, what does it perform? Hills suggests that cultural theorists perform an act of intellectual distance, not through elitist objectivity but via an amplification of 'passionate engagement' with texts that transcends fan culture and at the same time orthodox 'textual analysis'; that cultural theory makes political its observations, and that it situates culture – what matters and how it comes to matter – as a site of struggle, but that it need not concern itself with any claims to be purely abstracted from the 'others' it must always-already partly consist of. It merely 'does' an act of transforming such others through engagement with critical theory.

How, then, might theory passionately and politically engage with culture and identity after the media? The examples Jenkins spends time with in his book *Convergence Culture* are interesting to think through in relation to the Habermas–Lyotard struggle alluded to above. Jenkins describes 'knowledge communities' and 'textual poachers' – consumers, critics, fans coming together and falling away from one another, generally online, in acts of interpretation. Resisting the 'Media 2.0' discourse, he maps a world of hybridity – old and new media converging alongside old and new ways of reading and writing (in their broadest sense). On the one hand his work is very easy to appropriate for media studies since he provides a wealth of examples and sets them in the context of various claims and counterclaims – thus doing theory to them – and this can be understood, discussed and then 'retheorised' by students easily enough within the orthodox idioms of undergraduate study. And yet it is difficult to pin down any sense of 'the media' from this account, which is really more concerned with politics, forms of writing and ideas about folk culture. Our argument is much broader than merely claiming Jenkins as somehow demonstrating a change that the subject must respond to – that much is obvious. Rather we are suggesting that we could 'go back' to all forms of scholarly engagement with media texts, from the advent of the printing press to the birth of cinema to the broadcast of the Coronation, and 'do theory' on the folk culture engagement with these things in the same way as we can more straightforwardly assess with regard to online gaming or YouTube 'mash-ups'.

For Habermas, Lyotard's paralogy (reformulating constantly new rules in the game of postmodern micropolitics) leads inevitably to an apolitical relativism. For Lyotard, the way that Habermas asserts the 'ideal speech situation' as the aspiration of consensus maintains the 'grand narrative' view of history and struggle. Jenkins's desire to think through conflicting ideas about participation in and through 'convergence culture', then, can be viewed either way. An utterance such as 'when people take media into their own hands, the results can be wonderfully creative; they can also be bad news for all involved' (2006: 17) can be read as equally 'adept' for either intervention – the assertion of 'bad news' assumes a collective sense of ethics with which we can judge digital exchanges, in keeping with Habermas's 'unfinished project' of modernity.

All of Jenkins's 'case studies' – the 'digital watercooler' as collective intelligence, audience backlash against *American Idol* mobilised by an online 'Vote for the Worst' campaign, digital transmedia layering as an element of mass media diegesis; the uneven relationship between the 'folk culture' of fans (now more explicit and 'knowable' in digital space) and 'big media' producers, peer learning in affinity spaces and the ways in which participatory culture reworks political campaigning – these all reaffirm the notion of the public mediasphere. At no point does Jenkins want to set up the 'textual poacher' as more than an agent in a proximal relation to 'the media' as an entity that exists. Our intervention will also resist such telos. Rather, we suggest that in maintaining the ideal of the media as a plausible collective term, 'convergence culture' reinforces the insulation between 'it' and its other (us), in keeping with Lyotard's 'initial forgetting'. Perhaps we might have been tempted to follow Baudrillard and name this book *'forget the media'*? Either way, our project here is to undermine the idea of the separation of 'the media' from everyone and everything else. And yet in describing such convergence as 'a kind of kludge – a jerry rigged relationship' Jenkins suggests a paradigm shift to a new order of uncertainty over public–private sphere culture. We will claim this for our Lyotardian reading of (after) 'the media' but 'remix' it to view this state of differential and fluid relations as 'more of the same'. The shift is merely that convergence has enabled such fragmentation to be visible – a new way of thinking or, as for Lyotard, a purposeful 'waste of time' (1992: 47).

> The 'post-' of 'postmodern' does not signify a movement of comeback, flashback or feedback, that is, not a movement of repetition but a procedure in 'ana-': a procedure of analysis, anamnesis, anagogy and anamorphosis which elaborates an 'initial forgetting'.
>
> *(Lyotard, 1992: 93)*

Crucially, for us, Lyotard's postmodernity describes an optimism for the project of modernity to continue unabated by its constraining preconceptions, as opposed to a temporal 'after' – the 'end' of the project – and in this sense, shares Habermas's perception of modernity as an 'incomplete project' (1990). So too we envisage the 'project' of engaging critically with culture as optimistically charged with continuing, liberated from its interest in 'the media' – a (perhaps unintentionally) positivist belief structure – in texts, industries, audiences, and in its ability to deconstruct the representation of things, people, ideas in those texts. But the split with Habermas arises from Lyotard's refutation of the notion of consensus as a human aspiration, arguing that such a reduction to a 'meeting point' in culture is an act of terror, the denial of difference. If, then, media studies has become a grand narrative, the emergence of 'convergence culture' has not yet been its undoing.

Taking the 'Media Studies 2.0' debate as a *differend*, we can identify the key idioms of each language game. While Merrin and Gauntlett are wrongly accused of claiming that power has shifted entirely to the 'prosumer' (in fact both are closer to Jenkins's view of hybridity between old and new), the notion of a 'making and doing culture' sets up a parodic sense of how things were, or at least what media studies was interested in, against a set of ideas for how 'transforming audiences' might be dealt with instead, whether this was the intention or not, as this response by Gauntlett to a criticism by Paul Taylor illustrates reflexively:

> The superior examples are all those activists and organisations that have used online collaborative and participatory tools to raise awareness of many vital issues, and to organise political action. Someone like Taylor can always say, as he does, that these 'have met with limited success' but – crikey! – everything has to start somewhere, and there are numerous well documented cases where online campaigns have made an impact, and brought people together to engage in real-world action. Measured against the task of bringing about the demise of global capitalism, their success has indeed been 'limited', but perhaps this is setting the bar rather high. Academics writing articles for specialist journals have also 'met with limited success' in this department.
>
> *(Gauntlett, 2009: 154)*

The challenge to this view tends to situate itself in relation to the sceptical response to postmodernism on the grounds of irresponsible relativism at worst or at best a naïve overstating of any shift in power dynamics. A differend always-already escapes argument precisely because to discuss it in between or outside of the idioms of either language game is impossible, either there is 'the media' or not, and it has changed or it has not. To liberate ourselves from the idea that there ever was 'the media', to view it as a logocentric construct shot through with the conventions of a metaphysics of presence, does not reduce our sensitivity to the fact that people exercise power through news agendas, for example, or equally that people organise themselves to oppose subordinating imagery (in the case of feminism). Instead it allows us to focus always on the 'micro' without recourse to an ideal of 'the media' as monolithic or as all-powerful. Ironically, perhaps, when refuting the discourse of derision that pervades around the subject, media educators very often speak of 'the power of the media' as a legitimising force for their academic practice, thus creating a self-fulfilling prophecy which is at once undermining and self-defeating.

Was this the 'spirit' of the Centre for Contemporary Cultural Studies (CCCS)? Might the work of the CCCS, highly formative in our own work to date, be the *problem*? Or at least, might the dissemination of the research into narratives about communication and power create a blind alley? The work of the centre very rarely explicitly dealt with 'the media', instead exploring the complexities of the interconnection of culture, the making of meaning and the living of lives. And yet several of the emerging studies have been framed, at least retrospectively or 'in translation', by a focus on text and audience – from *Jackie* to *Nationwide* to *Crossroads*. Our hypothesis is that in the power granted to 'the media', the focus on the complexity of social practice has been lost in translation. Thus in the socio-cultural practices of *subject media*, the essential principle of the CCCS, that people are the object of study (returned to by the Media Studies 2.0 argument) was obscured by a reductive conception of power and subordination.

Gloss on resistance

But the purpose of this book is to begin the project of thinking through pedagogy for cultural analysis, and indeed for media studies (renamed or not) 'after the media'. For example, in rethinking the subject to pay attention to cultural events, as opposed to texts, we will tentatively imagine some different concepts. *Grand Theft Auto in the Suburbs*, a reworking of play sequences from *Grand Theft Auto IV* in the 'real world' of (presumably) the producers, posted on YouTube and played back by hundreds of thousands of viewers, seems to us to present something interesting in our thinking through 'after the media'. Working through theoretical concepts from the vertical discourse with students and imagining new rules for the game, we arrived at this emerging framework for thinking about *Suburbs* as an event. Crucially, this is only one response to *Suburbs*, one reception, one imagining. The concepts arranged in this way by students would not be fixed for the next

TABLE I.1 Towards a new conceptual (non) framework

	Reception	Playback	Collaboration	Convention	Discourse
Context	Meme, industry sanction (below the line marketing and viral homage not resisted, homage remixes by peers, academic discussion.	Hundreds of thousands of views + see reception. Mass audience playback.	Group creation + see reception for community dissemination/homage (see Michael Wesch on this form of media exchange).	'Backwards' logic/ conventions reworked, plays with real/ gameworld, violence more pronounced when juxtaposed?	Collective consumption, the 'event game', the discourse of pastiche – online 'knowing', play.
Event	Non-commercial but commercial benefit to game industry (not needed, though)...	Advertising on YouTube set against democratizing 'free platform'.	Comments, meme, homage, signifying chain.	Establishing conventions for remix-homage.	The discourse of convergence culture as event.
Diegesis	Comments on YouTube are diegetic or extra-diegetic? Discuss!	Is playback reception or a post-reception contribution?		Hybridity, convergence culture, media literacy.	Parody reformulation. Our world. Blended reality.
Paratextualdiegesis	Heavy intertextuality + double-determination (extra-diegesis + online remix community) – hip hop, gangster genre, migration, crime, franchise history.		Comments, meme, homage	Martinez research on playback aspirations as sub-genre.	Effects debate.
Frivolity	High frivolity in production, exchange and reception.	Playback is act of frivolity + viral exchange – meme status – becomes shared partly comedic 'moment' (in space, not time).	At level of frivolity, collaboration between game creatives and remix 'prosumer'.	Use of conventions from mixed genres for comedic homage is highly conventional now. Blended world conventions emerging – e.g. 'professional' sound over prosumer action.	Emerging 'norms' for remix parody and comments – YouTube subcultures realised through discourses.

moment of analysis or reflection. More important yet is the 'horizontal discourse' at work here. The context is not a public sphere category as there is no commercial organisation or public service institution to identify with an agenda that can be known and learned.

Likewise the nature of the event is 'up for grabs' and the blended nature of diegesis with its outsides forms a substantial part of the framework.

Students would next create another link in the signifying chain, a parody/ homage to or departure from *Suburbs*, with an open brief. As we will work through later, here we understand them to be oscillating between peripheral and full participation (Lave and Wenger, 1991), but the apprenticeship they serve is not craft or skill determined, but rather they are apprentices in theorising their culture. Media studies is here to facilitate 'mastery' in a meta-language which gives voice to reflexive negotiation of identity – a kind of 'culture literacy'.

Bearing witness

What does this reframing do to this event? In making the singularity of the event of reception prominent, the grid above can only be used 'under erasure' – as a snapshot, it captures only but cannot boast permanence. It is not a 'reading', but an attempt to stop the chain of signification for long enough to theorise and in so doing create some 'tagging' to concepts and ideas external to the document.

There has been a widespread acceptance that new media technologies (essentially broadband internet exchanges) have accelerated and amplified the practices of what Hills calls 'textualisation' and describes thus:

> This implies that culture is not automatically made up of bounded, unitary texts which are necessarily special or ordinary: rather, it is created through how producers and consumers do different things with texts, including breaking the world in to certain textual, symbolic bits in the first instance.
>
> *(Hills, 2005: 27)*

Do we need a notion of 'the text' at all? The model above strains to retain at least a boundary between textual and extra-textual, diegetic and non-diegetic, but the relations between them, as discussed by the students, are so erroneous to be only of interest in terms of how they are so – in other words the exception (textual boundaries made unstable) becomes the norm. Once again, at the risk of repetition, our proposal is that it has always been so – reception has always transgressed textual and diegetic limits, but this fundamental lifeworld practice (of fluid thinking about culture) has been largely ignored by *subject media*, or at best been annexed to content. Likewise, frivolity – significant to fandom and 'textual poaching' – is framed in a value system that despite itself 'others' such a response as somehow more active, more interpretive and more different from the implication of a more typical range of reception modes. After the media, the digital tools at the disposal of the audience merely offer an archive of the always-already frivolous reception of culture, whether realised through playback, intervention or just through unknowing what 'the media' encode. In short, *subject media* falsely believes it has been working with de Certeau's reading-poaching theory (1988) for all these years, yet the impulse in the model above to reduce the complexity of *Suburbs* to lingering binaries that, in thought, exercise power must be a site of adversion for us to, as Lyotard implores, 'work without rules, in order to establish the rules for what will have been' and to 'produce new presentations – not to take pleasure in them but to better produce the feeling that there is something unrepresentable'.

Address on the subject

> They never taught us nor allowed us to say our multiplicity. That would have been improper speech.
>
> *(Irigaray, 1992: 207)*

The chapters that follow are the work of three authors approaching the question from different directions and employing different strategies to think about the study of culture without recourse to the idea of 'the media' as hitherto so powerfully constructed in discourse and exercised in social practice to exclude. As such the rest of the book is dialogic as we work through this 'reimagining' in three ways, with more or less of a shared language game. In the early chapters we engage with the classical orthodoxy of text-centric approaches to studying 'the media', arguing that the spirit of the CCCS has been distorted or at least fractured by the colonisation of its methods by analytical approaches that insufficiently bear witness to the agency of people in life. Here we explore the status of power, genre and representation after the media. Next we move on to consider the hybrid context of current theorising around identity and performance, politics and history, with a systematic attempt to disrupt the grand narrative of media studies in so doing. And in the later chapters we establish a set of starting points for a 'pedagogy of the inexpert' – for the study of culture and identity after the media, engaging with questions of narrative, audience and technology while avoiding the conceit of 'knowing'. Crucially, here we turn on ourselves as members of a subculture – a community of agents framed socio-culturally in discourse, defined by how we explain ourselves, mediated by what we think culture might be and how we can imagine it differently.

In the detail we 'poach' an array of events, old and new. Beginning with power, we explore the institutional power that *subject media* has exercised, perhaps despite itself, and move on to engage with public service broadcasting in the age of the 'mediascape', the 2010 UK election campaign and the decline of press power, and a discussion of the TV show *Extras* in contrast with the 1976 film *Network*. In our consideration of genre, we work extensively with Derrida and then offer something towards an 'application' to *Glee*. Representation – as studied in contemporary media education – is examined with analysis of ten examples of its centrality across age ranges and national contexts, with Lacan and Zizek's different versions of 'the real' as our framework. Next to politics, where Baudrillard, Williams and the remake of *The Prisoner* help us to think through a (new) politics for cultural studies, and on to identity, where first we put *subject media* on the couch to interrogate its own idealised identity, map out the Gauntlett/Buckingham differend, and then work with Butler, Foucault, Hills and Zizek to suggest a pedagogy with paratextual agency and parody liberated from the margins and placed centre stage.

History is perhaps the chapter most 'abstracted' from media studies as currently configured – tellingly, in the domain of our central argument – and here we work together ideas from Foucault and Stuart Hall (among many others and in relation to the 'trappings' of modernism) as a way into looking at *Life on Mars* and *Watchmen*. In the chapters on audience and narrative we disseminate the outcomes of a range of research with people, with specific attention to *Grand Theft Auto IV, The Wire, Richard & Judy,* and young adults discussing their own status as 'readers' – of all kinds of culture. In each case some 'classic' audience theories and conceptions of literacy and storytelling are 'remixed' for after the media. Technology is considered through a critical response to how Lister et al frame the 'new', along with a sustained exploration of how McLuhan looks in the age of the iPad and how we might put Jenkins' *transmedia learning* to work – a question we also answer with regard to 'audience'. The 'outro' chapter – pedagogy of the inexpert – sets out some proposals for ways of working with students – always our primary concern.

Of course *subject media* is itself the sum of a set of tensions, contradictions and counter-discourses. We may set up something of a 'straw man' and unravel the logic of our own argument along the way by reducing our own object of study to the same monolithic status that (we accuse) it ascribes to 'the media'. Equally, resistance is a feature of discourse, and as such there will be plenty of practice – perhaps especially in 'the academy' (though this is for debate) – which escapes the normative reach of *subject media*, we concede. And yet our thesis – controversial or not – is that cultural studies has resisted the 'common sense' of *subject media* far less than it might think – or it might seem – and that media studies has departed from the exclusive and alienating 'moral supervision' of English education far less than it tells itself. At the heart of the problem is the idea of 'the media', and so we will devote the rest of this book to undermining it.

1

POWER AFTER THE MEDIA

> The knowledge which is preferred and privileged at any given moment is so simply because influential members of the concerned community have subscribed to it.
>
> *(Crowley, 1989: 46)*

Elsewhere, we have described three 'myths for media teachers', which sum up much that is both questionable and 'common sense' about media studies as a subject (McDougall, 2004):

1. During a discussion about whether media studies is a 'valid' subject, sceptics concede that 'the media' are incredibly important and powerful, and that young people need to be 'aware' of it, or be *media-literate*.
2. Justifying the study of soap opera to a parent, the media teacher explains that the student is never 'just watching' *Dr Who*, that the subject matter may be far more 'popular' and 'accessible' than, say, a Shakespeare play, but the tools of critical analysis are the same. The parent is amused but seems convinced.
3. In England, the *Times Educational Supplement* publishes a report on the intention of an exam board to introduce a topic within the A-level Media Studies specification on computer games and the representation of conflict. Various national newspapers follow up this lead, with varying degrees of scepticism as to the academic legitimacy of such analysis. The *Independent* includes the item in its editorial, suggesting that the power of the gaming industry justifies such classroom attention.

These stories present a subject that feels the need for self-justification, as if, like Kafka's Josef K, it has been convicted in its absence of an unspecified crime. Unfortunately the subject seeks its validation unwisely. What is patterned across these tales are assumptions about value which form part of a discourse wherein various kinds of power are exercised. In attempting to site itself credibly, media studies almost inevitably finds itself constructed and positioned in a limiting way within this discourse. Where media studies does relate to power, though, is as a form of resistance to the tangible power of 'the media', and acquiescently as a unquestioned response to the economic power of the gaming industry, which is required to seek no further validation.

If we are to attempt to reconceptualise media studies 'after the media' we must first acknowledge this starting point and its construction by discourses of schooling and formal education rather than by notions of what can be known in the world. Subjects as academic disciplines are produced by contingent cultural practices as forms of identity, knowledge and legitimation. *Subject media* is a technology and a discourse constructed from and framed by its entire history, and in particular the inherent tensions between its 'spirit' (a sort of Barthesian myth constructed by its participant community) and its 'word', how it performs itself (being taught, assessed and managed). This discourse is necessarily concerned with the exercise of power both within and beyond its formulations which relate to not only the status of the subject but also its proposed and performed content and its project of emancipation and empowerment of learners.

This chapter represents the first play in a systematic deconstruction of *subject media* which is the first stage in a reconceptualisation of the media studies 'project'. We will argue that framed as it is within the patronage of *subject English*, *subject media* has become, in the age of the iPads, more and more untenable since its 'system' has become irreparably uncoupled from the lifeworld (Habermas, 1984: 153). This is not a matter of embodying significant contradictions, but rather about failing to make these competing discourses a central object of study (Fraser, 1990). This has led progressively to a focus on 'the media' which has become less and less convincing, at once both refuge and ambush, poison and cure. Our 'ounce of civet', as Peim's was for an equally ailing and arguably more entrenched *subject English*, is cultural theory, but this time ingested rather than merely juxtaposed. A central paradox of *subject media* is that media studies, though informed by poststructuralist theory to a point, in so much as representations are taken seriously as constructions for analysis, is still immersed in a way of thinking about the world wherein 'the media' is given agency to send 'messages' to 'the audience' within the workings of 'ideology'.

Our address comes from a cultural studies viewpoint, ironically one of the original wellsprings from which media studies would emerge – in the United Kingdom at least. Stuart Hall's identification of the four distinct components of this intellectual departure remains useful:

- Cultural studies moved away from behaviourist stimulus-response approaches to media influence.
- The notion that media texts are transparent bearers of meaning was rejected in favour of a semiotic approach.

- An active view of audience was taken, looking at varied decodings and the importance of political and social motivation.
- British cultural studies broke with the notion of a monolithic mass culture and mass media.

(as described by Schulman, 1993)

In finally calling time on 'the notion of a monolithic mass culture and mass media', we are keen to pursue how, where and by whom power is being exercised 'after the media'. This takes us partly into the dynamics of an increasingly participatory culture where power and resistance are continually negotiating spaces wherein new dispensations can be formulated. Only by seeing these negotiations in the fullest cultural contexts can we genuinely hope to find space for an emancipatory pedagogy. There is a vertical discourse that needs to be disrupted if the expertise of media studies students is not to add a sharp sting to the taste of their disempowerment by a dominant discourse. Such a discourse requires them to render this expertise in a language 'other' to their experiences in a model that is every bit as monologic as that ascribed to the once thought monolithic mass media.

Reissue, repackage, repackage: power and the Industrial Revolution

What haunted us later
was not the cool dispensing
of sacrament
in the burnished doldrums
but something more exotic –
that sense
of a slight shift of cargo
while becalmed

(Pauline Stainer, Sighting the Slave Ship)

The Hellenists taught us that the household in classical Greece was watched over by two deities; Hestia, the goddess of the hearth, at the shadowy, feminine centre of the house; and the outward-looking Hermes, god of the threshold, protector of exchanges and of the men, who monopolised them. Today the television and the computer have replaced the hearth. Hermes has taken Hestia's place.

(Auge, 2008: viii)

This chapter might well have been titled 'Industry after the media' save for the fact that, such has been the speed of industry's fall from grace as an essential media studies focus, it might have seemed incongruous in our revised list of concerns. This is not to imply that media industries have ceased to exist, though many are reformulating business models or that media ownership is no longer an issue in economic terms. It is rather to register a decisive shift of emphasis for many who see the 'proper' focus of media studies as the ways in which media create, negotiate and circulate meanings across a globalised world. In this pragmatic and semantic domain the industrial model has run out of steam. Various kinds of power might still be readily available to the Murdochs and Berlusconis of the post-digital media landscape but the power to make sense of the world on our behalf is nostalgic. This was confirmed in the United Kingdom some few expedient months before the 2010 General Election when Murdoch's prize UK tabloid, the *Sun*, declared for David Cameron's compassionate Conservatives. In 1992 a narrow Conservative victory was widely put down to the *Sun*'s virulent campaign against Labour leader Neil Kinnock which included the polling day headline 'If Kinnock wins today will the last person to leave Britain please turn out the lights.' This was followed a day later with the equally famous 'It was the *Sun* wot won it.' In 2010 it was a non-event, eclipsed by the rumour that Simon Cowell was going to host the first presidential-style televised debates between party leaders. Throughout the 1980s the *Sun* was a *cause célèbre* and liberals worried about the presence of Rupert's fat fingers in the minds of UK voters. Singer-songwriter Billy Bragg articulated the concerns of the broad Left in the song 'It says here':

> If this does not reflect your views you should understand
> That those who own these papers also own this land.
>
> *(Bragg, 1983)*

Even to the most diehard Marxist–Leninist this now seems untenable. Murdoch will always be a hate figure but his major current concern is finding feasible ways to drain revenue from on-line content in the form of a paywall. This is not to suggest that hitherto 'media moguls' are faced with a choice between finding new revenue streams and strengthening their ideological hold on the free world, or that forms of right-wing corporate dominance have suddenly become meaningless. However, it does imply that their equally important symbolic power is on the wane as their desire to contain and define the news agenda becomes less feasible. Little more than a decade ago a respected commentator like Anthony Giddens was able to make the following statement without compunction:

> The media ... have a double relation to democracy. On the one hand the emergence of a global information society is a powerful democratising force. Yet, television, and the other media, tend to destroy the very public space of dialogue they open up, through relentless trivializing, and personalizing of political issues. Moreover, the growth of giant multinational media corporations means that unelected business tycoons can hold enormous power.
>
> *(Giddens 1999: np)*

Little more than ten years later and we find 'television, and the other media' in a somewhat bewildered state, trying to keep track of that 'public space' that they would once, according to their detractors 'tend to destroy'. Emily Bell of the *Guardian* predicted an 'apocalyptic' period for mainstream traditional media. 'We are standing at the brink of what will be two years of carnage for western media. Nobody in my business has got a grip of it yet,' said Bell. This doesn't sound like a media capable of destroying anyone save perhaps itself. 'We are' said Bell, 'at the meeting point now of a systematic down turn and a cyclical collapse' (Oliver, 2008).

Bell went on to predict the demise of perhaps five national newspapers, 'the regional press heading for complete market failure' and no commercial UK-owned broadcaster except for the BBC. And all this in the context of having to meet the online need to produce differentiated content amongst what Bell called a 'hurricane of knowledge and publishing' caused by the growth of self-publishing online, such as blogging' (ibid.).

The BBC are an interesting exception here since it can be argued that the changing landscape has made the job of this well-funded public service broadcaster (PSB) significantly easier and its position in the market place significantly more secure. The provision of differentiated content across a range of platforms supported by an unparalleled archive and an active iPlayer makes the public service more transparent somehow. The PSB commitments are almost synonymous with the iPlayer's categories by which we might search content, despite the elusive nature of the internet viewing service in relation to the licence fee, of course. The blog, meanwhile, is an index of the unforeseen consequences of the digital age, the kink in innumerable fine theories about where we are and where we are going. It is the unwelcome splash of water in the face of the determinist agenda. To the technological determinist Neil Postman, technological change is the driver since each stage of development provokes its own mindset. He famously exemplified this in the following way:

> To a man with a hammer, everything looks like a nail.
> Why stop there?
> To a man with a pencil, everything looks like a list.
> To a man with a camera, everything looks like an image.
> To a man with a computer, everything looks like data.
>
> *(Postman, 1998)*

But what about the woman with a broadband connection? This problematic yields immediate clues: To a woman with broadband, everything looks like a social network. It is this shift of intellectual cargo that provides us with things to explore. Whereas all the other models lead to a new point of focus, this shift is of the focus itself. Suddenly this feels like an act of emancipation rather than appropriation, a restoration of something essential. The German philosopher Karl Jaspers, writing on the eve of Hitler's rise to power, detailed our responsibilities in this regard: 'Philosophic truth sees all human beings as possible others with whom it remains our task to communicate' (in Myerson, 2003: 146). With technologies able to provide the means, are we simply relearning who we really are?

Certainly for Bell, the sea change is clear and explicit. She talks of 'the age of representation', where media organisations offered what they thought readers should know, being brought to an end essentially by the blogosphere. Thus we are entering an 'age of participation' where content will be much more audience aware and interactive. The notion of news, for example, as a conversation rather than an exposition, gives some indication of the shift. As early as March 2010 with the release of a nine-minute video to promote Lady Gaga's single 'Telephone' on YouTube (which prompted some 20 million hits), commentators were declaring the effective demise of MTV (with a history lasting from 'Thriller' to 'Telephone').

Manchester United fans wearing gold and green in semiotic resistance to the corporate workings of their US owners provide a 'mutation' in the sense that de Certeau uses it when he talks of active reading; 'This mutation makes the text habitable, like a rented apartment' (de Certeau, 1988: xxi). In the corporate world of top-level sport where club owners sell audiences to media corporations, this is beyond frivolity. Discordant messages do not please sponsors – let alone owners – particularly when the messages themselves lack the conciliatory tone we expect from corporate communication. Once fans might have stood around braziers and disrupted programme sales, now they 'flame' on websites that ensure that the action is both local and international. This same impulse and organisation put Rage Against the Machine into the UK music charts at Christmas 2009 in order to prevent what had become the obligatory *X Factor* 'Christmas number one'. Even US TV's highest paid performer and *X Factor* franchise owner Simon Cowell had to concede that 'the people had spoken' and the mode of address was both pointed and nihilistic. Not only was the point made specifically by the band's name, but equally and simultaneously this was a demonstration of raw power. Jon and Tracy Morder conceived of the response as mirth, Tracy pointing out: 'It was one of those little silly ideas that make you laugh in your own house.' Ultimately though it went, in Jon's words 'stratospheric', earning Rage Against the Machine a record for downloads in a single week on a song that was not actually 'released' or physically available anywhere (accessed at http://news.bbc.co.uk/1/ hi/8423340.stm).

It's good to talk: the audience speaks back

Struggling for credibility in all this is any notion of a monologic 'meanings-imposed' approach. The simple truth is that any text, what Bakhtin would call a 'living utterance' – 'cannot fail to become an active participant in social dialogue' (Lillis, 2003: 197). The need to have dialogue not only with but also about texts has been made self-evident by an almost infinite variety of online communities. Dialogue is not an option any more than 'the digital age' is something happening only to someone else. The Media 2.0 agenda is underwritten by this uncertain shift: 'The view of the internet and new digital media as an "optional extra" is replaced with recognition that they have fundamentally changed the ways in which we engage with all media' (Gauntlett, 2007). In a world where school students use YouTube as a search engine and the construction of knowledge is conceived as a wiki, 'authority' is at least under pressure. It is a world where Lily Allen can launch a career from her MySpace and ultimately prompt 19 million downloads often of unfinished/developing songs (she ended up with 448,000 friends). The film criticism site Rotten Tomatoes may still discriminate between 'top critics' (the professionals) and the rest (amateurs) but the commodity value of professional opinion is under threat when so much is given for free.

While these arguments are almost inevitably overstated as a description of any given moment or situation, they surely have profound implications for those of us involved in and concerned about education. What begins as 'a slight shift of cargo, when becalmed', if ignored, may well in time have serious implications for what for now seem fairly robust cultural articulations of 'authority': reputation, expertise, institutional warrant. We are seeking these here but are also aware of the challenges and dangers inherent in these 'articulations' becoming merely defensive and as a result entrenched. In embracing the 'inexpert' we better maintain 'expertise'. Authority is not to be abandoned or anarchy embraced but the continual renegotiation of 'curriculum' and by implication the terms of engagement is, as ever, crucial. This may lead to a genuine democratisation of knowledge or to a selective fulfilment of Hesse's dystopian nightmare Castalia, the ultimate 'academy' and each for good or ill (Hesse, 2000).

At the end of Ray Bradbury's futuristic parable *Fahrenheit 451*, the hero – book-burning fireman Guy Montag – escapes into the woods to join a community of scholars. Each of these has the responsibility for one significant book (be it literary, cultural or philosophical) where 'responsibility' means they have had to memorize it. Less dramatic but equally engaged are the communities of practice that have sprung up on the internet, whether they be based around fandom or scholarship or simply social communication. In the face of a new knowledge culture an old idea re-emerges, that of community, for some the very antithesis of modernity. Communities, to some degree, conceived in literal terms, are indexes of a world subsumed and consumed by the media on behalf of a dominant elite. As literal places they can be, and literally are, breached, overrun. As virtual communities however, these things must change and the first thing that slows, then goes, is 'the growing mobility of the media as they conquer space' (de Certeau, 1988: 165).

This is what Fiske has been campaigning about, for many years, for this shift from a fixation on the identity and integrity of the text towards the contexts of its production, distribution and 'performance'. Ideas about unlocking the meaning of texts by perceptive critics are replaced by ideas about meaning as action: how texts work for those who use them. The media academic as much as the media executive is wrong-footed by a process Fiske was addressing over 15 years ago:

> The ways that people use the text quite often surprises the academic critic and academic analyst. For me the important thing is, rather than trying to

understand what the text is, is trying to understand how people use it, how it works rather than what it is, how it is put to work and how different social formations will try to put texts to work quite differently.

(quoted in Muller, 1991)

Fiske does not discount the various contexts and power discrepancies or the needs of media industries, but a quarter of a century later the medium has quite simply caught up with his message and his overplayed hand looks stronger and stronger:

Texts are always put to work socially. They are a very important in commercial life as well, in fact in any form of life. Texts are always bought and sold, they are always part of the way that money circulates socially as well, and one has to look at that side of it.

(quoted in Muller, 1991)

Part of the movement to de-text media studies is the desire to remove ever cleverer readings of largely mundane texts which are ignorant of or indifferent to the ways in which these texts are used by their respective audiences. Even polysemy has become an unedifying spectacle, demonstrative rather than resourceful. Fiske wants texts to be 'semiotic resources', open to different kinds of utilisation and exploitation. He wants us to understand that interpretations are neither neutral or equal, that they are active interventions which 'interfere' with texts:

The first thing, obviously is that there is no single meaning of a text. The second thing is that interpretational criticism is part of the struggle for meaning. Interpretation is not a neutral, a naïve or an objective art. It is part of the process so we need to be explicit that the way in which we are interpreting is a politicised and theatrical way and that it contests other ways.

(quoted in Muller, 1991)

And so we return to de Certeau's 'exorbitant art', reading, which for Fiske is very much involved with identity 'as a social construct, as the relationship between the social formation and the individual'. This is not an abstract notion but rather an activism that Fiske sees as the basis of hopes for a 'semiotic democracy'. It is an argument clearly strengthened by certain kinds of readings of the impact of the Internet:

Audiences are no longer passive receivers of media texts. They have outgrown the models proposed in 'active reception'. Audiences are learning how to be the media, how to net-work.

(Ross and Nightingale, 2003: 161)

Jenkins, also writing in 2003, attempted to find balance in the contesting views:

> It would be naïve to assume that powerful conglomerates will not protect their interest as they enter this new media marketplace but at the same time, audiences are gaining greater power and autonomy as they enter into the new knowledge culture.
>
> *(Jenkins, 2003: 280)*

The final years of the decade have served only to underline how difficult protecting one's interests is. In the United States in 2010 use of social networking sites increased by 277 per cent, giving further credence to Fiske's focus on identity as a key context:

> That's where identity is and its very much involved not only as a way of producing certain readings of the text but equally importantly certain readings of the text are used to produce identity. There is a mutual relationship between the identity and reading.
>
> *(quoted in Muller, 1991)*

For Gee this notion of active use is central to the act of reading:

> In the end, 'to read' is to be able to actively assemble situated meanings in one or more specific 'literate' discourses. There is no reading in general ... at least none that leads to thought and action in the world.
>
> *(Gee, 2000: 204)*

Perhaps an interesting way to exemplify 'this new knowledge culture' and shifting role of the reader is to consider not reader renegotiations of media output but rather reader responses to media academics and cultural theorists. This is Fiske's point above, that 'the ways that people use the text quite often surprise the academic critic and academic analyst' (quoted in Muller, 1991). But what about when the roles are reversed? The controversial Marxist philosopher and cultural commentator Slavoj Zizek stirred things up in March 2010 when he launched an attack on 3D special effects blockbuster *Avatar*. In a piece provocatively entitled 'Return of the natives' Zizek accuses the seemingly politically correct film of 'brutal racist undertones'. The article is wide-ranging, addressing Hollywood's creation of couples and their function in films like *Reds* (Warren Beatty, 1981) and Cameron's other box office smash *Titanic* (1997) before rounding on *Avatar* for a brutal racism covered up by 'its technical brilliance'.

> *Avatar*'s fidelity to the old formula of creating a couple, its full trust in fantasy, and its story of a white man marrying the aboriginal princess and becoming king, make it ideologically a rather conservative, old-fashioned film. Its technical brilliance serves to cover up this basic conservatism.
>
> *(Zizek, 2010)*

Apart from exposing his attitude towards not only *Avatar* but also, perhaps, the blockbuster 'project', Zizek is also activating problematics around notions of 'new' and 'old-fashioned' which somewhat cleverly seem to condemn the film for both its newness and 'oldness'. In doing so he is offering an active reading whose status, like *Avatar*'s in his eyes, comes largely from its energy (plus a residue of reputation and clear perspective). He 'finds' the film easily:

> It is easy to discover, beneath the politically correct themes (an honest white guy siding with ecologically sound aborigines against the 'military-industrial complex' of the imperialist invaders), an array of brutal racist motifs: a paraplegic outcast from earth is good enough to get the hand of a beautiful local princess, and to help the natives win the decisive battle. The film teaches us that the only choice the aborigines have is to be saved by the human beings or to be destroyed by them. In other words, they can choose either to be the victim of imperialist reality, or to play their allotted role in the white man's fantasy.
>
> *(Zizek, 2010)*

Here, at one level, is an indisputably 'expert' reading, which inhabits an established critical discourse and apparently adds value to our appreciation of this popular and accessible text. Zizek offers a concise, though fully energised postcolonialist analysis of the film's narrative structure from information that might have been found in a cinema listings plot summary. This is not in itself a problem: there are equally interesting things to say about *Hamlet* once you learn it is the story of a lad whose mother has remarried and who is visited by his father's ghost. However, Zizek goes further, and where he goes may be helpful in developing our ideas about both 'inexpertise' and the use of texts: not necessarily clarifying but at least problematising them. Zizek's claim is for 'an array of brutal racist motifs' and for a stab at what 'the film teaches us'. Both of these are legitimate concerns, though his interest is less textual than contextual:

> At the same time as *Avatar* is making money all around the world (it generated $1bn after less than three weeks of release), something that strangely resembles its plot is taking place. The southern hills of the Indian state of Orissa, inhabited by the Dongria Kondh people, were sold to mining companies that plan to exploit their immense reserves of bauxite (the deposits are considered to be worth at least $4trn). In reaction to this project, a Maoist (Naxalite) armed rebellion exploded.
>
> *(Zizek, 2010)*

Here the analysis of text is dragged towards Zizek's own political agenda in a way that Fiske would understand, though it contradicts his point about ordinary people being less interested than academics in what a text is: preferring to think about what they can do with it. Fiske, you will remember expressed just this sentiment:

> For me the important thing, rather than trying to understand what the text is, is trying to understand how people use it, how it works rather than what it is, how it is put to work and how different social formations will try to put texts to work quite differently.
>
> *(Fiske, 1994)*

Zizek's reading attracted a flurry of media interest but only 14 managed a response when the *New Statesman* published it online. Among them was this dismissive but not entirely thought-through response:

THE OLD MAN

04 March 2010 at 13:18

Don't be so silly. Have you no serious things to think about?

More significant though was the interestingly titled 'emperorsclothes' who took Zizek to task on a number of points from a number of perspectives:

EMPERORSCLOTHES

07 March 2010 at 19:45

Other comments above cover some of the inaccuracies and evasions of Zizek's attack on Avatar (Mar 5th). But if you have not actually seen the film, as he boasted was the case at a talk on March 3rd (at Cardiff University) then these become explicable. And there's no easier way to win over one kind of academic audience, it seemed, than to fire a cheap shot at the biggest recent Hollywood blockbuster, and to admit to 'of course' not having seen it.

In another part of his rambling talk he criticised Marx for an over simple contrast between the ideological and the real – exactly what he then performed in a right-on claim to know members of Maoist anti-colonial struggle in India who were said to be the reality of the struggles Avatar fictionalises.

In fact members of one such struggle, the Dongria Kondh tribe fighting the mining corporation Vedanta, did bother to see the film, and sent a letter to Cameron, the director, appealing for support. They saw its resonances (OK, highly profitable), and its potential as a focus for anti-corporate struggle of this kind (and were presumably sceptical about Cameron actually picking up the challenge). But to enjoy the anti-'war on terror'/anti-corporate and eco-sympathetic traces in the film (as well as the pleasures of the technologically inventive, melodramatised, action adventure form it takes) you need to have actually seen it. It seems Zizek is above such a petty need for evidence.

This response raises all kinds of issues, not least about the 'state of mind' of media studies. This is not a 'case study' in the kinds of 'inexpert' readings that might form the basis of meaningful work in the media classroom, but it does reinforce at least that 'meaningful' readings and 'expert' readings resist synonymity. If anything the case merely, and refreshingly, reminds us of both the 'advantage' of textual engagement and the danger of merely using texts as pretexts for other agendas. In media studies as an assessed subject this often manifests itself in terms of bloodless technical analysis designed only to display knowledge of everything but the text itself. This often masquerades as the application of theory to practice. Practice should be made of sterner stuff: more passion, more commitment. Zizek at least provokes a debate.

The double issue of not seeing the film and being lionised for it return us to the doubts about the 'discipline' which surfaced at the beginning of this chapter. It would seem less likely that Zizek would admit to not having read Kafka's *The Trial* (a text he often returns to). In a subject that validates students' own choices it is inevitable that 'teachers' (and Zizek is an effective, charismatic teacher) will lack knowledge or confidence, and we will suggest later how this might be turned into an advantageous pedagogic position when we develop 'the pedagogy of the inexpert'. However, the extra issue exposed by this response to Zizek reminds us that in media studies with regularity the 'inexpert' imposes his judgement on the 'expert'. For while media studies has an excellent track record when it comes to granting access to media examples drawn from students' own experiences, it is less convincing when it comes to responding to these in a non-judgemental way – this is a kind of 'false consciousness' since it leads students to only deal with their chosen examples of everyday media texts and technologies in the technical register of the teacher's construction of the discipline.

The power of the media in everyday life

Beyond the effects-based models of media communication this also asks significant questions of Ball-Rokeach and De Fleur's media-system dependency model. This is the notion that there is an interdependence between media, political and economic systems such that 'the capacity of individuals to attain their goals is contingent upon the information resources of the media system' (Ball-Rokeach, 1985: 487). The argument then goes that as the world becomes more complex so people turn increasingly to the media to understand it. The point of breakdown is 'the information resources of the media system' which presupposes some degree of delineation. The blogosphere provides both information and a challenge to 'the media system', in fact to the idea of it. In this case the medium is not the message, rather it is the quality of contact and relationship that is at issue. Dependency, like determinism, depends to some degree on a system of control, or at least a system you can control.

Baran and Davis (2009) point out that the assumption is that 'the more a person depends on having his or her needs met by media use, the more important will be the role that media play in the person's life, and therefore the more influence those media will have on the person' (Baran and Davis, 2009: 273). However, there is an apparent conflation here of 'the role that media play' and 'the role that *the* media play'. The point is that 'media use' is now just as likely to be about 'producing' and 'participating' as it is to be about passively receiving.

Given that the original work on media dependency focused on three sets of explicit needs, it would be interesting to speculate to what extent these are met these days 'through media' rather than 'from the media' (where these designations are our own). Later versions propose 'selective influence', recognising a differentiated audience, a world of different takes but trying to hold on to notions of our dependency. Certainly as a set of industries, 'the media' as a system is locked into an economic and political 'landscape' but this argument is damaged by the existence of resistant, alternative systems which circumvent and intersect this landscape.

It was de Certeau, as poacher in chief, who intimated that a change was going to come. In fact, more than that, he had never bought into the idea of 'narcotyzing dysfunction' offered by the critical theory of Horkheimer and Adorno. Chapter XII of his *The Practice of Everyday Life* is a dozen pages of significant analysis and a potential primer for what is happening everywhere now. It is prefixed by Lyotard's assertion that 'to arrest the meanings of words once and for all, that is what Terror wants', thus siting the investigation in that 'thoroughfare of woe', the mainstream (de Certeau, 1988: 165).

De Certeau is keen to explore what Keats called 'the fierce dispute betwixt damnation and impassioned clay', but here 'damnation' like Lyotard's 'Terror' is self-interest and ideology as much as it is 'the dark'. In doing so he constructs a more than plausible image: a narcotised mass audience grazing on popular culture laced with dominant ideology while its betters range free and 'snack' selectively on the more succulent buds of culture. This perhaps prefigures what Mark Paterson labels as 'savvy' and 'sucker' consumers in his *Consumption and Everyday Life* but it also enshrines a model that was sacrosanct to media studies as a developing discipline (Paterson, 2006: 161). De Certeau prepares us meticulously for his punchline. 'The masses rarely enter these gardens of art,' he points out. He then draws out the accepted wisdom:

> But they are caught and collected in the nets of the media by television (capturing 9 out of 10 people in France), by newspapers (8 out of 10), by books (7 out of 10, of whom 2 read a great deal and … 5 read more than they used to), etc.
>
> *(De Certeau, 1988: 165)*

Here is the lesson of critical theory as formulated most substantially in Horkheimer and Adorno's 'The dialectic of enlightenment' and in the latter's *The Culture Industry*, both of which are dismissive and suspicious of mass culture (and ultimately the mass media). 'Films, radio and magazines', they suggest, 'make up a system which is uniform as a whole and in every part' (Horkheimer and Adorno,

2001: 71). This system, ideological in character, gives even to those who disbelieve: 'The triumph of advertising in the culture industry is that consumers feel compelled to buy and use products even though they see through them.' Furthermore Adorno, in 'Schema of mass culture', writes off mass media output in one short contemptuous sentence: 'Mass Culture is unadorned make-up' (1991: 61). Painted metaphorically thus, it is perhaps not surprising that the contributions of consumers hold so little sway in critical theory and mass participation in itself is no argument:

> A technological rationale is the rationale of domination itself. It is the coercive nature of society alienated from itself. Automobiles, bombs, and movies keep the whole thing together until their leveling element shows its strength in the very wrong which it furthered. It has made the technology of the culture industry no more than the achievement of standardisation and mass production, sacrificing whatever involved a distinction between the logic of the work and that of the social system.
>
> *(Horkheimer and Adorno, 2001: 41)*

De Certeau may eschew 'automobiles' and 'bombs' but he nevertheless paints a vulgar picture of the consumer as 'patsy' for an overwhelming impoverishment of everyday life:

> Instead of an increasing nomadism, we thus find a 'reduction' and a confinement: consumption organised by this expansionist grid takes on the appearance of something done by sheep progressively immobilised and 'handled' as a result of the growing mobility of the media as they conquer space. The consumers settle down, the media keep on the move. The only freedom supposed to be left to the masses is that of grazing on the ration of simulacra the system distributes to each individual.
>
> *(de Certeau, 1988: 165)*

And having established all of this he makes his play (as we make ours): 'That is precisely the idea I oppose: such an image of consumers is unacceptable'(op. cit.: 166). He goes on to establish the premises by which he declares reading 'a misunderstood activity'. He begins with a focus: 'Today the text is society itself'; and for us the interest heightens with 'It takes urbanistic, industrial, commercial and televised forms.' He problematises the transition to 'the technocracy of the media', prophesied by Horkheimer and Adorno, which he says 'did not touch the assumption that consumption is essentially passive'(ibid.). De Certeau is uncompromising, insisting that 'the text (society or otherwise) has a meaning only through its readers' and dismissing the notion of a text's 'literal' meaning (Hall's 'dominant-hegemonic) as 'the index and result of a social power, that of an elite'. Dominance is addressed here but not reciprocated by dependence. Reading, for de Certeau, is active, an act of resistance, 'a silent production' (ibid.).

> He insinuates into another person's text the ruses of pleasure and appropriation:
> he poaches on it, is transported into it, pluralizes himself in it like the internal
> rumblings of one's body. Ruse, metaphor, arrangement, this production is
> also an 'invention' of the memory. Words become the outlet or product of
> silent histories. The readable transforms itself into the memorable.
>
> *(de Certeau, 1988: xxi)*

The 'invention of memory' is vital to our understanding of how power has
shifted, since when these 'ways of operating' (victories of the weak over the strong)
meet the opportunities offered by technology, many of de Certeau's provocations
become completely comprehensible. Having identified reading as 'the exorbitant
focus of contemporary culture', 'an epic of the eye', he establishes a more telling
context:

> learning to read is not a result of learning to decipher: reading meaning and
> deciphering letters correspond to two different activities, even if they
> intersect. In other words cultural memory (acquired through listening, oral
> tradition) alone makes possible and gradually enriches the strategies of
> semantic questioning whose expectations the deciphering of a written text
> refines, clarifies or corrects. From the child to the scientist, reading is
> preceded and made possible by oral communication, which constitutes the
> 'multifarious' authority that texts almost never cite.
>
> *(de Certeau, 1988: 168)*

Here is a model of situated literacy where 'the autonomy of the reader depends
on a transformation of the social relationships that overdetermine his relationship
to texts'. If the text is society itself, we should not be surprised that meaning
is socially and culturally determined. This 'transformation' is a necessary task
and one that for five or more years the blogosphere has been progressively and
more than adequately addressing. Here is the articulation of a politics of reading,
since 'reading is thus situated at the point where social stratification (class
relationships) and poetic operations (the practitioner's construction of a text)
intersect: a social hierarchy seeks to make the reader conform to the "information"
distributed by elite (or semi-elite) reading operations that manipulate the reader by
insinuating their inventiveness into the cracks in a cultural orthodoxy'. He is
always aware that he may be overstating the 'reader's impertinence' since 'the
media extend their power over his (the reader's) imagination, that is over
everything he lets emerge from himself into the nets of the text … his fears, his
dreams'. At the same time he is unequivocal in his faith in 'every subject's ability
to convert the text through reading'(op. cit.: 172). This 'mutation' is central to an
oft-quoted segment:

> This mutation makes the text habitable, like a rented apartment. It transforms
> another person's property into a space borrowed for a moment by a transient.

Renters make comparable changes in an apartment they furnish with their acts and memories; as do speakers, in the language into which they insert both the messages of their native tongue and, through their accent, through their own 'turns of phrase,' etc., their own history; as do pedestrians, in the streets they fill with the forests of their desires and goals.

(de Certeau, 1988: 172)

Networks of practice: a lesson from history

Much is made later in this book about the fact that changes in technology can only be meaningfully understood within broader social and cultural movements – specifically urbanisation. Thus there is a guerrilla aspect to both blogger and graffiti artist: both are involved in acts of reclamation which are at the same time constructed discourses of resistance. These are images of groups – not individuals – reclaiming the 'space' which they feel belongs to them and which is vital to their sense of both freedom and identity. Whether this is about mobilising support against power corporate institutions or sharing your critical opinions of the latest Hollywood 'horrors' (in either sense) there is a sense that some small part of the lifeworld is being reclaimed, and as Marx himself suggested, 'Every emancipation is a restoration of the human world and of human relationships to a man himself' (Marx and Engels, 1978: 46). It is about thwarting, or at least obstructing 'the growing mobility of the media as they conquer space'(de Certeau, 1988: 168).

However, in order to thwart, or even modestly obstruct, a rampant mass media intent on colonising every aspect of this world and the next (the 'other country' of the imagination), something had to change. The unitary understanding of the mass media as a manipulative instrument of Western cultural imperialism and/or the ideological state apparatus *par excellence*, reached its apotheosis in the 1970s. This was the period when people started to get really worried about 'the media', particularly television, a sure sign of its perceived importance. It was a period obsessed with effects (and causes) and an uncritical quantifying of content. Statements that still crop up regularly in discourse about media and its contexts have their origin in this period: for example the 'fact' that US children have seen on average 400 screen deaths before high school (Gerbner, 1970). To be 'plugged in to 'the media' was your essential access to social life.

The media were then about institutions and corporations – as can be seen from the sci-fi of the period – which dreamed of multinational corporations and conspiracy theories. One film epitomised these anxieties, classifying the questions and modelling potential solutions, for which it was much lauded and awarded. *Network* (1976, directed by Sidney Lumet, screenplay by Paddy Chayefsky), which incidentally does much to unwittingly support our arguments about genre as cultural categories, developed in Chapter 3, is a 'tale of the West' though its 'frontiers' are explicitly those of (ad)venture capitalism: media, advertising, marketing, ideology. Peter Finch, in his final film, is a former achiever, like John

Wayne in *The Shootist* (1976) or Clint Eastwood in *Gran Torino* (2008) (or even *Unforgiven*, 1992) returning for one last fight, as 1976's version of the gunslinger, the network news anchor.

Howard Beale (Peter Finch) is two weeks away from dismissal on the back of falling ratings, that cancer of a corporate media career when he explodes into action: promising the 'real' in the form of his own suicide and then publicly taking the mass audience to task for the state of debate about all of this. Rather than the end this has quickly become a new beginning, with Beale recast as the 'mad prophet' of the media age (reminiscent of the almost contemporary Vaughan, nightmare angel of the expressways, in JG Ballard's novella *Crash*). The internet is currently awash with accounts and video clips of Beale's most famous speech which ends:

> HOWARD (ON THE SET): Stick your head out and yell. I want you to yell: 'I'm mad as hell and I'm not going to take this any more!' (Chayefsky, 1976: sc. 99)

However, far more pertinent to us is his performance as 'the mad prophet' in which he confronts the narcotised state of the mass audience:

> HOWARD: But, man, you're never going to get any truth from us. We'll tell you anything you want to hear. We lie like hell. We'll tell you that Kojak always gets the killer, and nobody ever gets cancer in Archie Bunker's house. And no matter how much trouble the hero is in, don't worry, just look at your watch – at the end of the hour, he's going to win. We'll tell you any shit you want to hear. We deal in illusion, man! None of it's true! But you people sit there day after day, night after night, all ages, colors, creeds – we're all you know. You're beginning to believe the illusions we're spinning here. You're beginning to think the tube is reality and your own lives are unreal. You do whatever the tube tells you. You dress like the tube, you eat like the tube, you raise your children like the tube, you even think like the tube. This is mass madness, you maniacs! In God's name, you people are the real thing! We are the illusion! So turn off your television sets! Turn them off now! Turn them off right now! Turn them off and leave them off! Turn them off right now, right in the middle of this sentence I'm speaking to you now! Turn them off!!
>
> *(accessed on 16 July 2010 at*
> *http://www.nealromanek.com/blog/2008/02/great-film-monologues-3-network.html)*

There is a counterscene to this, a response from Arthur Jensen, his boss (played by Ned Beatty). This scene is memorably set in a lavish meeting room which Jensen dubs 'Valhalla'. They sit at opposite ends of an enormous table and Jenson significantly draws the heavy curtain before he launches into:

JENSEN: You have meddled with the primal forces of nature, Mr. Beale, and I won't have it, is that clear?! ... You are an old man who thinks in terms of nations and peoples. There are no nations! There are no peoples! There are no Russians. There are no Arabs! There are no third worlds! There is no West! There is only one holistic system of systems, one vast and immane, interwoven, interacting, multi-variate, multi-national dominion of dollars! petro-dollars, electro-dollars, multi-dollars!, Reichmarks, rubles, rin, pounds and shekels! It is the international system of currency that determines the totality of life on this planet! That is the natural order of things today! That is the atomic, subatomic and galactic structure of things today! And you have meddled with the primal forces of nature, and you will atone! Am I getting through to you, Mr. Beale?

(Chayefsky, 1976: sc. 152)

Here is the power of the markets channelled through the most awesome propaganda force in the 'whole godless world' an economic and ideological invasion: 'There is no America. There is no democracy.' Here is a pitiless imperial impulse, Debord's 'Spectacle' revealed, as he said it would be, as 'the flip side of money' (Debord, 2005: 24) and at its centre, ironically, the network, the organisation, the 'web'.

Fast forward over 30 years to the Christmas special of *Extras*, first broadcast in the United Kingdom but exported globally, which provided the final episode of the much-celebrated Gervais/Merchant sit com. Here Andy Millman (played by Ricky Gervais), extra turned writer-cum-actor, offers his 'wake up and smell the coffee' monologue on celebrity (and reality television) from the slightly ironic context of *Celebrity Big Brother*. Like Beale he is urging people to tune out, switch off and drop back in!

ANDY: I'm just sick of these celebrities just living their lives out in the open! Why would you want to do that? It's like these pop stars, who choose the perfect moment to go into rehab. They call their publicist before they call a taxi and then they come out and do their second autobiography: this ones called 'love me or I'll kill myself'. Oh, kill yourself then. And the papers lap it up. They follow us round and make people think we're important and that makes us think we are important. If they stop following us around taking pictures of us, people wouldn't take to the streets going 'ooh, quick, I need a picture of Cameron Diaz with a pimple'. They wouldn't care, they'd get on with something else. They'd get on with their lives. You open the paper and see a picture of Lindsay Lohan getting out of a car, and the headline is 'Cover up Lindsay, we can see your knickers!' Of course you can see her knickers, your photographer is lying in the road, pointing his camera up her dress to see her knickers! You're literally the gutter press. And fuck you the makers of this show as well! You can't wash your hands with this. You can't keep going 'oh, it's exploitation but it's what the public wants' No! the Victorian freak show never went away, now its called 'Big Brother' or 'American Idol' where in the preliminary rounds we wheel out the bewildered to be sniggered at by multi millionaires. And fuck you for watching this at home. Shame on you. And shame on me.

(Gervais and Merchant, 2007)

And yet for all their similarities as diatribes against the unacceptable, they are not the same: everything has changed. What Beale is exposing is the 'spectacle', the illusion, the apparatus, the conspiracy, the implications of McLuhan's medium as message. He is attempting to wake the passive consumer. Gervais (rather than Millman) on the other hand is opening up the processes through which his own celebrity is being constructed in an interactive age that makes it both so much more and so much less. In other words in a serious way he is addressing the 'extras', the marginal differences between 'extra' and 'star', between also-ran and winner.

The 'harm' here is more than personal but less than ideological, more social psychological than political. *Big Brother* too, when juxtaposed with *Network* speaks of a renegotiation of terms, a different kind of surveillance. It is *Network* that is by contrast Orwellian, and paradoxically contains the seeds of its own dissipation. The network is a symbol of the importance of communication and connectedness. It is an electronic highway, sending messages to the far-flung corners of the empire and sometimes even getting them back. However, it is also a resource, and out there and open to use (like real highways). It is a web, a matrix, a series of potential interactions. Ultimately the network would be betrayed by its own technologies: its provinces in revolt using the networks against itself. These appropriations are of the same order as those physical appropriations of urban space by skaters and squatters.

Meaningful spaces: an analogy

If we are to understand the provenance and implications of the virtual spaces created by the digital revolution we must first understand the ways that physical three-dimensional space is produced, regulated and controlled. A key thinker in this regard is the Marxist philosopher Henri Lefebvre, whose book *The Production of Space* was the first to conceive of space as a social product. Lefebvre sees the social production of urban space (in other words the subjecting of it to rules and conventions) as essential to the reproduction of a capitalist society. In fact he argues that 'the penetration of and into space has been as historically important as achieving hegemony through the penetration of institutions' (2003: 212).

Though the internet does exist to some degree like the Wild West, an even mix of danger and opportunity, creating moral panics is a last-gasp strategy from institutions who do not know what else to do. Pretty much all attempts to control, police or even exploit these 'spaces' have proved unsatisfactory. In this fragmented space anything goes, but this is not about an absence of boundaries but rather about the ability to make your own. As Marc Auge suggests, 'our ideal ought not to be a world without frontiers, but one where all frontiers are recognised, respected and permeable' (2008: xiv). It is not far-fetched to suggest that at its best that is what the blogosphere offers, while all around it the mastiff snarl of media operations who keep buying more of the 'infinite pie'.

The points that Lefebvre makes about the conception of space as a social product refer to cyberspace just as readily as any other 'variety' if not more so. These spaces are also:

> reconstituting a complex process: discovery (of new or unknown spaces, of continents or the cosmos) – production (of the spatial organisation characteristic of each society) – creation (of ouevres: landscape, the city with monumentality and décor).
>
> *(Lefebvre, 2003: 209)*

They are also archly exposing the discrepancies between the 'society under consideration' and its space, between the ideological state apparatus formerly known as 'the media' and its influence and control.

The age of ideology is not over. However, models of competition and control are now 'redundant', woefully inadequate in an age of participation vanguarded by an almost infinite number of internet communities. It is worth repeating what Lefebvre thought his work 'began to elucidate': 'The concept of space links the mental and the cultural, the social and the historical.' It does this by creating communities, and by allowing communities to be created, literally communities of practice, whose first 'practice' is construction: founding the community. Community is a vital idea for a number of reasons, not least because it had come to represent the very antithesis of modernity and as such was dismissed by the postmodernists as a modernist metanarrative of sentimentalised brainwashed banality. In the context of supermodernity, however, that energetic attempt to salvage something from the excesses of postmodernist deconstruction, community is a key term describing as it does a collaboration around the principal act of 'meaning making'.

Interestingly the opposition of 'community' and 'modernity was predicated on the problematic designation of community as what Anthony Cohen calls 'a nostalgic, bourgeois and anachronistic concept' (1985: 12). Cohen argues that in this formulation community was ascribed those features of social life that modernity lacked, thus creating an idea that by design could not survive 'industrialisation and urbanisation'. This is not a hundred miles away from Tolkien's sentimentalised notion of the Shire as an ideal community threatened by Saruman's foundries in *The Lord of The Rings*. Nevertheless communities were 'addressed' by industrialisation and its implications, which did sometimes mean that they were bypassed, disordered or even destroyed (semantically or otherwise). Online communities are on the whole better protected, more flexible or both.

What they certainly share with the physical communities explored by the anthropologist Cohen, and with places and spaces as defined by the supermodernist

Auge, is identity and function. These are also viable descriptions of communities both online and physically situated (Auge, 2008: 63). Cohen describes the 'consciousness of community' as 'encapsulated in perception of its boundaries which are themselves largely constituted by people in interaction' (1985: 14). Auge may argue that all frontiers should be 'permeable', that 'a frontier is not a wall, but a threshold', but sometimes 'people in interaction' offer significant barriers. Even on fansites that seem the epitome of Jenkins's original 'textual poacher' work there are unspoken boundaries, which are often too high to breach.

This gives a pointer to the arguments that Cohen is making in his book *The Symbolic Construction of Community*, principally that community, as a symbolic idea, is chiefly concerned with symbolism. 'Community', he reminds us, 'is where one learns and continues to practice how to "be social"' (1985: 15): it is where we acquire culture (and communities are where we acquire cultures). This is vital to our reconfiguration of media studies as an area of study simply because it is centrally about where we acquire and develop our capacity to make meaning: 'When we speak of people acquiring culture, or learning to be social, we mean that they acquire the symbols which will equip them to be social' (1985: 16).

Here is a process of empowerment which reinforces the argument that new digital media have unwittingly retooled a supposedly passive mass audience. What we may well be getting from our online 'communities of practice' is symbolic equipment: where once we got answers we now get the means to make questions. For whereas the 'age of representation' implied a kind of determinism, the 'age of participation' is seeking intensity rather than conformity: 'Culture, constituted by symbols does not impose itself in such a way as to determine that all of its adherents should make the same sense of the world' (Cohen, 1985: 16).

This absence of authority unsettles academics and media organisations as it must once have worried a government on the Eastern seaboard looking West and dreaming of an America that could be governed. Some still feel they can fight a rearguard action, ignoring the palpable facts of 'wikinomics' as described by Tapscott and Williams (2007). This is not about winning or losing the argument, it is about newly having to rely on arguments. The new road is built and people are using it: 'mass collaboration changes everything'. It's not about 'capturing' meaning any more but about making it: 'Millions of media buffs now use blogs, wikis, chat rooms and personal broadcasting to add their voices to a vociferous stream of dialogue and debate called "the blogoshere"' (Tapscott and Williams, 2007: 1). Our various communities provide us with symbols, and as Cohen has pointed out, 'Symbols do not so much express meaning as give us the capacity to make meaning' (1985: 16). In the beginning, after all, was 'the Word'.

Clifford Geertz could not have predicted how apt his metaphor would prove to be. 'Man', he proclaimed, 'is an animal suspended in webs of significance he himself has spun', unaware that in fifteen years the webs would be 'worldwide' (Cohen, 1985: 17). These webs, of course, constitute culture. Geertz also defines the nature of our response as 'not an experimental science in search of a law but an interpretative one in search of meaning'. Here again is a denial of culture as something imposed and an affirmation that it is best demonstrated in 'the capacity with which it endows people to perceive meaning in, or to attach meaning to, social behaviour' (ibid.). The 'meaningfulness' is in the passionate act of interpretation rather than the dissection of (dead) texts. All communication in this sense is therefore determined in every sense by our responses. Once we perhaps may have been convinced by the singularity of it but we can no longer be lured back to 'mono' for anything but an indulgent moment of 'nostalgic, bourgeois anachronism' – staying home with Hestia is no longer an option.

We have traced, in this chapter, the development of a meta-awareness of how we can more clearly see, through new configurations of space – enabled by technology – how power and the idea of 'the media' have been confused and confusing with regard to notions of 'passive' consumption and 'active' engagement. In other words, it is not so much 'the age of representation' but rather an era where we can see representation played out online and archive it. Moving away from the idea of 'the media' will allow for the study of the symbolic webs we spin for ourselves – and why we do so. Next we turn our attention to the most self-fulfilling concept of all – genre.

2

GENRE AFTER THE MEDIA

Are genres really 'out there' in the world, or are they merely the constructions of analysts?

(Robert Stam, 2000: 14)

This chapter does not take issue with textuality or textual analysis as such, nor does it subscribe to the view that 'genre' is a redundant critical tool or even necessarily 'under erasure'. Rather it agrees with Jason Mittell's position which he expresses clearly when specifically examining television genres: 'genres do matter a great deal but not in the ways that scholars have generally used them' (2004: viii). Mittell goes on to usefully describe genres as 'cultural categories', in other words 'produced with particular discursive formations which usefully locate genre within specific sites of discourse' (Harbord, 2002: 80).

Like us Mittell approaches genre from a post-structuralist perspective. In his case this means conceiving genres as 'discursive practices' after the manner of Foucault's discursive formations. This is predicated on the notion that 'genres are not textual properties' (Mittell, 2004: 12):

> Specifically I contend that television genre is best understood as a process of categorisation that is not found within media texts but operates across the cultural realms of media industries, audiences, policy critics and historical contexts.
>
> *(Mittell, 2004: ix)*

Mittell does not dispute that media experiences are classified and organised into genres, nor that these practices are, as it were, media-wide, covering but not necessarily connecting producers, audiences and critics (by a golden thread!). However, the connections Mittell makes are of a particular kind, with 'particular concepts like cultural values, assumed audience and social function' (ibid.: ix) The fact remains that for all the progressive work being done in the Academy both currently and across the last 40 years (Tudor and Ryall were making some of these points from the 1970s onward), fixed genre labels remain a central plank of *subject media* as witnessed by specifications, programmes of study and the plethora of traditional genre study publications. In this way the story Mittell tells, 'before I discovered the field of Media Studies', of a heated but friendly debate with his friend Wendy about 'whether *Northern Exposure* is sitcom or drama' is liable to still be the central significant focus of genre studies. In this pursuit of decisive classification, the equivalent perhaps of fixing butterflies on pins, *subject media* differs little from *subject English*, that store of traditions that Peim (2000) hoped media studies might mend. The chief difference, though, in this labelling 'phallusy' is that *subject English* has the more impressive labels, bathetically pitching Auden's use of the sonnet form in 'In time of war' against the way *Talk Sport* uses the generic conventions of the radio phone-in show.

Much of the rest of this chapter constitutes our attempts to suggest how genre may be reconceptualised in a media studies operating 'after the media'. We do this by offering a case for and an active reading of Derrida's seminal but neglected provocation 'The law of genre', a much referred to but very rarely discussed ur-text of post-structuralism. This Derridean *tour de force* which seeks (darkly) 'to make light of all the tranquil categories of genre theory' performs its theme by 'putting to death the very thing it engenders' (Derrida, 1980). Here in the 'blink of an eye', in the fragile transience of the hymen we encounter the redemptive feminine challenging the opposition of the laws of nature and history imposed by phallocentrism: replacing 'the law' with 'la loi' (in French 'the law' is feminine). There is an exuberance here that is also vital for post-structuralist genre studies. It offers the experience of genre as 'participation without belonging', an act that carries with it the inherent dangers of impurity, anomaly and monstrosity which in itself becomes a powerful model for our role as textual adventurers in a dispensation which accounts meanings as endlessly deferred. We exemplify this by attempting to perform the television musical drama *Glee* in this critical 'key'.

Derrida's extremism (which may equally connote integrity, diligence and insanity) also makes clear so many of the issues for a reconceptualised genre in a surprisingly similar way to the way the increasingly hybrid nature of genre classifications has called into question the principle of generic 'label fixing'. Derrida addresses hybridity implicitly as a function of all texts, not as some simple amalgamation but rather as a full-blown 'breeding' of potentially dissimilar stock, as dissimilar, if you like, as masculine and feminine and as a productive act which forgoes 'intercourse': offering invagination rather than 'classification'. Here we are back to Mittell's (and Foucault's) 'discursive practices', designed partly to 'upset their taxonomic certainties' but also to 'summon up these classes' so that 'laws' themselves can be examined. For it is a common thread of our general argument that opening the processes through which judgements are made to scrutiny is a vital part of the reconstituted media studies. As Mittell so rightly says, 'analysing genres must consider the processes and practices of categorisation, not just the elements which fall under categorical rubric' (2002: xiv). Only then might we approach the law of the textual event', 'an account without edge or boundary', a genuine 'jouissance'.

Prologue

Madness is law, the law is mad-ness.

(Derrida, 1980: 81)

This account of genre 'after the media' is as we have indicated partly inspired, in spirit at least, by Derrida's elliptical, irreverent and at times darkly ironic 'account of an accountless account', 'The law of genre'. This 'principle of contamination', this 'law of impurity', this 'parasitical economy' is a welcome provocation in a critical region that seems sometimes overrun with complacency and insularity (ibid.: 59). It is not as though the area is short of interesting critical work or enlightened reflections on progress. It is just that these are partly obscured by a configuration of genre that conflates notions of genre as a process of categorisation with genre as specific collections of texts in the context of a simplistic model of media producers and their audiences. This model is a model of dependency but one where neither the focus of interest nor the source of significance is either a function or a product of that dependency.

In genre, therefore, we have the critical concept that is most predicated on the singularity of 'the media' as an idea and a concept which has continued to parade its one-dimensionality even in the face of those who would wish to see genres as 'ubiquitous, multi-faceted phenomena' (Neale, 1999: 28). The result is a spectacular absence of any kind of professional critical consensus, though much of the more interesting work shares key notions like multi-dimensionality and situatedness. The term was first used by Aristotle more than 2,300 years ago. This lineage is, of course, another of the problems since it encodes notions of high culture at the earliest point of the genre story and ultimately presents the study of popular culture as one of literature's hand-me-downs. Moreover, post-Romantic literary theory had rejected the 'generic' as the antithesis of art, establishing value in advance of evaluation. Thus a fixation on the genericity of media texts sets up a binary opposition with the 'uniqueness' of genuine art work, where value 'can in part be defined by its desire to be uncaused and unfamiliar, as much as possible unindebted to any tradition, popular or otherwise' (Braudy, 1992: 444). It is easy in this context to see how critics keen to value media texts saw the benefit of building value through accumulation rather than intensity, whether by notions of authorship or genre. It remains an influential strategy in film and television studies where products can be packaged both materially and discursively to pass themselves off as disguised literary texts.

Derrida, though with his own agenda, suggests that genre is 'a bit too rashly' assumed to be an artificial conception ('of techne ... still more narrowly of poetry')

(1980: 58). He is concerned about the relationship between nature and history, a relationship often made implicitly antagonistic by genre theory. His exemplification of a set of difficult premises, presented in an opaque legalese with evidence taken from an obscure modern French text, offers much to go on, not so much in the text as of it. Like Eliot's notes to *The Wasteland*, the protesting is too much, bringing to light the madness of genre. Like Neale, Derrida understands that there is not really a problem with genre, save for the fact it defies categorisation (its form is paradox).

> The genre has always in all genres been able to play the role of order's principle: resemblance, analogy, identity and difference, taxonomic classification, organization and genealogical tree, order of reason, order of reasons, sense of sense, truth of truth, natural light and sense of history.
>
> *(Derrida, 1980: 81)*

It is a challenge that in the thirty years since its conception has been barely recognised and rarely addressed in a subject that has raised genre-study to a position of dominance. The fact that Derrida also claimed that 'there is no genreless text' (ibid.: 65), seemingly confirming genre's importance as a tool of analysis, does no harm despite the fact that this aside is unrepresentative of the argument of the piece. Now that we are potentially freed from the thrall of 'the media' as a unified or even unifying field, what of genre? Certainly Derrida's opaque *tour de force* seems a reasonable site for rallying the progressive forces in genre studies to construct a new dispensation. If anything genre study needs transfiguring rather than reconfiguring. This is not the same as the call for a 'trans- or post-generic' media of the sort that Paul Watson makes (2007). Genre is not dead but equally comes the suspicion that it has never been fully and critically alive. The last thing it needs are new categories or even new forms of categorisation.

The search for ever more restrictive generic categories is very clearly part of the culture of fandom. As such it deserves consideration as part of the broader discursive practices that it informs and is informed by, a set of practices to critically examine: often a system of attachments, allegiances and exclusions. Musical sub-cultures are classic and often almost exclusively male: not the music but rather the 'cognoscenti' (those who classify). For heavy metal, for example, Wikipedia cites 30 separate sub-genres:

> Alternative metal Avant-garde metal Black metal Christian metal Crust punk Death metal Doom metal Drone metal Extreme metal Folk metal Funk metal Grindcore Glam metal Gothic metal Groove metal Industrial metal Metalcore Neo-classical metal Nu metal Post-metal Power metal Progressive metal Rap metal Sludge metal Speed metal Stoner metal Symphonic metal Thrash metal Traditional heavy metal Viking metal

By contrast the appropriately liveried 'Metal Crypt' offers only twelve (nine 'secure' and three problematic ones) but does so with the following anchoring

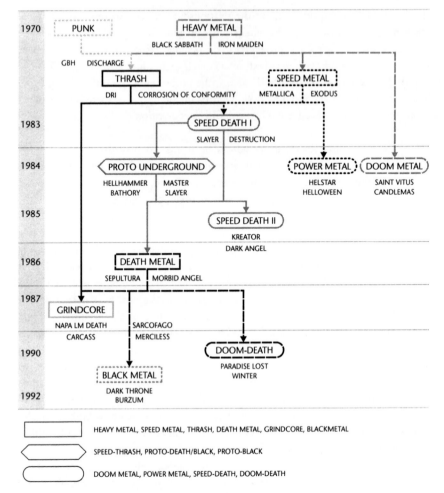

FIGURE 2.1 Heavy metal genres

Source: Back Legions Archive at anus.com

statement: 'Brief Description of Metal Genres, as they are used as a reviewing and classification tool'. It admits, as perhaps all genre labellers would, that 'This cannot be a comprehensive listing of all the genres ever named or postulated', but the question is, where do you go from there? For fanencyclopediadom the answer is always 'Forward with increased determination', but we are more concerned that in the midst of so many trees the wood might be lost. It is easier then for us to appreciate those attempts that have a little more perspective. Considering Heavy Metal, 'in our time' ('as the hawk sees it or the helmeted airman' are Auden's memorable words). the Back Legions Archive (at anus.com) offers something much more useful: a genealogy:

This aspect of the textual event is question rather than answer, multiple rather than hybrid, multi-modal and multi-dimensional. It is about participation rather than belonging, performance rather than production, allowing rather than describing. The fact that texts exceed our expectations reinforces this and defines it as an act of emancipation, and emancipations, as Marx suggested, return the world to us (Marx and Engels, 1978: 46).

This process works itself out through the contradictions of form and content, of expectation and performance, of purity and contamination all across the rainy, stony world, for genre is indeed ubiquitous and 'in nature'. What follows is no structured survey of 'genre today', nor is it like Derrida's piece 'a re-reading of the entire history of genre theory' (1980: 59). Rather it is an engagement in four 'waves' with Derrida's arguments and significant circulating narratives of genre within the subject, always with the desire to maintain the problematic.

He do the police in many voices

> Genre is what we collectively believe it to be.
>
> *(Tudor in Neale, 1999: 18)*

> Every text participates in one or several genres; there is no genreless text.
>
> *(Derrida, 1980: 65)*

The problem of genre is that in most senses it is not really a problem. 'Genre' is in itself an imprecision, a rough category though always promising more, a hint of genus, and something more scientific, but genre has not yet had its Linnaeus. Dix suggests that 'Genre usefully breaks up the generalised stuff of narrative into recognised patterns organised by choices', but this is hardly the description of the operation of a powerful critical tool (1980). When Alan Williams (1984) asked, 'Is a Radical Genre criticism possible?' his answer was more Aristotle than avant-garde, returning as he did to literary style modes of address: narrative, experimental and documentary. Certainly the absolutism of the 'golden thread' argument, that genre gave the clearest account of the dependent relationship between producers, texts and spectators, has substantially less purchase in a context where hybridity is the order of the day. Like cultures, genres develop and decay unless unnaturally preserved 'out of time'. This is partly a matter of recognising that the approach Altman labels 'semantic' (1999) has run its course. It cannot any more be feasible for the following to function as a serious critical response: 'to call a film a Western is thought of as somehow saying something interesting and important about it' (Tudor in Neale, 1999: 18). This recognition that the taxonomies are of limited use is a vital confession. It does not stop descriptive work on genre classification from going on, but it does relegate this work to its proper subsidiary function, and in doing so relaxes the domination of, for example film criticism, that Jim Collins suggests genre theory has 'enjoyed' (2009). And that is fitting, perhaps, if in this way genre theory came into media studies via film studies and then left by that route.

This crisis, if that is the word, is precipitated by what Tudor calls the 'empiricist dilemma'. This is partly the head-on collision that a dominant structuralist/

semiotic approach to genre has had with history and with notions of the 'interpretative community'. The Todorovian 'natural selections' approach which believes in 'naturally' occurring evidence of generic identity offers a challenging analogy: that the 'organic' essences of media genres are comparable to the 'whiteness' of swans:

> a hypothesis which is based on the observation of a limited number of swans but which informs us that their whiteness is the consequence of an organic characteristic would be perfectly legitimate.
>
> *(Todorov in Altman, 1999: 6)*

In fact Todorov is to go much further with 'this general scientific truth', which he argues 'applies not only to the study of genres but also to a writer's entire oeuvre, or that of a specific period' (ibid.). Leaving aside questions about how exactly the whiteness of swans approximates to, for example, the essential formats of television game shows and who will be responsible for defining well-known genres, Todorov's approach has more fundamental problems.

First, there is a central paradox (Tudor's 'empiricist dilemma'). If genres are 'scientifically' established by the gathering of evidence across a number of texts, how do we, in principle, know either the critical criteria or the relevant texts? Tudor nails this one:

> These writers, and almost all writers using the term genre, are caught in a dilemma. They are defining a western on the basis of analyzing a body of films that cannot possibly be said to be westerns until after the analysis.
>
> *(Neale, 1999: 18)*

Moreover a focus here on inherent qualities, which are assumed to be naturally occurring within the genre text compounds a traditional fixation with form which goes back to Aristotle. In this way genre becomes an unwitting (though often willing) substitute for Saussure's 'linguistic community' as a context for 'meanings'. This conveniently allows the meanings of texts to be discussed without reference to specific audiences, as if genres were neutral constructs. Even the mythic readings of genres prompted by the work of Levi-Strauss offer only negotiations of 'audience needs' found in the narrative structures of the texts themselves rather than out of active readings of them. And with the 'interpretative community', as Rick Altman calls it, goes History (Altman, 2003).

Altman makes clear the inevitable issues associated with a structuralist approach to genre: the search for pattern, 'the figure in the carpet', is scrutiny not interaction. A science, as Aristotle himself was aware, can only be as accurate as its subject, in this case of its subjectivity.

Preferring narrative to narration, system to process and histoire to discourse, the first semiotics ran into a set of restrictions and contradictions (Altman, 2003: 29).

Genre, home of the metanarrative

The notion of 'the golden thread', the expediency of which has done more than most to maintain genre as a key term for a complacent generation of media students, is of course predicated on that notion of 'the media' that this book intends to put out of its misery. It explains Stam's concern about the 'Hollywoodcentric' nature of genre criticism as a criticism that starts with producers and production (in Dix, 2008: 164). Genre is something 'the media' do, either for us or to us depending on whether you prefer the 'ritual' or ideological' model of the producers' relationship with their audiences.

The troubles with genre study start with it being very old and yet not moving on, and continue through its problematic relationship with 'history' – its own and ours. Altman is generous when he says that 'The debate over genre has consistently taken place in slow motion' (1999: 1). In some cases it has barely taken place, and establishing a critical consensus has proved impossible or at least irrelevant. Among the discipline's significant approaches and key concepts, genre has proved most resistant to genuine dialogue.

Given that it is the function of criticism to enable a full-scale dialogue to take place about how, in Terry Hawkes's words, 'all of our experience is coded for us ultimately by our total way of life' (1977: 104), genre is at times more than just a disappointment. To understand how, it may be useful to consider the descriptions that Habermas offers of genuine communication (or 'communicative action ' as he calls it) and of the 'systems' we create to enable and support it. Genre criticism, like all of the approaches offered in this book, operates as what Habermas would understand as a system, a way of connecting people up who are going through the process of reaching understandings about the world. Habermas talks also of 'relief mechanisms' which 'either condense or replace mutual understandings in language' (Myerson, 2003: 157). He is referring primarily to communication media, but this is also a more than adequate model of critical approaches in all disciplines: they distil and organise the state of a discourse in order to make better spaces in which genuine communication can occur. This makes perfect sense – clarifying the 'issue' of genre should make engagement with texts and their worlds (theirs and ours) more productive.

However, Habermas foresaw a danger with systems, which is also a potential reading of genre study. He argued that systems have a tendency, if unchecked, to take on lives of their own, to become ends in themselves. Habermas calls this process 'the uncoupling of system and lifeworld', by which he means that systems become divorced from what they are meant to be serving – our shared sense of the significance of human actions. Thus rather than allowing us better access to an open interaction with mediated experiences, a system like genre merely occupies us in rule-governed activities – in empty formal exercises and in the categorising of rather than engaging with experiences. The fact that much genre work operates independently of audiences as interpretative communities and thus notionally outside a substantial historical context compounds this. In such a state, systems become, according to Habermas, 'pathological' – harmful to those endeavours that they are meant to be relieving and enabling.

Moretti stresses the hypothetical status of genres, calling them 'temporary structures' and stressing the historical dimension. He argues that genres are 'of their time' and regularly replaced: 'a genre exhausts its possibilities – and the time comes to give a competitor a chance' (Dix, 2009: 182). For Moretti this is a matter of representation rather than popularity/audience response. Genres quite simply lose the ability they once had to represent 'the most significant aspects of contemporary reality'. Thus they remain 'Janus-like creatures with one face turned to history and the other to form' (Dix, 2009: 178).

We are dealing with judgements that are not regulated by categories. In Lyotard's terms, 'I judge. But if I am asked by what criteria do I judge, I will have no answer to give' (1985: 14). This negotiation is strongly evident in the work of Ryall, who argues (2007) for a tighter reading of genre as a critical concept in order that genre might perform its primary function: the defining of limits and establishing areas of liminality. Ryall seeks not purism but rather a working model, however crude – for him this boils down to the 'consciousness' of genre in the minds of makers and spectators. This is a step beyond classification, it has to do with how an individual text 'plays' in a specific set of contexts (Ryall, 2007: 101–3).

These contexts are cultural, since genre is a situated concept. They are also personal, professional, aesthetic and social, and are collectively contributing to a common cultural consensus. Tudor argues that 'Genre notions are sets of cultural conventions', the collective responsibility of those whom Altman calls the 'interpretative community' (distributers, reviewers and critics alongside directors, writers and audience members). Put simply, 'Genre is what we collectively believe it to be': the focus is cultures, not texts (which is an emancipation of sorts). It is also a reminder that, in Steve Neale's words, 'all instances of discourse are encountered in some kind of context', which is another way of saying – as Gee does – that 'there is no reading in general'. Thus genre remains indispensable because we have made it so.

This to some extent 'respools' the 'golden thread' narrative which we rehearsed earlier though with a very different focus and flavour. Rather than 'the media' (and what it does to us) we have a focus on enculturation and what Gledhill calls the 'intertextual relay' between interpreters and texts (Dix, 2009: 172). Rather than genres as sets of conventions and simple expectations, they become, in Altman's memorable phrase, 'an always incomplete series of superimposed generic maps' (Dix, 2009: 171). The plurality of this is key, though not merely as a way to address hybridity – that particular bane of structuralists and semioticians.

Rather this 'series' of 'maps' reminds us of the self-reflexivity and performativity of texts, which, according to Derrida, always exceed our expectations of them. For better or worse the meaning of a text lies in its 'narration' in its telling itself, and of itself: As Hawkes says 'narration equals life … absence of narration is death' (1977: 100). It is in these moments only that Derrida's much quoted dictum, 'there is no genreless text' is true, since the generic identity is an aspect of the text's performance rather than its identity. There is no membership, no 'belonging' but equally no performance is possible without the text submitting to the state of 'being generic'. Thus though texts may flaunt individual genres, they cannot, for Derrida, take liberties with the law of genre.

The law of the law of genre

> Making genre its mark, a text demarcates itself.
>
> *(Derrida, 1980: 65)*

It is pertinent to note that the most often quoted segment of Derrida's critical set-piece is 'there is no genreless text', or its companion 'a text cannot belong to no genre'. In either case it is a single clause in a lengthy and dense dissertation on genre. In addition, there may be recourse to 'Every text participates in one or several genres' and a discussion about hybridity or bricolage (ibid.). These are particular readings. The much-quoted region is archly a moment of simplicity in the midst of a particularly elliptical passage in which Derrida explains how the 'mark' of genre, its specific trait, while identifying a text is nevertheless not a component of what it identifies, how it 'belongs without belonging'. And all this in the blink of an eye: 'The eyelid closes, but barely, an instant among instants' (ibid.).

It is at this moment that Derrida breaks off to deliver these palatable moments of clarity that have proved so quotable. They are presented as an aside with a good deal of affectation. 'To formulate it in the scantiest manner', he quips/teases, 'the simplest but most apodictic —'and then declaims, 'I submit for your consideration the following hypothesis.' He is clearly waiting for us to bite, working as he is both in and out of the genre of defence speech, of philosophical discourse, of critical essay, leaving open the possibility that is always there, demonstrating his theme. There are barely three sentences before the paradoxes begin again to pop. 'A text cannot belong to no genre, it cannot be without or less a genre. Every text participates in one or several genres, there is no genreless text; there is always a genre and genres, yet such participation never amounts to belonging' (ibid.).

The study of genre in *subject media* has a track record for 'cutting and running' with critics more interested in staking their claim than exploring the terrain. A careful edit might epitomise what this important theorist thinks about genre. Thus we get little of 'it cannot be without or less a genre' and practically nothing of 'participation never amounts to belonging'. Instead we get a blanket endorsement of all manner of genre studies merely on the basis that all texts are genred and therefore theoretically await classification. Thus Derrida's problematising of genre-study is reduced to a casual remark about 'one or several genres' which in itself is subsumed into an often superficial free for all surrounding a supposedly postmodern sensibility which is hyperconscious, intertextual and hybrid.

Derrida is insistent that his role is merely to provide witnesses in the form of exemplary texts, though he further raises the stakes by adding that 'I am convinced fundamental rights are bound up in all of this', and ultimately that 'the law itself is at stake' (1980:). And so it goes on his experience that 'does not constitute a text ipsofacto as 'literature''' this 'rereading of the entire history of genre-theory'. And all the way the form remains 'in the way', insisting almost on a process of rearticulation but certainly ironising and problematising so as to enable and insist on a symptomatic reading. In calling ingenuously for 'a common trait' identifiable in 'a given textual event' and then casually conflating 'genre, type, mode, form', Derrida is subtly forcing us to confront fundamental issues about genre in a new light, a context in which genre is perhaps now merely subject rather than 'subjector'/ruler. He has already pointed out the 'benefits' of these genre identifications since they are 'authorizing us to determine, to adjudicate whether a given text belongs to this genre or perhaps that genre'. Derrida's response to this is encoded in 'This may seem 'trivial' (1980: 64).

What then about the absence of generic marks? Derrida submits this as an 'axiomatic question', and then proceeds to explore it in the most impassioned sequence of the speech. Even so it functions more than adequately as a survey of much of the interesting work being dug out of that overworked pit, genre. Rather than prescription we get licence; rather than constriction we get opportunity. Derrida offers two broad guidelines or understandings for authenticating 'discursive art' in the contexts of genre:

- a recognition of the multi-modality of texts: 'it is possible to have several genres, an intermixing of genres or a total genre, the genre 'genre' or the poetic or literary genre as genre of genres'.
- a recognition of the multi-dimensionality of genre: 'this (generic) re-mark can take on a great number of forms and can itself pertain to highly diverse types' (Derrida, 1980).

The deconstruction here is of 'techne', of the explicit and artificial 'norms and interdictions' which Derrida evokes from the beginning. We are challenged as much by what is stripped away as we are by the intense dexterity of the reasoning. The effect of the generic code and its mark, Derrida argues, enables participation but prevents belonging. Ergo, 'genre-designations cannot be simply part of the corpus' (Derrida, 1980: 65). Rather they are a function of the situatedness of the text and how it performs. And this is where Derrida is: with text in context in the act of becoming. This designation 'gathers together the corpus and, at the same time, in the same blinking of an eye, keeps it from closing, from identifying itself with itself'. Derrida writes of 'an inclusion and exclusion with regard to genre in general' being placed 'within and without the work, along its boundary' like a two-way hinge. 'Genre in general is a debilitating idea in the context of an idea that only pages before was drawing limits as soon as it was 'sounded': 'the word "genre", the figure, the voice' (Derrida, 1980: 65).

To some extent we are talking about a regendering of genre, or at least a regendering of 'the law', and that is the final paradox of the Derrida intervention.

He alerts us to the extra levels of subtlety in French over genre and gender: 'the semantic scale of genre is much larger and more expansive than in English and thus always includes within its reach the gender' (1980: 74). These are not propositional but illocutionary and perlocutionary issues, matters of force and effect. The patriarchal nuances of 'heavyweight' intellectual interventions with a concern for 'the law' here reach their apotheosis and then emasculation. This law of which Derrida speaks is no law of appropriation, of classification of taxidermy, it is no imposition. Rather it is '*la loi*' – a spirit of licence, flexibility madness: it is chiasma, membrane, boundary, hymen. Classifications are for users, not authorities: 'fandom' as Jenkins rightly points out 'generates its own genres' (Dix, 2009: 174). But it does so at no one else's expense, as a matter of empowerment rather than power. In undermining the 'power over' practised by media institutions and academic critics alike, Derrida is offering a recognisably feminist model for empowering himself and all of us, the power to engender meanings in flexibly generic arrangements.

Having returned genre to nature, Derrida is able formally to free it from the tyranny of form, whilst maintaining its central position in the way texts read and are read. He is also offering a powerful model of genre as a multi-dimensional phenomenon, twenty years before Neale declared it as a prerequisite for a serious examination of genre in Hollywood. And yet, in its clinging to an 'applicable' law of genre in its conceptual frame, media studies – with *subject English* – looks still upon the most (theoretically) barren of landscapes.

Finding the glee in *Glee*

> When *Glee* works – which is often – it is transcendent, tear-jerking and thrilling like nothing else on TV.
>
> *(James Poniewozik, Time magazine)*

> Before long, issues of pregnancy will assail both generations, giving birth to subplots that become so credulity-straining it's hard not to yearn for another song to relieve them.
>
> *(Brian Lowry, Variety)*

But what does this mean in practical terms, as shaping, leading or enabling discussions about media products and practices? Take *Glee*, for example, the stand-out television hit of the 2009–10 season. Here is a show conceived as a film, rescripted for television, picked up by Fox within 15 hours of receiving the scripts and then picked up for a third series only moments after the first series had finished airing. Add to this all songs from the show available on iTunes before transmission, regular compilation albums, all of which contributed to the fact that in 2009, the *Glee* cast had 25 singles chart on the Billboard Hot 100, the most by any artist since the Beatles had 31 songs in the chart in 1964 (wikipedia). The season one finale, 'Journey', was watched by an estimated 13.7 million on US television, doubling the number it had at its mid-point hiatus. It has generated all manner of 'critical chatter'; reviews, appreciations, Gleek clubs (fandom), reminiscences, all manner of marketing opportunities. But what are we to make of it?

> *Glee* is a musical comedy-drama television series that airs on Fox in the United States. The pilot episode of the show was broadcast after *American Idol* on May 19, 2009, and the first season began airing on September 9, 2009. On September 21, 2009, Fox officially gave the series a full-season pick-up. *Glee* aired its mid-season finale on December 9, 2009 and returned from a four-month hiatus on April 13, 2010, picking up the remaining nine episodes of the season. The spring premiere had an estimated 13.7 million viewers, nearly doubling in followers on its return.
>
> *(wikipedia)*

> From Ryan Murphy, the creator of 'Nip/Tuck,' comes GLEE, a new comedy for the aspiring underdog in all of us.
>
> *(Fox site)*

> All the episodes, we're writing them thematically .... And also, with every episode, we do between five and eight music numbers, and my goal is to really try and give the audience something for everybody. We have a hip-hop. We have an R&B. We have a top 40. We have country.
>
> *(accessed on: hollywoodchicago.com/news)*

> @JKoscheck
> This episode is calling Journey so it was both a journey of how they came to Regionals and so they sang Journey songs! :)
>
> *(YouTube)*

> @sherbear158 but if they had won what would have been the point of them getting a second chance the next year. them loosing made you want even more to stay and watch the rest of the episode and see what happens to them.
>
> *(YouTube)*

> 'It's a 9 p.m. show, it's not designed for 8,' he said. 'But it is designed for families to watch together. This is a different genre, there's nothing like it on the air at the networks and cable. Everything's so dark in the world right now, that's why 'Idol' worked. It's pure escapism.'
>
> *(Ryan Murphy interview on Variety Entertainment News,*
> *posted: Wed. 23 July 2008, 6:00 pm PT)*

The new series, 'Glee,' a high school musical that casts both a sceptical eye and a dreamy gaze on the world of competitive show choirs, will have its debut on Tuesday in one of the most coveted time slots on television: after the final performance episode of 'American Idol.'

(Edward Wyatt, 15 May 2009)

'I wanted to do a sort of postmodern musical,' he said. 'Fox was not interested, and neither was I, in doing a show where people burst into song. People do sing, of course, but there are rules: the singers will have to be onstage rehearsing or performing, or a song will come in the form of a fantasy in a character's head'.

(Ryan Murphy, www.nytimes.com/2009/05/17/arts/television/17wyat.html, accessed on 12 December 2010)

It's very easy to find generic classifications of *Glee* and to be drawn into engaging discussions with them. The Internet Movie Database (IMDB), which has 'genre' as a prompt (rather than up for discussion) declares *Glee* 'Comedy | Drama | Music' and the *See more* tab alongside 'Music' leads to a revealing list of thematic 'connections', dubbed 'Plot keywords' for *Glee*:

High School ★ Teacher ★ Gay Teenager ★ High School Principal ★ Infidelity ★ Cheerleader ★ Audition ★ Musical Performance ★ Indian American ★ Coach ★ Marriage ★ School Counsellor ★ Dance ★ Teenage Girl ★ Teenage Boy ★ Outcast ★ Gay Interest ★ Teen ★ Singing ★ Boyfriend Girlfriend Relationship ★ Geek ★ Glee Club ★ Student Athlete ★ Competition ★ Wheelchair ★ Multicultural ★ Friendship

(IMDB)

This is revealing because it confirms a tendency to see the meaning or at least the substance of a text as a 'culmination' of its content 'elements', with genre at worst merely seen as a set of headings to be given to specific content lists or sublists. It does not attempt to enter the discussions captured above within and between the various constituencies that *Glee* might impact: creators, producers, fans, critics, cultural commentators, encyclopedias, even those who do not watch the show (who for a show this popular and talked about are often themselves positioned by it). Nor does this desire to classify by content take account of any of the other issues that a simple trawl of responses reveals: issues of scheduling, of genealogies outside of established generic codes (*Glee*'s hitching' onto *American Idol* in more than just a launch slot), of contemporary socio-cultural values (the cult of the underdog), of socio-historical contexts and movements (the postmodern musical, the dynamics of 'family' entertainment), even ideas about the meanings of traditional genres may have interest (Dyer, 1992: 18 on the utopianism of the musical for example). The point is to engage and engage the text in these circulating discourses which ultimately work to site texts and provide them with tentative generic identities.

We are moving dramatically from dealing with pre-categorised texts, in order to confirm they are what you think they are, to engaging with what Mittell calls 'culturally circulating generic practices that categorize texts': means not ends. Put simply, it is the arguments about 'genre' that are at issue here, including our discussions about what it does rather than what it is, for as the playwright Bertolt Brecht maintained 'Zeigen ist mehr als sein' ('to show' is more important than 'to be'). If we are to engage meaningfully with both the concept 'genre' and a range of contemporary, often hybrid, texts we need to embrace this paradigm shift. Mittell sums it up this way:

> By regarding genre as a property and function of discourse we can examine the ways in which various forms of communication work to constitute generic definitions, meanings and values within particular historical contexts.
>
> *(Mittell, 2004: 12)*

This equally means considering genre not as a singularity but as a multiplicity, a series of contingencies which become more or less feasible. *Glee* has a postmodern sensibility in its broad use of parody and pastiche, in its joyous participation in the implosion of cultural forms (there is no homage here to the classical Hollywood musical), in its cultivation of a hyper-reality. *Glee* taps a contemporary sensibility. Particularly in its use of real-life celebrities as themselves (in the way Ricky Gervais used them in *Extras* to deconstruct their celebrity) and the paratextual reality of twenty-five singles in the charts, the show has made it its business to explore notions of simulation and of simulacra, images without originals. When we engage critically with the show, as we must, these are the energies that emerge, of a text with multiple identities teeming with ideas and fully integrated if unstable.

This is where Derrida comes in to help us to go the extra yard. In inviting us to deconstruct the text Derrida is effectively allowing us to address its hybridity as so much more than a combination of one thing and the other. In a dispensation where everything is deferred, so too everything is fully engaged. There are no half measures here. There are no musical dramas where neither music nor drama are explored but rather a kind of alchemy where generic identities form part of a broader engagement with context, where participation is never half-hearted, nor classification ever enough (or possible?).

A simple example might suffice, though a highly charged one: *Glee*'s season one finale, 'Journey', and specifically Quinn's labour and subsequent birth unwittingly played out to Queen's song 'Bohemian Rhapsody' as performed by their rivals. At this point and at various points throughout each show all the elements converge and 'are frolic'! At these points everything is at stake as the text is striving to both be contained and break free of its structural and linguistic limitations. In Derrida's terms the dangers are 'anomaly, impurity and monstrosity', easily transplantable to any show that takes significant risks (or plays it safe), but also for Derrida there is a world to win. For within Derrida's dispensation *Glee* is, crudely variety show and melodrama and satire and broad comedy and maybe even musical: all of these, all of the time. These are grafted – not combined or merely mixed. Five to one and one to five, in the blink of an eye: all or nothing. No, all and nothing.

Derrida's claim that 'every text participates in one or several genres' is a useful starting point here since it implicitly takes issue with Ryan Murphy's rather contrived intention to write a 'sort of postmodern musical'. Both Fox and the writer, Murphy implies, wanted 'rules'. For Derrida this is both unavoidable, since genres are negotiations of rules and paradoxical, since for him 'The law is mad, is madness'. As 'Journey' (and all of its 'journeys') comes literally to its end, so its identities play themselves out in a moment-by-moment continual renegotiation of their identity. Even the relationship between diegetic and non-diegetic elements remains unstable.

This text is interested in the energy generated by *High School Musical*, by *The X Factor* and *American Idol*, by reality television, by YouTube covers and tribute bands, by iPods and the politics of inclusion. These elements are folded in and 'cooked on gas'! Here is a plausible 'talent' competition with 'real' celebrity judges judging fictional characters underscored by the 'history of pop' soundtrack, which itself at the time of broadcast was riding high in the charts. Here two school Performing Arts groups compete: the pumped-up, barely legal-sounding 'Vocal Adrenaline' vies with 'our Team', a promise of 'New Directions'. This competition happens across a series of generic contexts which each increase or lessen the chances of 'a result'. Queen's 'hybrid' chart outrage of 1975 provides an astonishingly extensive experience since its multiplicity adds to the fun and horror of it. As the song itself changes genres in the blink of an eye, so it moves evenly inside and outside the action as both pure performance and sometimes spiteful commentary.

In the sequences which describe pregnant cheerleader Quinn's arrival at the hospital ward, which seem to visually awaken memories of everything from *ER* to *Carry On Nurse*, the Queen lyric sets an ironic tone by juxtaposing being born and dying. It also sets the formal karaoke (complete with pink shirts) going on back in the hall into a particular context, though not with the intention of undermining it. Ultimately two genres are being more than juxtaposed: their narratives and themes are shared within our experiences: hope for Quinn and New Directions meets in our hopes and expectations: two into one will not go.

Rather than a resolution the sequence chooses to instead offer a collision (or maybe 'elision') as Quinn screams 'shut up' and 'you suck' before succumbing to the intrusive pain at the very point the soundtrack and screen are filled with Vocal Adrenaline's virtuoso phallocentric lead guitarist. The intrusion of the 'rock video' and black comedy is almost bathetic and then is indeed bathetic, as the talent show audience pay glo-stick homage to 'Rock as cock' just as Quinn reaches the next stage and prepares to evacuate the invaginated denouement to the scene, episode and season. The different intensities and modes are here emblematic of the vacillation of the text: 'easy come easy go!' Quinn or win? And all this is stylised, its mode dramatic over realistic every time.

For us as for Quinn there is a significant release. In the best traditions we are returned to our world as 'mere' spectators: left at the back of the auditorium with Rachel ahead of us, providing a glee-less 'New Directions' point of view. The song ends 'Any way the wind blows' but by then we don't need a weather forecaster to know which way the wind is blowing. Quinn is unconvincingly recently 'birthed' but more than convincingly happy and *Glee* is once more merely a 'hybrid', a formal bricolage of generic features. And we are sent off to think and reflect. Only here, up to our necks in text but also fully immersed in the wider world, the cultural context, at the point where our ability to say it in words deserts us do we fully experience the text as performed (and particularly) and performing at what Derrida calls 'this flood-gate of genre'. And at that 'moment when genre is broached, at that very moment … the end begins'.

In this chapter we have dealt with the reliance of genre on singularity and what we can only describe as the strange privilege granted to the concept in media education. Removing 'the media' from genre is relatively straightforward, providing we can situate bricolage as a starting point. Oddly, whilst at first it might seem obvious that a focus on multiplicity would render genre redundant, in the working-through of this a reversal occurs, lending to genre a purpose and a clarity in its very dismantling and resurrection in the guise of the 'textual event'. Having arrived at such an unexpected destination, in the next chapter we ask the same questions of representation.

3

REPRESENTATION AFTER THE MEDIA

The notion of 'representation' is one of the founding principles of media education. The media do not offer us a transparent 'window' on the world, but a mediated version of the world. They don't just present reality, they re-present it.

(Buckingham, 2003: 57)

Representation is an enclosure built on the strength of an exclusion.

(Bennington, 1988: 14)

Buckingham's statement is unproblematic as a description of the 'order of things' in media studies which, in its proximal relation to *subject English*, has stoically preserved the concept of the representing text. Bennington, interpreting Lyotard, helps us to consider how this 'founding principle' has aided us in avoiding our 'jouissance' – the inevitable encounter with the absence of our 'real' – the exclusion. As such, media studies fails to bear witness to that awkward part of the modern (the postmodern) – the acceptance of the 'something missing', and again, we will argue that the idea of 'the media' is the obscuring apparition. Media studies has ignored the 'incommensurability' of representation (Belsey, 2005: 127) and thus the always-already retrospection of itself, of the rules of its scrutiny – of 'the media' and the world 'they' represent.

To put it simply, reality is never directly 'itself'; it presents itself only via its incomplete-failed symbolization and spectral apparitions emerge in this very gap that forever separates reality from the real, and on account of which reality has the character of a (symbolic) fiction.

(Zizek, 1999: 74)

Back to culture

In *Cultural Studies Goes to School* (1994), Buckingham and Sefton–Green explicitly accounted for ways in which young people in schools were able to explore the politics of identity through various pedagogic strategies aimed at 'making sense of the media'. Here, then, was a range of examples of the integration of cultural studies and media education, English and interventions as responses to 'mass' culture. The main argument made is for a removal of the insulations and classifications surrounding categories of culture and textuality, and therefore that whether a subject is called media studies, English literature or cultural studies, its practitioners ought to deal with the culture which students are engaging with and distance themselves from models of 'enrichment' based on outdated and conservative agendas for cultural reproduction. We agree, and if anything feel that *After the Media* is returning to this argument with the advantage of 'Media 2.0' (see Chapter 7) having eroded these insulations for us. At the same time, we are not postulating a binary which would serve to locate the enrichment discourse at the furthest point from an alternative, more 'progressive' approach – this would serve as a grand narrative and undermine our project. Rather, the place of media taste within the lifeworld of students must also be a matter for reflection, and subject to challenge and being made unfamiliar through critical work.

Buckingham and Sefton–Green deal explicitly with representation in an account of research conducted with students in a Tottenham school (in London, England) who were engaging, through production work, with theories of stereotyping set against the creation of positive images of minority groups. The students' refusal to engage in 'serious' academic discussion of their own highly parodic work (Slutmo) in relation to theories of gender representation by disclaiming it as 'having a laugh' (1994: 190) is a central discussion point in the account. The female student, Zerrin, who constructs, and accounts for in a highly personal evaluation, 'Slutmopolitan' is too complicated for the academic insulations that frame her work and the attendant measuring of the reflective mode:

> Broadly speaking, we would argue that the experience of the Slutmopolitan project gave Zerrin an unrivalled opportunity to explore issues of gender and sexuality on both a personal and wider social level. Yet what is puzzling is the extent to which the project 'empowers' Zerrin – whatever we might take that to mean. And what is even more difficult to ascertain is the kind of 'media learning' that might be going on here (and the relationship of that learning to any kind of empowerment). If Zerrin cannot disentangle the levels of parody and power explicitly in her own writing, what can one claim for the educational value of the activity? Of course, this question raises a secondary one: the educational value for whom?
>
> *(Buckingham and Sefton-Green, 1994: 198–9).*

Quite a lot of what we want to argue about *subject media* as a distortion is laid bare in this reading of Zerrin's learning. There are two issues of framing. The first is 'popular media' which provides an objective to be learned about, and thus an ideal for Zerrin to respond to. This is awkward precisely because Zerrin resists the compulsion to neatly account for her own creative material in relation to 'the media' but instead reveals her own complex tapestry of identities which, as Gauntlett shows in his recent work on metaphor and identity (2006), are at most partly influenced by magazines in a dialogic context with a range of other determinants and negotiations. Second, the failure to coherently separate the representation from the subject (the 'me' from the category represented – women in the media) speaks loudly to the idea we started with (from Lyotard) that we are dealing with a fetishised exclusion – the outside, the objective, the Real:

> Her account makes it almost impossible to distinguish between her subjective investment in the project as a piece of self-expression and her objective interest in the project's avowed intent, which is to parody women's magazines.
>
> *(Buckingham and Sefton-Green, 1994: 200)*

As Buckingham and Sefton-Green theorise, this parody as performative but elusive to academic discourse bears witness to Butler's arguments and reveals most clearly the ways in which teachers place more value on certain modes of expression – the ones they can most clearly understand using the idioms of particular language games – than others. In the end these researchers were forced to distinguish between empowerment at the level of the energy students showed in engaging with questions of identity, and the ability of formal education to allow this to 'make any difference' – in the sense that cultural studies was mobilised for social and political change. It seems clear that the idea of 'representation' and the compulsion to account for creative, playful and highly parodic activity in relation to this rather narrow idea (that 'the media' represent people and things in particular ways and that students can choose to 'reinforce or challenge' this through their own) is delimiting. Parody as a starting point allows for a dismantling of the assumptions and internal logics of both discourses of textual value and of existing student media culture.

The real

Media students usually experience the concept of representation chronologically, from ideology through structuralism to postmodernism. The notion, then, that representation might be an unsatisfactory tool to be working with is reduced ultimately to a kind of extension activity for those still paying attention. Pragmatically, it is also clearly much simpler to separate representation from reality and to comment on the relationship between the two. This also reinforces the idea that 'the media' are powerful – they can influence how we see the world – and legitimises a derided discipline. Ironically, the double determination of this discourse unravels itself – the derision rests on the notion that the media are powerful (and thus education should be an antidote to them). For Lacan, the real is absent to the subject but exists – it is external to us, but we believe in it. Media studies, then, is Lacanian in the sense that 'the media' are fetishised as being responsible for the absence of the real – we live in a media-saturated hyper-reality, and we must account for this academically and by theorising the media that we create. The desire to unmask reality may be impossible, but the aspiration lingers – beyond representation, there is something to represent. Behind Kafka's door there is an absent law, but the absence of it makes it imaginable if unreachable.

> The lesson of modernism is that the structure, the intersubjective machine, works as well if the Thing is lacking, if the machine revolves around an emptiness; the postmodernist reversal shows the Thing itself as the incarnated, materialized emptiness.
>
> *(Zizek, 1999: 43)*

The real of media studies must be what justifies itself in all its symbolic manifestations, and these, being compelled to avoid the painful suggestion of non-reference, must look to an absence beyond 'the media' and media studies itself. Like English, this is presented as a scrutiny of the mediation of the real, of everything through and beyond symbolisation, either as straightforwardly as is done by Barthes (1977) on signs, or in a more complex and fluid account, what Hills (2005) calls 'textualized agency'. Either way, media studies understands itself in various ways as the other of 'the media'. Subject media wrestles with this question of what to be, with its *dasein* – its specific modes of being in practices. Elsewhere, we have explored the dynamics of this Lacanian view of subject identity in relation to the arrangement of media in English as a curriculum strand:

> We can characterize the difference between Symbolic and Real and the effort to address the Real as the operation of desire at work in the subject. To cut a long story of interpellation and professional identity short, it is this relation that motivates the determination of the subject and the affiliation to specific versions of subject identity by practitioners.
>
> *(McDougall and Peim, 2007: 304)*

The Lacanian distinction between the symbolic and the real locates the latter as beyond or outside of the former, the crude, unrefined (but elusive) reality that escapes the mediation of experience. Language situates us in the symbolic order, forever knowing that the real is there, but outside of any experience that we can represent. Subject media desires the assertion of an ideal on behalf of a perception of the desire of the other. Extending this model of symbolising the absent, we can say that there are three 'moments' in the attempt to wrestle with the absent real here. The real of students' culture (the pleasure of media consumption and response) is symbolically reordered into the language game of education. The 'irruption' of media studies into cultural studies is reconciled through a renegotiation of how popular culture is understood in relation to the idea of 'the media' and the signifying practices of 'media texts' are ordered through the application of theoretical concepts in order to legitimise discussion.

Dealing with representation after the media will be to move from Lacan's 'take' on the real to Zizek's. There is a certain convenience in the way that Zizek has used film to do this, but it is necessary to extend the use of popular culture as a 'way in' to Lacan, beyond the relatively canonical products of Hitchcock to a more contemporary videogame, to understand more fully the implications of the status of the real for the study of media representation. Zizek explains the construction of Vera Miles approaching the Bates Motel in *Psycho* (1960) in terms of the combination of subject in motion viewed objectively with a subjectively viewed look at the object (the house) as an 'exemplar' of Lacan's use of view and gaze as a dialectic frame of reference. The anxiety created by Hitchcock through this technique is the sense that the house is already looking at the approaching woman but cannot be seen doing so – absent but in her senses. This gaze of the object cannot be subjectified since this would denote the gaze of another subject – another character, within the conventions of film thrillers. The status of the Bates Motel is aligned to that of the law in Kafka's parable, deconstructed by Derrida, elusive to subjectivity but powerfully objective in absence.

Oscillating (wildly)

> For Derrida, the Dialectic of representation is any conceptual logic, based in binary opposition, with or without a mediating third element, which through negativity and the contradiction of identity and difference brings about a representation, a mimesis productive of Universal Truth, thereby erasing the movement of difference.
>
> *(Jardine, 1985: 131)*

The lip service paid to poststructuralist theory in the broader field of *subject media* does the same violence as the cultural politics of English teaching, as traced by Peim. Thus, as already asserted, we argue that Peim's optimism for media studies as the other of English has been unfounded. How is it that media studies has been unable to think of difference differently, how has it failed to think the unrepresentable when we could be forgiven for assuming that its status, derided, on the margins, like Foucault's 'ship of fools', would afford it the space to resist the 'freezing' scientific impulse of structuralism?

Clearly we are not suggesting that Derrida's *Of Grammatology* (1976) be placed on the reading lists of undergraduate media modules, nor should it become the subject of PowerPoint presentations to cohorts working on animation projects. But the 'spirit' of theories associated with postmodern and post-structuralist writers ought to inform the way that the media curriculum is framed, with particular regard to the privileged status granted to the concept of representation.

Lyotard's most compelling 'model' for reimagining justice through the singularity of the event is the 'differend' – an interaction in which one discourse can only be regulated through the idioms of the other. Just as for Lyotard, a citizen of a communist state constructs a 'differend' the moment they deny that the state is communist, so does a student of media when they deny the existence of 'the media' as a regulatory principle in the academic discourse.

Archives

And so to an exposition on the meta-narrative of representation in media education. We shall select a range of ten very different arrangements of pedagogy to do this – the Canadian version of 'Media Literacy' (as framed by a Jesuit priest); a best-selling textbook used internationally by school and college media students; an article in the UK publication *Times Higher Education* treating the study of 'popular' culture as a curio (in 2010); two contrasting examples of higher education media courses in the United States – a 'pure' production degree and the Comparative Media Studies programme at MIT; a policy statement by the UK regulatory body Ofcom which acts as a framing device for cross-curricular media literacy work (with particular impact on primary education, given the protectionist discourse of the regulator); an undergraduate university module from London on Media Representations of Identity; a US account of a teacher's media literacy work in the classroom and at home with her children; a Danish Ph.D. student's research into videogames and the awkward nature of an object of study that has to be played to exist; and an 'unseen' analysis of a *Doctor Who* extract (discussed in the context of Hills's research on 'fanwork'). These are chosen to maximise engagement with the broadest range of contemporary forms of media education, but of course in being chosen they are not representative, more performative – of ideas and modes of social practice. However, they are tied together by their location on a continuum – the first examples (from 1) are the most strongly classified representatives of 'subject media' and its reductive operations, the latter (to 10) are the most 'after'.

In all cases, the question here will be – what happens if you take the idea of 'the media' out of the equation? And the agenda for so doing is far from frivolous, if we find that the idea of representation by the media of reality in one way or another is, itself, an exercising of power, or to go further, as Jardine (1985: 118–19) claims, 'it has been denounced as complicitous with a violence as old as Western history itself'. The denial of dialectical mimesis in articulations of representation is key to patriarchal, phallocentric and repressive regimes of thinking based on presence and absence. To question the centrality of such a construct in media studies is more than a clever post-structuralist trick with language, rather the gesture is obligatory if we are to return cultural studies to its intended objective – media studies has 'frozen' the dialectic in order to impose a model, with good intentions, but has failed to return to the question in good enough time. At a simple level, we can deride the absence of Derrida and Lacan from 'subject media' in relation to the presence of Althusser and Todorov. This is not to say that the latter two should be removed, but only that they should be accompanied (or chaperoned).

(1) Literacy as protection

Pungente, Duncan and Anderson (2005) describe Canadian media literacy education in celebratory fashion in a compilation of North American reports, contextualised by an opening statement from a Chicago high-school student which apparently serves to 'cement' the need for media literacy education as a rationale for what follows:

> The media can persuade anyone to do something or to think a certain way. It can promote drugs and violence, or it can preach good education and hard work. We learn from the media and we also get sucked into the media. It covers everything – campaigning, fashion, education, and most importantly, life. When I say life, I mean anything that can ever happen to you, from the clothes you wear to regular days at school to walking home from somewhere.
>
> *(Griffin, 2005: 1)*

Doubtless, this is an articulate and reflective statement from a high-school student and we have no intention of being critical. But the insertion of this (the extract here is from a longer piece that deals with the influence of the media on teenage identity in much more detail) at the start of this book without comment is problematic. Its premise (and conceit) – that 'the media' are something to be concerned about and that 'they' can exercise power in the form of persuasion on 'us' is firmly reproduced in Pungente et al's theoretical declarations, which are unreferenced and abstracted from any paradigm or research evidence, such as 'the media construct versions of reality'; 'media messages contain ideological and value messages' and 'each medium has a unique aesthetic form', to identify but three of a much longer list of assumptions (2005: 151) about how 'the media' work and why we must tell students about this so they can know it as well. Importantly, in relation to our objectives, these Canadian agents – including Pungente, a Jesuit priest whose status as such, combined with his work as a broadcaster (within 'the media') has been viewed by many as a potential conflict of interest – root their work firmly in the Birmingham tradition:

> Canadian teachers are, like most informed media educators, participating in an eclectic circus. We are enthusiastic pragmatists, selecting from a rich menu of critical, cultural and educational theories and filtering them for classroom use. There seems to be a consensus about contextualizing media education within the frameworks of the British-inspired cultural studies, an interdisciplinary approach to the construction of knowledge that problematizes texts and representations of gender, race and class.
>
> *(Pungente et al, 2005: 15)*

While Canada is established as a developed nation for media education, there is no formal, assessed qualification in compulsory/further education for studying or producing media 'texts', or exploring industries or issues. England, then, is seen as something of a nirvana by media educators in British Columbia. In the later 1960s, secondary courses set up around 'screen education' were established (similarly to the origins of media studies in England), but no broader study of the media followed until 1987, when Ontario became the first Canadian province to introduce media education in the curriculum, but not as an examined subject. In 1980, the National Film Board worked with a group of teachers of a film literacy programme, manifested in a magazine for teachers on film 'appreciation' and production. In 1984, the Jesuit Communication Project was established, and since then, a great deal of media education activity in Canada has been dominated by Pungente, who has more recently established a strong relationship with the CHUM broadcasting institution, perhaps problematically. In order to be granted a broadcast licence in Canada, an institution must demonstrate a degree of public service activity, and the involvement in media education satisfies this criteria. There are mixed feelings about Pungente's role amongst Canadian teachers. On the one hand, he is an energetic enthusiast for media education, and there is a great deal of activity in Canada (workshops, conferences, a bi-annual summit on media literacy) that would not happen without his involvement. But on the other hand, critics see his close relationship with a major broadcaster and his refusal to take a critical stance on 'the media' in terms of institutional and commercial practices as closely connected. Pungente hosts a television show, *Scanning the Movies*, which is analytical but avoids judgement, leading many to assume that the lack of critique is a result of corporate pressure.

The political and symbolic violence done by the kinds of well-intentioned 'pragmatics' articulated by Pungente above is written into the genealogy of media education and, by unravelling the inconsistencies and 'tricks of light' in such a horizontal discourse, this book will go against the grain of the enthusiastic and philanthropic language game spoken by Pungente. For if we stop for a moment to explore the symbolic power exercised in the objectification of 'the media' and compare it with the category of 'literature' so beloved of English teachers, and yet so alienating and exclusive to many of their students, we can observe a shared effect of social practice which is almost diametrically opposed to the political intentions of 'Cultural Studies 1.0'.

> The idea of literature as a special category worthy of attention in itself, with its own special qualities and specific effects, and its very own modes of engagement is really a very dubious affair. Teachers of English have believed, in a necessary ideological move, that literature really does exist – in itself, somehow – and that it really does have intrinsic qualities that make it worthy of study in itself. They have maintained, one way or another, that literature is generally very good for you, if you're lucky enough – or sensitive enough – to appreciate it. If you're not able to appreciate it this is likely to be due to

innate insensitivity or poor social conditioning, or maybe the general decline
of culture into technological mindlessness and media intoxication.

(Peim, 1993: 176)

Media texts, a term we use under erasure (preferring less 'frozen' ways of
thinking about performance and exchange), are complex and fluid in relation to
who makes them and how they are used and circulated in relation to all the other
aspects of everyday life. The delimiting effect of the idea of 'the media' that
represent is equally essentialist to the idea of representing an external reality. The
preserving of the category '*the* media' as a taken for granted entity to be studied,
that is separate from us – from people – is part of the same 'necessary ideological
move' that Peim observes English teachers making when they decide to believe
that there really is such a thing as literature. Elsewhere (Kendall and McDougall,
2011) we have discussed the discursive operations of the *Richard & Judy Book Club*
as a book club which intervenes in the cultural activities of readers in a seemingly
emancipatory gesture which ultimately serves to reproduce and reinforce the
'schooled' conception of literature as an exclusive and alienating category to be
admired and appreciated from a distance:

> It seems that the Richard & Judy Book Club potentially offers a different
> framing to traditional classificatory relations of reading because of its
> relatively weak indexing to schooled regimes of 'distinction' and the
> subsequent lack of insulation. Here potentially is a much 'freer' paradigm
> within which ways of being as a reader and thinking/talking about reading
> might be re-thought. The book club offers the potential to be about
> 'undoing', yet the readers' notes, as a pedagogical technology (in Bernstein's
> terms) seem to undermine the potential for reflexive ways of thinking about
> reading and the practice of reading together for pleasure because they 'steer'
> (back) towards a more conventional paradigm of reading/being a reader.
>
> *(Kendall and McDougall, 2010)*

The same degree of conservative undermining of apparent potential to disrupt
the order of things is apparent in the ways that 'the media' are framed for study.
The shift, of course, is that the enrichment discourse that circulates around
literature asserts a value judgement – that studying literature is culturally 'healthy'
(in comparison with the other cultural material we have access to, which are,
either explicitly or by inference, devalued). But a different version of the same
discourse asserts a negative value on 'the media' – we need to study them because
they are potentially harmful or at best distracting. In this neat and seemingly
neutral (but extraordinarily powerful) move in the game, *subject media* is constructed
as an annex to *subject English* – a different route to the same, ultimately exclusive,
transference of categories. And, operating entirely within the idioms of this
language game, when cultural studies turned its lens onto 'mass media' it wandered
down a blind alley and compromised beyond repair its ability to theorise everyday

life adequately, becoming little more than a complicit agent in the preservation of a hierarchical view of literacy which is still very much reproducing itself today in the streaming of 'less academic' students into media classrooms and the proliferation of a protectionist model of 'media literacy' (demarcated as other than traditional literacy and often reduced to little more than online competences and 'e-safety').

(2) Teachers, parents, protection

Crockett (2005) describes media literacy as a 'tool' for the promotion of critical thinking and values. In keeping with the language game in which Ofcom works, images of students being 'bombarded' by the media are conjured up in her account. What is different, though, is this report's deliberate merging of teacher and parent identity (these are often problematically divided in media education, especially with reference to videogames):

> As a parent, I am especially concerned about the value messages, unrealistic body images, and false representations of 'reality' to which my children are exposed. I want them to recognise values that are important to us as a family, and recognise when these values may be skewed by the media.
>
> *(Crockett, 2005: 270)*

Hills's 'network of discourse' (see the discussion of 'fan-work' that follows) is immediately relevant here. While a general value system of respect for diversity and social justice is inferred in the account, there is no more specific mapping of which particular values (that exist 'before' contact with 'the media') are to be compared with the distorting actions of media. Nobody is going to argue against the importance of discussing body image, advertising and other powerful aspects of culture with the author's children, but how this relates to a public sphere consensus about literacy is never addressed. Throughout all of the examples of both the classroom and family media literacy work, the problematic ideal of enlightenment and truth/falsehood dominates. The media do things. 'They' have commercial agendas and these carry with them representational biases. Everyday life is affected by this, but seems to exist outside of it. It seems odd that such a profoundly uncritical, untheoretical view of contemporary culture and identity should form the basis of this project:

> 'For me, the heart or crux of media literacy is to lessen children's vulnerability and increase their abilities to make responsible media choices. It is about teaching them to think critically'.
>
> *(Crockett, 2005: 270).*

(3) University (production)

The International Academy of Design and Technology in Detroit provide a degree in Digital Media Production (http://www.iadtdetroit.com/programs/digitalmedia.asp). This course is at the other end of media education's meandering spectrum from the media element of GCSE English in the United Kingdom, sitting as it does at the far extreme of the theory/practice divide, if such a distinction can be maintained in the age of convergence culture. The value of the course is described in the promotional material as 'what can't be learned from books', thus securing the precepts of this opposition between thinking and doing, heads and hands (see Elliot (2000) for a theoretical analysis of pedagogic discourse in media theory/practice – or autonomous and vocational – modalities). There is no reason to think that a student on this degree programme will come into contact with theories of representation at any time, as the skills and competences required to graduate are constructed entirely in relation to discourses of technical attributes, the ability to generate economically viable material and to adopt professional ways of working as defined by contemporary business practices. Media education has for a long time dodged this issue – that the 'outside world' would pay little attention to the nuances of distinction between a film studies degree with no production work involved and this course, and yet the experience of students will be almost entirely different. We can use Bernstein's theory of pedagogic codes, as Elliot does, to work through this problem.

Bernstein (1996) asserts that pedagogic modalities are crucial realisations of symbolic control and cultural reproduction. Elliot argues that the seemingly commonsense polarity/relations at work between these two models (preparing for work/critical thinking) is confused, in the sense that the assumptions underlying the philosophy of each modality can easily be dismantled and exposed for the ironic illogic of their own internal givens. The vocational course is conceived within the market-oriented modality (education for work), while the academic route resides within the autonomous modality (critical thinking). The liberal-humanist model of education makes a virtue of a strong separation (or classification) between work and education. This autonomous modality is more involved with broad cultural economy than the acquisition of vocational exchange value. For Elliot, this modality has an arrogance in its claim to the moral high ground and indifference to its own social stratification.

The market-oriented modality, on the other hand, attempts earnestly to deny the barrier between work and education – this is a necessary evil to be obscured and eroded at all costs in the name of economic purpose – 'what can't be learned from books'. However, the illogic of each modality can be understood simply by consideration of the ways in which vocationalism exists to mobilise a 'widening participation' agenda by extending the curriculum – by the recontextualising principle working to insert the horizontal discourse of work into the vertical discourse of curricula. However, by its very desire to deny the opposition between vocational life and learning, this code serves to reproduce the unequal distribution of the economic and symbolic hierarchy which alienates and denies access to the 'widened participators'. At the same time, the autonomous modality asserts its 'otherness' to the social and cultural marketplace while simultaneously situating itself entirely within the economy and circulation of cultural capital.

In 1984 Paul Willis wrote 'The new vocationalism' during the Thatcher era in the United Kingdom, when new government initiatives in dealing with unemployment were being introduced amidst much controversy. Willis and his colleagues were concerned about the policy drive to subordinate schools to the needs of industry, in order to produce better, more disciplined and vocationally skilled workers. Willis's account focused in particular on misplaced assumptions about the relationships between work, teachers and pupils:

> The new vocationalism has drawn much of its credibility from its apparent bridging of this previous gap. On the other hand, just because we might find ourselves agreeing with an analysis which suggests that the conventional curriculum offers very little to working class youngsters, we should not assume that a near compulsory period of post-school training, or a vocationalising of the whole curriculum, will offer much that is better – or indeed that pupils will not reject such 'relevant' offerings with the same power that they sometimes use to undermine conventional schooling. Nor can we simply assume that the popular support of parents, who see their children at least getting something that looks like training and holds the possibility of jobs, will be unequivocal, or will not evaporate in the face of cheap labour schemes with a gloss of 'skills training' followed by prolonged unemployment.
>
> *(Willis, 1984: 223)*

Bernstein's ideas about recognition and realisation are also useful in this discussion. On a theory course, students' recognition that certain modes of critical thinking are legitimate does not necessarily enable the realisation of such autonomy, and the very notion of required autonomy is itself problematic to say the least. On the other hand, students following a practical course recognise the craft and creativity of production but this does not predetermine their ability to create. It would appear that an application of Bernstein's ideas about discourse, in keeping with our borrowing from Foucault and other 'thinkers', would suggest that the dynamics of space, framing, assessment and coding perpetuate the very traditions, both symbolic and empirical, that media teaching seems to want to challenge. In relation to the lack of an explicit study of media representation by students in Detroit, the stark issue is the maintenance of the abstracted nature of 'the media' in this equation. The autonomous modality and the vocational modality both preserve the boundaries between people and the media. Whilst the one modality offers enlightenment through a new way of looking at the media, the other offers students a door into it. Whilst both recontextualise the study of popular culture and seek to legitimise it in different ways, neither are concerned with dismantling the idea that it exists. Media educators' complicity with the exclusive categories of both undermines their emancipatory desires.

(4) Textbook

Lacey (2009) cites a wide range of influential theorists to formulate a user-friendly 'toolkit' for media students analysing representation, drawing together semiotic, generic, ideological, feminist and Marxist approaches, culminating in the relatively straightforward idea that:

> All media texts re-present the world. Many seek to inform audiences, and many try to do so in an honest a fashion as possible, albeit it in a way that will inevitably be influenced by the dominant ideology. Many, however, are designed to benefit the producer and so will represent the world in a way that suits them and not the audience.
>
> *(Lacey, 2009: 189)*

It is very important to state clearly here that the intention is not to be critical of Lacey's contribution since it meets its objectives of providing media students in further and higher education with an overview of key concepts extremely well – these concepts are taken for granted precisely because they are 'handed down' by curriculum, specifications and assessment criteria. However, even the briefest deconstruction of the essentialising boundaries at work in the statement will lead us to observe some fundamental problems with contemporary media education when framed (or frozen) in this way. First, the idea of a media text which re-presents the world does three things. It assumes a boundary around a single text which exists as 'knowable' in a proximal relation to 'the world', and – by the 're' – a temporal space between the world and its mimesis in representation is offered as a precept for judgement. The text, then, is a kind of transcendental signifier which escapes (or resists) difference, it can present an absence clearly enough for the media student (or academic) to say how it accounts for what it purports to stand in for – oscillation suspended. Media studies, viewed in this way, is phallocentric – presence (of the text that stands in for absence) is 'inside' the curriculum. The use of the 'unseen text' in examinations is a rich example. In the (usually darkened, quasi-cinematic) examination hall a video extract is screened, reproducing the conditions of the cinema where the darkened interior stands in for the external reality. Zizek's analysis of the screen as (partly) 'sublime object' resonates, but the curriculum retains the binary of the text which represents the world, and the media student is obliged to be complicit in this metaphysics of presence. In the following sentence the text is given agency as it 'seeks' an effect which we can judge with a moral compass – a text can have integrity, or be dishonest in this reading. Audiences and texts are both, however, in a subordinate relationship to ideology (another of Zizek's sublime objects) in a statement which reproduces the 'turn to ideology' we have traced in cultural studies – which we see as a wrong turn. Finally the binary relationship between producer and audience hinges on the idea that the way the external, absent world is represented can serve either one or the other. Boundaries then, are preserved intact, without question, between text/world, producer/audience, producer and audience/ ideology. We do not need to turn to Derrida, Lacan or Cixous to view this as problematic – Zerrin's creation of 'Slutmo' breaks open this model by its elusive dialectics and deferral of educational function. Again, we make no judgement here about the work – Lacey's project in this textbook is to facilitate students' learning about the concept of representation as it is always-already constructed in modernity, and as such he is compelled to work with the raw material in this way. We take the book as an artefact of the archaeology of knowledge that constructs the conditions of possibility for media studies.

(5) Regulation

Ofcom, the UK regulatory body for broadcast media and telecommunications, can be viewed as an agent in the New Labour project to replace regulation with responsibility. In this configuration, its version of 'media literacy', a much used but largely untheorised term, is shot through with protectionist discourse.

> As explained in our statement, there is no single agreed definition of media literacy.
>
> We have defined media literacy as: 'the ability to access, understand and create communications in a variety of contexts'.
>
> Media literacy has parallels with traditional literacy; the ability to read and write text. Media literacy is the ability to 'read' and 'write' audiovisual information rather than text. At its simplest level media literacy is the ability to use a range of media and be able to understand the information received.
>
> At a more advanced level it moves from recognising and comprehending information to the higher order critical thinking skills such as questioning, analysing and evaluating that information. This aspect of media literacy is sometimes referred to as 'critical viewing' or 'critical analysis'.
> *(Ofcom, 2008: http://www.ofcom.org.uk/advice/media_literacy/of_med_lit/whatis/)*

The status of these statements might appear profoundly distinct from that of an academic textbook, and yet there is a reciprocity in the formulation of representation, influence and being critical. Ofcom has given hitherto-absent credence to media education in the United Kingdom through the development of a Media Literacy strategy, created in collaboration with academics and industry professionals, and disseminated through the convening of regional Media Literacy Task Force groups. This national body liaises with European media literacy groups, UNESCO and, through international media literacy research seminars, academics from New Zealand, the United States, Canada and Australia. This media literacy agenda is fraught with confusion and a reluctance to adequately 'theorise' media literacy in two ways. First, the structural arrangement of the agenda by a regulatory body inevitably provides, intentionally or not, a protectionist agenda; and second, this protectionist impulse is amplified by the dialogue with international groups for whom such a 'risk reduction' approach is unproblematic.

Klimmt attempts a 'normative model' of game literacy and explicitly connects this to the emerging international media literacy agenda:

> While there is a broad consensus about the importance of preventing negative effects of game violence, other equally relevant dimensions of media literacy that competent gamers need to develop in order to meet the challenges implied by the recent developments of the digital game sector have received less attention.
>
> *(Klimmt, 2009)*

According to Klimmt, these dimensions include the development of 'resilience' to effects, self-regulation of time spent and investment of energy in online gaming ('affordances') and the management of game time in relation to 'real-life tasks' ('inertia effects'). While this intervention takes the debate forward by offering a more informed set of 'competences' exhibited by gamers (for example the management of 'social affordances'), its protectionist premise is undermined by a failure to engage with the relationship between 'coping' and performance, and 'knowing' as a trait of criticality.

Returning to Ofcom, the repetition of the reductive description of cultural material as 'information' seals the conception of literacy as being a set of competences. What is surprising is the credence given to Ofcom's project by media educators who, drunk on legitimation, have been prepared to bracket even the most basic theories of reception in order to mobilise this discourse of protection and 'consumption skill'.

(6) Notes on the 'popular' (still)

> Bowling Green State University is the only university in the United States to implement a graduate department devoted to the scholarly study of popular culture. By expanding literature course offerings to include the research and analysis of detective fiction, romance fiction, westerns, and other so-called genre fiction; and by developing coursework on popular film, popular television, popular music, and folklore and folklife, the Department of Popular Culture in 1973 opened students to a consideration of cultural forms that they were familiar with in their everyday lives, but had not reflected upon critically. Through the consideration of popular materials, students confronted issues concerning the relationships of commerce to art, the popular media to society, and the popular use of the mass media.
>
> *(http://www.bgsu.edu/departments/popc/page16730.html)*

This extract from a university website offers little to us apart from another example for the brief history and critique of cultural studies we provide in the introduction to this book. Indeed, we might consider this a rather 'classical' example, with the oppositions maintained between media and art, media and literature, and with the reinforcement of the boundaries imposed by the words 'popular' and 'mass'. However, the attention paid to this course by an article in *Times Higher Education* in April 2010 is indicative of the way that power struggles over what counts as knowledge in the academy have developed very little since the inception of the Birmingham School. At the same time as we are attempting to move beyond the study of 'the media', the popular discourse around the study of 'everyday life' is as conservative as it has ever been, it would appear:

> Bowling Green is the only American university to have a department of popular culture – the term itself is said to have been coined by the late Ray Browne, distinguished university professor emeritus in popular culture, who co-founded the programme in 1973. Dr Browne, who initially had trouble persuading colleagues that popular culture was a serious academic discipline, died last year at the age of 87. But the field he pioneered is thriving. 'When the programme first started, highbrow academics looked down on it and didn't see it as a legitimate form of study,' said Matt Donahue, instructor in the department and one of its 10 full-time faculty members.
>
> Dr Donahue teaches about and performs popular music, dabbles in decorating cars with everything from papier mache to ceramic tiles, makes documentaries about pop music and automobile art, and likes to address people as 'dude'. 'A lot of folks in the academy get their information from books. I take great pride in the fact that I'm involved in creating popular culture,' he explained. Dr Browne, he said, 'went through the shit to make this happen. Shakespeare, classical music and so on were the only valid forms of study. Now it's become hip to study popular culture.'
>
> Although there are no hard statistics, a growing number of US universities are adding popular-culture components to conventional disciplines – offering a history of rock'n'roll class via a music department, for example, or including a history of television course as part of a communication curriculum.
>
> *(Marcus, Times Higher Education, 1 April 2010)*

It is easy labour to map the discursive markers at work here in delimiting the discussion – the entire piece is an exercise in othering culture and the attention drawn to markers of alien activity – 'dude', creating culture as part of teaching, the word 'hip'. And yet the complicity is telling in the reinforced notion of an emancipatory project and a quasi-sub-cultural identity, neither of which are in themselves necessary for the pursuit of designing a course. And so it is not sufficient to identify how this article represents the social practices involved in students and staff at Bowling Green engaging with this course. Rather we must, following Foucault, consider how the discourse speaks both writer and the written. According to Schulman, in an article which has arguably acquired the status of an 'official biography' of the Birmingham Centre:

> Birmingham cultural studies was designed to address an intellectual (and political) void in a highly stratified society whose higher education system was constructed along traditional disciplinary lines. It is a measure of how much cultural studies has succeeded in modifying the climate of higher education in Great Britain that the void which motivated its inception is no longer so glaringly apparent.
>
> *(Schulman, 1993: 14)*

Perhaps, and yet the closure of the Birmingham school, the mutation of cultural studies into – at undergraduate level and A level – media studies and the existence of Marcus's article in 2010 might lead us to question such a linear account. We will argue that these claims for the 'effects' of the Centre for Contemporary Cultural Studies (CCCS) in terms of 'touching the void' in Schulman's terms are overstated most precisely as a result of the way that the study of 'media representation' (two concepts joined together in a 'perfect storm' set in train by modernist arrangements of presence and absence) has undermined the political desire of cultural studies.

(7) University (theory)

Media Representations of Identity is an undergraduate module at Kingston University, London. The module summary, aims, learning outcomes, curriculum content, teaching and learning strategy and assessment strategy are framed by the Quality Assurance Agency, a supremely panoptical arrangement whereby academics self-regulate the articulation of learning and teaching under the assumed gaze of the regulator, the 'already being looked upon' effect that Zizek attributes to Hitchcock's camera. A key distinction between the theoretical premise of *subject media* in higher education and in schools is marked here – essentialist categories are questioned, and one of the module aims is to 'outline and examine theoretical frameworks and debates related to representation in media texts' (2010: 1). In comparison with Lacey and Ofcom there is a complexity here – representation is a matter for debate – studied as a 'concept', as opposed to a concept to apply and a set of influences and agendas to 'see through' with critical eyes and ears. 'The media' are absent from the module, and yet representation is still conceived of as existing 'in media texts'. On the whole, the space between the starting point of this arrangement of learning and the other examples is about more than just undergraduate study being more 'difficult' – while the assessment focus on 'the analysis of ways in which media representations construct, confirm and contest formations of identity' does conform to the notion of 'media representations' and identity as distinguishable constructs, there is no recourse to abstracted notions of 'the real world' or 'audience'. The problem here is the idea of the text. In other words, in comparison with Lacey's 'toolkit' and Ofcom's protectionist project, the complexity of cultural exchange and identity-play is born witness to in Media Representations of Identity, but still the possibilities for the political intentions of cultural studies here are obscured by the retention of the model of the media text as being capable of doing something to/with what is separate and absent in this configuration – identity. The strength of the exclusion holds.

(8) Ontology

Iversen (2008) offers an interesting shift in videogame analysis, suggesting that each game 'in itself' is a 'bastard phenomenon' – born from conception by game and 'media text'. Part of this framing is imaginable in relation to Hills's discussion of performative theory, if we adapt the notion of singularity to think about each gaming experience as an event as opposed to a text or a game (so we remove these models and boundaries in so doing). Iversen's theoretical framework requires the following considerations:

> Considering the computer game's particular mode of being, some of the methodological challenges that arise on this basis are being addressed. This includes issues such as the relation between interpretation and configuration, between fixed and unstable elements, and between game and player.
>
> *(Iversen, 2008: 36)*

What is at stake here is more than a paradigm shift for game studies only, leaving intact the study of representation in more conventional media texts. Rather, we suggest that this way of seeing ontology in relation to a cultural form which preserves no distinction between object of study and played experience ought to work as a model for analysing all cultural material as always-already 'thrown into the subjective'. As Iversen has it, 'there is no escaping the player'. If we extend the idea of the player to all reception, so that all reading is playing, we arrive at a distinctive and more enlightening ontology for studying culture 'after the media'. We begin the important work of eroding the binary opposition that has been constructed between the text in its abstracted form and the player. Students are urged not 'just' to watch the film, but to analyse it, as though it is possible to distinguish these actions. As we have argued, this preservation of the object and the denial of the player in the ontology of media studies is predicated on exactly the same logic as the educated appreciation of literature.

(9) Fan work and exam work

In June 2009, English media students at AS level were required to write about an extract from *Doctor Who* in an exam, assessing how the clip sets up particular representations of gender. Five categories were selected for scrutiny, and these were published in the specification so that teachers could prepare students to work with them – camera, editing, *mise en scène*, sound and effects. The task for students is then to figure out how these technical decisions on the part of producers lead to symbolic representations for viewers. Hills (2010), in his fan-critical academic work on the programme, suggests a discursive approach for looking at *Doctor Who*:

> Though a text like Doctor Who may seem to have obvious 'frontiers' in space and time, such as the bounded minutes of its broadcast, or its sell-through existence as a DVD, in Foucault's terms the text of Who is inevitably caught up in a system of references to other ... texts ... it is a node within a network .... It indicates itself, constructs itself, only on basis of a complex field of discourse. It is thus as a node within a network of discourses that I will think about Doctor Who.
>
> *(Hills, 2010: 15)*

So, is any cultural product outside of this description – as a 'node within a network of discourses'? Clearly not. And so, in this example we can see the constraints of media studies as it has been constructed and played out for students (and their teachers). The earnest and, in the cause of liberal humanities more generally and the politics of cultural studies more specifically, well-meant desire to look at television in relation to power struggles over gender, ethnicity, class, age, sexuality, ability/disability works against itself by reducing the operations to the realm of 'producer intent' – it denies the player, the way that any viewer of *Doctor Who*, or any other television show is living inside the network. What is distinctive about *Doctor Who*, of course, is the very clear ways in which it blurs fan–audience–producer boundaries through both its 'authorship' and the ways in which it encourages fans to remix and rework it online. But, like videogames, all it does is make more visible the limitations of the idea of television shows as objects of study more generally, and thus the constraining force of the concept of 'media representation' as external to the rest of life, thought and culture.

(10) Comparative (media) studies – almost there?

This programme, made famous by Henry Jenkins, is perhaps the most straightforward example of the 'crossroads' we are at, in the sense that on the one hand the course dispenses with much of the orthodox thinking about 'the media' we have been discussing, but on the other its maintenance of boundaries around each medium (in order to compare them) seems contradictory. Module CMS100 is described here:

> Introduction to Media Studies is designed for students who have grown up in a rapidly changing global multimedia environment and want to become more literate and critical consumers and producers of culture. Through an interdisciplinary comparative and historical lens, the course defines 'media' broadly as including oral, print, theatrical, photographic, broadcast, cinematic, and digital cultural forms and practices. The course looks at the nature of mediated communication, the functions of media, the history of

transformations in media and the institutions that help define media's place in society. Over the course of the semester we will explore theoretical debates about the role and power of media in society in influencing our social and cultural values and political beliefs. Students will also have the opportunity to analyze media texts, such as films and television shows, and explore the changes that occur when a particular narrative is adapted into different media forms. To represent different perspectives on media, several guest speakers from the MIT faculty will also present lectures. Through the readings, lectures, and discussions as well as their own writing, students will have the opportunity to engage with critical debates in the field as well as explore the role of media in their own lives.

(http://student.mit.edu/catalog/mCMSa.html#CMS.980)

It appears that the academic study of (partly) mediated life is much less restricted at MIT by the view that it is necessary to study theories of 'the media' before we can deconstruct the idea that underpins them. There is no 'the' in media here. If this is accepted, then studying culture 'after the media' is no longer, at best, marginalised as a postgraduate activity – in the same way as critical theory is often bracketed in this way (as an option or extension work, 'too difficult' for mainstream learning). On the other hand, the option for students to 'explore the role of media in their own lives' is positioned at the very end of the summary. The reproduction of the discursive separation of 'consumers' and 'media' appears at the beginning. This is important, not because we think it undermines the progressive work of the programme at MIT, but because it does very little to challenge the archaeology of knowledge of media education.

In order to 'unthink' this, it is necessary to separate the power that is exercised in this way of articulating the idea of the media from knowledge and from institutions. Here we are firmly in Foucauldian territory. Just as Deleuze explains (1999: 63) that for Foucault, there is no state, only state control, so for our purposes, there is no media, only media power (as discursively manifested – in statements, including ours):

> Power-relations are the differential relations which determine particular features (affects). The actualization which stablilizes and stratifies them is an integration: an operation which consists of tracing 'a line of general force', linking, aligning and homogenizing particular features, placing them in series and making them converge. The integrating factors or agents of stratification make up institutions, not just the state, but also the Family, Religion, Production, the Marketplace, Art itself, Morality and so on. The institutions are not sources or essences, and have neither essence or interiority. They are practices or operating mechanisms which do not explain power, since they pre-suppose its relations and are content to 'fix' them, as part of a function that is not productive but reproductive.
>
> *(Deleuze, 1999: 63)*

So if we add, next to Art, 'the Media' to Deleuze's list, we can say that the various social practices discussed in this chapter are all part of such integrations; that each serves the reproductive function of the idea of media power and that we, media educators, are complicit in this actualisation. To think differently about culture, to resist the discourse, it is necessary to traverse diagonally in between life, culture and the idea of the media.

Thinking awry

The 2010 videogame *Heavy Rain* is a hybrid event (or rather, each play of the game is such) bringing together the conventions of thriller films with ludic videogame experiences. Technically, this is constructed by a form of design-control which liberates the movement of the character from the perspective of the camera. This decoupling has apparently profound effects:

> Heavy Rain is the first game that has made me feel. I felt with the protagonists, and i wanted to do my best to help them out. As you can read from any review, the main plot of the game is to save a child who has been kidnapped by an evil killer. Through its amazing visuals and storytelling techniques, the game manages to make you really want to save the poor kid. He isn't just a bunch of pixels on the screen, he's a real kid that you want to do your best to help. But the question then becomes, how far are you willing to go to save him? The game involves a bunch of moral choices. Some of them are aimed at making you feel the pain of the protagonists, but most of them are aimed at making YOU, the player, think and feel. And it works. It works so very well. At one point during the game i actually had to put the controller down, and think. Should i do this? Am i a bad person if i do this? I mean, i just want to help the kid. Eventually i made the choice, picked up the controller and clicked the right couple of buttons. But that moment of thought stuck with me. Had i done the right thing?
>
> *(RasmusBoseruphttp://www.pixelgameninja.com/2010/02/heavy-rain/)*

Unlike *Psycho*, we cannot pause the film and watch over again the same frames in order to make the judgement Zizek makes about the absent real in the form of the objectified gaze on the subject. Mulvey (2006) makes the case for a reworking of Barthes's theory of the punctum (1993) in relation to the pause facility on the VCR, but we have accelerated from that discussion into 'convergence culture' and the impossibility of pausing signification. *Heavy Rain* cannot be observed in the same way since, like any videogame, it only comes into being as an experienced event by the unique actions of the player. While it might be argued that such an event can be converted 'back' to text for analysis – walk-throughs, gameplay sequences, Machinima – the very apparent translation at work in such textualisation serves, if anything, to further exemplify the event as orthodoxy. Consistent, though, is our argument that all this merely allows us to observe more clearly what has always-already been the case – reception is the 'text'. But the gamer quoted above is claiming something more, and we can evaluate this in obvious relation to Zizek. Boserup is always aware of a law, always deferred, never on-screen but always an objectified 'thing' to consider. The 'feeling' afforded by the change made in the design of the product is less about genre and representation – though this is how media studies will account for it, as a convergence of games/films and an intense representation of themes through immersion – and more about a kind of encounter – with the boundaries of the symbolic and the real. And yet the gaming community will reject such affordances, precisely because the pleasure of the gaming experience is its liberation from the real. The moral panic over violent games, in particular, misses the central point that the 'effect' of *Call of Duty* is to provide a space where moral observation is painlessly absent, where nothing is felt to be real. Of course, *Heavy Rain* is no more or less 'real' than anything else in culture, but the dynamics of the intervention made by the designers will be to reimpose the absent real (the objective gaze on the playing subject) on the edifice – the elaborate conceptual structure – of the gameworld.

In this chapter we have discussed a wide range of current examples of work students are doing with the concept of representation in media studies. We have covered such a broad tapestry of material in order to show how a diverse range of learning and teaching contexts can be, if we are not careful, bound together by an unhelpful essentialist view of representation as something that is done by one group of (elite) producers with an impact on the rest of us. We have suggested that the idea of 'the media', of 'the text' and of media literacy as an enlightening tool for seeing (for the first time) what is being 'done' (with some knowable sense of the real) might helpfully be reimagined through sustained attention to networks of discourses and of events in which the act of 'reading' is seen as an act of playing. In this way the field of 'game studies' with its ontological shift to media as lived experience might serve to inform the whole of media studies in the twenty-first century, to bring us to our jouissance. Next we turn to the most divisive concept in the inventory of subject media – ideology.

4

IDEOLOGY AFTER THE MEDIA

All the basic assumptions of British Cultural Studies are Marxist.

(John Storey, 2009: xvi)

It is part of the intention of this chapter to reclarify the political project of media studies and media education 'after the media'. So much is assumed in this respect that it is worth taking time out to unpack some of the issues both here immediately and across the chapter. Despite Baudrillard's claim that 'There is no theory of the media', there have been no shortage of attempts to theorise its study. Drawing on the substantial work of Buckingham, Masterman and Bazalgette among others, elsewhere we have offered five overlapping and conflicting 'viewpoints' on media education which will be helpful to us in this regard. Standing out is the first:

> 1   Media education is more political than other subjects because it deals with the everyday cultural consumption of learners.
>
> *(McDougall, 2004: 45)*

This sits very easily with assumptions about the subject area's radicalism, which seems still to add vehement energy to those who seek to deride it. Growing out of a mix of impulses and developments, media studies was certainly delivered with a radical energy largely provided by those in literature and humanities who wished chiefly to have the opportunity to subject popular texts to a rigorous and serious critique. It is to be remembered, as Schudson points out, that 'the celebration of popular culture and popular audiences in the universities (*and beyond; my bracket*) has been a political act: it could not have been otherwise' (Schudson, 1987: 562).

> 2 Media studies is not a form of English but an alternative approach due to its delivery through concept before text.
>
> 3 Representation is the central concept for media learning.

Michael Schudson refers to Giametti's claim that the two most important decisions a teacher makes are: a) where to start from and b) what to start with (Schudson, 1987: 558). With this in mind it is easy to see how the best laid plans of *subject media* 'go oft awry', particularly when the pressing contexts of assessment and achievement add their conservative contributions. In some senses the claim that *subject media* puts concepts ahead of texts comes to grief largely on the priority of one such concept, representation, which ensures in practice that textual analysis will wag this particular dog. From there a depoliticisation of the subject is almost inevitable, whatever good is intended. And, ironically none of this is helped by the absence of a media studies canon (a motherlode of bona fide texts like *subject English* has) since free choice becomes a byword for a certain kind of cautious expedience. The concentration on representation implies a discussion about values and assumptions, discourses and stereotypes, but it all too often becomes a presentation of 'classic cases'. In this context a 'good' resource is often one that unequivocally deals in problematic representations, often involving girls in bikinis on computer magazines or even more fatuously the depiction of girls in 'lads' mags'. And we should not let the triviality of this conceal the more serious issues. First, *subject media*'s over-fascination with female gender representation makes its own statement in 2010, particularly when under examination, so much of it is either uncritically politically moralistic or else predictable, unchallenging and offensive.

However, its underlying assumptions are even more concerning and undermining for a media studies that still seeks an active contemporary role and sees itself as 'more political than other subjects'. If this job begins with the ritual washing of the 'ideology' of representations to reveal the untainted truth beneath, *subject media* may be less radical than we thought (and less contemporary in thought than it is in action). As such we see the possibility that media studies could be considered a reactionary attempt to fetishise the real by re-establishing its presence as 'truth' obscured by media representation. In this sense media studies would in itself be an example of what Baudrillard calls the hyper-real. It is this inherent conservatism and abiding inability to convincingly assimilate theory that needs to be addressed.

If politics is the art of the possible, it is for us to respond in possibilities. When 'the media' was conceived singularly, operating on us all as passive victims with 'mind-gas' ideology, the project was simple like an episode of the old *Doctor Who*: travel to planet 'text', wake up the native victims, show them the truth and then lead them against the instrument of oppression. Now we know they are awake already, the game changes somewhat. You are still aware that things are not quite right, but this is more like an episode of 'Nu-Who' and therefore you are required to act a little more grown up: consider the evidence, recognise that you yourself are a factor, think contingencies rather than causes.

This is what the chapter tries to do: to productively pick its way through the debris of the 'old' thinking to, it is hoped, appreciate the opportunities offered by the active audience, the renewed importance of culture and the stimulation given to the area by postmodernist and post-structuralist agendas. It means this chapter is an extended debate about how and where we site ourselves as a way of demonstrating that the most important step we need to make is making these debates, these judgements about judgements, part of the substantive subject of our enquiries. For example Cary Bazalgette writes about the tensions between media teachers as consumers of media and as agenda setters (arbiters of 'taste') (1991, 1992). While *subject English* conceals these judgements behind canonical 'law' it is for media studies to celebrate the interplay of ideas: taste, pleasure, subjectivity, inequality, power.

---

4 Media studies should foster 'critical autonomy'.
5 The nature of media audiences and their responses to texts should be explored more.

Williams put it well when he wrote:

> We need to say what many of us know in experience: that the struggle to learn, to describe, to understand, to educate, is a central and necessary part of our humanity. This struggle is not begun at second hand, after reality has occurred. It is in itself a major way in which reality is formed and changed.
>
> *(Williams, 1962: 11)*

Let the struggle begin.

Strategic illusions

> The class experience is largely determined by the productive relations into which men are born – or enter involuntarily. Class-consciousness is the way in which these experiences are handled in cultural terms; embodied in traditions, value-systems, ideas and institutional forms. If the experience appears as determined, class-consciousness does not …. Consciousness of class arises in the same way in different times and places, but never in just the same way.
>
> *(E. P. Thompson, 1980: 9)*

> What used to be called art has been surpassed by and in the media.
>
> *(Hans Magnus Enzensberger, 1986)*

In his 'Requiem for the media' Jean Baudrillard claims that 'there is no theory of the media', and further suggests that therefore 'the 'media revolution has remained empirical and mystical' to all shades of opinion (1986: 124). Baudrillard is particularly concerned to address the 'strategic illusions' of the left, which he otherwise describes as 'schizophrenic', but his general critique is a powerful one. Given that we ourselves are also proposing a requiem of sorts, these arguments may be worth pursuing.

What did Baudrillard mean by 'empirical' and 'mystical', and to what extent does the hyper-extended 'media revolution' we are currently experiencing still exhibit these qualities? Certainly 'empirical' and 'mystical' are unlikely bedfellows, which is much of the point: not exactly opposites but certainly at odds. On the one hand we have something that is measurable and scientific, like the strength of your broadband connection or the impact of televised violence on small children. At the same time we are offered our addicted love for the popular media and hopes or fears for a liberating or uncertain future. Neither leaves us wiser. Rather we seem left some way between indifference and awe. We cannot accept that our lives are determined but cannot dispute our vague feelings of unease.

Certainly we have critical distance if we need it but as long as we are prepared to merely denounce mass-media culture as an ideological manipulation we are hardly seeing any trees for the wood. To be fair, although regrettably elitist, those great reprovers of mass culture from the Frankfurt school were arguing about more than cultural decay. Adorno and Horkheimer more significantly were concerned about what today is often referred to as 'one size fits all', what they see as the instrumentalisation of reason through a mass culture that is progressively homogenous, predictable and standardised. By the exercise of what Adorno dubbed 'identity thinking', reason is used to classify people and ultimately systemise and control them (Adorno, 1991). This, after all, is what George Orwell in *Nineteen Eighty-Four* (1949) really meant by this memorable image: 'If you want a picture of the future, imagine a boot stamping on a human face – for ever.' It is the threat of O'Brien, who speaks these words and who elsewhere clarifies the situation:

> We control matter because we control the mind. Reality is inside the skull. You will learn by degrees, Winston. There is nothing that we could not do. Invisibility, levitation – anything. I could float off the floor like a soap bubble if I wish to. I do not wish to, because the Party does not wish it. You must get rid of those nineteenth century ideas about the laws of Nature. We make the laws of Nature.
>
> (Orwell, Nineteen Eighty-Four, 1949)

Isaac Deutscher (1984) analysed Orwell's response to totalitarianism in the novel. His conclusion is that, as a rationalist and socialist, Orwell could not deal with the horrors of torture and state terror, and this led instead to an emotional, almost mystical response; that he came, in Deutscher's words, to 'view reality through the dark glasses of a quasimystical pessimism'. Orwell came to see the problem as a function of that greatly problematical discourse 'human nature', and therefore as dangerously apolitical (Deutscher, 1986: 119–32).

This notion of our being rationalised into generic experiences through which our less rational desires are efficiently serviced certainly has some face validity as a response to mainstream Hollywood film, or the shopping mall or theme park. So too does Marcuse's notion of the 'ideology of consumerism' and of the creation of 'false needs' (2002). When the economist J. K. Galbraith describes advertising as 'a relentless propaganda on behalf of goods in general', he is acknowledging this ideology of consumerism, how the general climate of consumerism impacts on, for example, the aspirations of consumers (1969). For Marcuse this flags up the potential tyranny of taste and the potentially corrosive influence of a notion of consumer choice that has become almost sanctified, and thus depoliticised. For the theorists of critical theory consumerism is a pseudo-reality offering pseudo-pleasure and pseudo-enjoyment in a controlled environment wherein meaningful political 'choices' are undercut by meaningless commercial ones.

In this sense politics functions chiefly as an absent presence. The action of hegemonic forces serves paradoxically to render 'politics' (now a thing in itself like 'religion') an aberrant and disruptive element within successful Western democracies, which guarantee your right to have 'politics' as long as you do not force it on the rest of us. Thus political opinions become personal possessions or habits which are given slots in the media schedules in the same way that golf is or culture. In this way politics becomes commodified and (de)politicised. All this is predicated on the elision of freedom and freedom of choice, whether this be fifty television channels or fifty-seven varieties of bean. And Marcuse argues that bastardised mass culture organises leisure in the way that capital organises work, where 'organise' suggests 'routinise', 'systemise' and standardise. Work and play, night and day the ideological machine grinds on, while we pass through like commodities attempting to discover our exchange value. There is much of this 'mythology' in Baudrillard's justly famous deconstruction of Disneyland, but also a little more:

> Disneyland is a perfect model of all the entangled orders of simulation. To begin with it is a play of illusions and phantasms: pirates, the frontier, future world, etc. This imaginary world is supposed to be what makes the operation successful. But, what draws the crowds is undoubtedly much more the social microcosm, the miniaturized and religious revelling in real America, in its delights and drawbacks.
>
> *(Baudrillard, 2009: 415)*

Rather than seeing the experience as 'various', as is no doubt intended, Baudrillard sees only an extension of the worklife it is designed to relieve and oppose. Never has a car park seemed so oppressive, so totalitarian:

> You park outside, queue up inside, and are totally abandoned at the exit. In this imaginary world the only phantasmagoria is in the inherent warmth and

affection of the crowd, and in that sufficiently excessive number of gadgets used there to specifically maintain the multitudinous affect. The contrast with the absolute solitude of the parking lot – a veritable concentration camp – is total. Or rather: inside, a whole range of gadgets magnetize the crowd into direct flows; outside, solitude is directed onto a single gadget: the automobile.

(Baudrillard, 2009: 415)

Here leisure is a routine like any other: to be endured with the fixed grin of the puppet mask. We too are on hidden tracks like the average theme park ride, watched over by the benevolent patriarch with the icy heart:

By an extraordinary coincidence (one that undoubtedly belongs to the peculiar enchantment of this universe), this deep-frozen infantile world happens to have been conceived and realized by a man who is himself now claimed to be cryogenized; Walt Disney, who awaits his resurrection at minus 180 degrees centigrade.

(Baudrillard, 2009: 413)

Ideology and the media

Sign becomes an arena of class struggle.

(Volosinov, 1973: 23)

Ideology is, indeed, a system of representation.

(Louis Althusser, quoted in Hebdige, 1979: 12)

What Baudrillard's scathing account has which the dismissive and elitist accounts provided by Horkheimer and Adorno consistently lack is an appreciation of 'the inherent warmth and affection of the crowd'. Critical theory addresses popular culture critically but cannot bring itself to appreciate it or even understand it. One aspect of this problem is the now untenable suggestion that the mass audience is a model of duped passivity, propagated by the absence of authentic experience. Notions of the active consumer clearly undermine such simple models of media manipulation, with their insistence on the ways in which dominant ideology works through texts to overcome our resistance. Introducing a new edition of Adorno's *The Culture Industry* in 1991, J. M. Bernstein pointed out that mass culture is simply 'more diverse, dynamic and conflictual than (his) theory allows' (Adorno, 1991: 20). It is also significantly less homogenous and mindless than its critics will allow.

This can slip very easily into what Mulgan calls 'the stale debate between a crude populism … and an equally crude elitism' (cited in McGuigan, 2009: 615). Here the refusal to entertain any criteria of quality is as intractable as the refusal to validate any act of consumption or everyday practice. The truth is that nothing is more damaging to the media studies project than this absence of a productive debate about popular culture, to some extent the discipline's *raison d'être*. Instead what is encouraged are technical readings of decontextualised texts, where theoretical perspectives become an end in themselves, the echo of an empty activity. In this way neither relativism not ideological credibility need to be compromised, only the discipline's most significant questions.

This is partly about reuniting media studies with the cultural studies project, at the centre of which according to Stuart Hall is 'the politics of culture or the culture of politics' (cited in Storey, 2009: xvi). For Fiske too, despite the reservations of other cultural critics, the 'culture' in cultural studies 'is neither aesthetic nor humanist in emphasis, but political': not about the 'old fashioned aesthetic sense of the text as a self-contained art object complete in itself' but of how it might be 'put to work socially' and 'bought and sold' (quoted in Müller, 1993). Readings of popular culture might then start with this sense of active engagement with both practice and theory. McGuigan in his 'Trajectories of cultural populism' (see Storey, 2009) cites Geoffrey Nowell-Smith to telling effect, explaining 'the term popular culture retains its value when one is talking about the people who make it popular – that is, when one is talking about the people who keep a particular cultural form going by being the public for it or by being its producers.' At the same time Nowell-Smith does not want us to lose sight of the wider cultural field which he offers up as two 'major realities':

1. Modern culture is capitalist culture
2. Modern culture also takes the form of a single intertextual field, whose signifying elements are perpetually being recombined and played off against one another.

(McGuigan, 2009: 615)

This seems like a more auspicious starting point than that offered by 'media manipulation' at a point where culture seems to have such a heightened significance when, as Murdock points out, 'the interplay between the symbolic and economic has never been so pronounced and demanding of critical attention' (in McGuigan, 2009: 616). This is partly where we came in. Baudrillard's 'Requiem' is taken from a longer piece on the political economy of the sign. Baudrillard rejects not only the media manipulation model but also the utopian socialist model perpetrated by Brecht and Enzensberger, which asks us to think of the media as 'fundamentally egalitarian' but 'perverted by the capitalist order' (Enzensberger, 1986).

For Enzensberger the challenge is to liberate the media from the control of the dominant classes, to transform their 'means of distribution' into a genuine 'means of communication'. Baudrillard is unwilling to accept the media as 'purely and simply a means of distribution' or 'the relay of an ideology' or as 'marketing and merchandising of the dominant ideology'. For Baudrillard 'it is not as vehicles of content, but in their form and very operation that media induce a social relation; and this is not an exploitative relation: it involves the abstraction, separation and abolition of exchange itself. He continues by pointing out that 'the media are not *co-efficients*, but *effectors* of ideology', and moreover that 'ideology does not exist in some place apart, as the discourse of the dominant class, before it is channeled through the media'. For Baudrillard ideology is 'the very operation of the exchange value itself' (1986: 128).

We will return to Baudrillard later. What we may be doing is at least resisting that 'custom of consumer capitalism', according to Judith Williamson, whereby our emotions are directed to objects rather than actions by seeing ideology as operating through cultural practices rather than residing in cultural products. Hall makes this point clearly when he writes, 'the meaning of a cultural form and its place or position in the cultural field is not inscribed inside its form'. As Storey points out, Hall's notion of 'articulation' (if meaning is not inscribed it must be expressed) is also influenced by the work of Volosinov, who also offers us a couple of steps forward, in terms of a plan of action. Firstly Volosinov stresses the multi-accentuality of texts and practices: 'that is that they can be articulated with different "accents" by different people in different contexts for different politics' (Storey, 2009: xvii). This makes texts, even signs, sites where meaning can and should be contested: 'Sign becomes an arena of the class struggle. This social multi-accentuality of the ideological sign is a very crucial aspect' (Hall, 2009: 132).

Notions of dominant ideology, even Althusser's, stress instead the uni-accentuality of cultural reproduction, whereas Volosinov sees this uni-accentuality as a product of a practice whereby a 'struggle over meaning' has been mastered. An unwillingness to engage in discursive practices around mastery would inevitably lead to a further confirmation of dominant practices. As signs and language make the struggle possible they must be pursued and struggled with in an arena wherein 'signifying elements are perpetually being recombined and played off against one another' (Hall, 2009: 133).

The analysis of culture

> Culture is the meaning of an insufficiently meaningful world.
>
> *(Guy Debord, 1994: 102)*

> the art is there, as an activity, with the production, the trading, the politics, the raising of families.
>
> *(Raymond Williams, 1961: 61)*

McGuigan sensibly points out that contemporary cultural objects are mainly commodities. Clearly this includes media products, many of which are significant determiners of our identities and foci of our passions and commitments. As a result critically reflective media studies students find themselves caught between celebrating media forms as creative expressions of identity and bemoaning them as agencies of ideological manipulation. This is what Steven Miles refers to as 'the consuming paradox': 'consumerism appears to have a fascinating, arguably fulfilling, personal appeal and yet simultaneously plays some form of an ideological role in actually controlling the character of everyday life' (cited in Paterson, 2006: 157). Judith Williamson makes a similar point, though with more concern in the introduction to *Controlling Passions* : 'what I am concerned with is the way passions are themselves consumed, contained and channelled into the very social structures they might otherwise threaten' (1986: 11).

In *Consumption and Everyday Life* Mark Paterson exemplifies and develops these arguments with specific reference to the creation of youth cultures, cultures which hold media products closest to their hearts. This comes in a chapter where Paterson has been talking about 'sucker' and 'savvy' consumers, and has asked in the youth culture context whether we are 'seducers or the seduced', concluding, 'Perhaps as in any sexual encounter, a bit of both.' The 'consuming paradox' is then explored via an invocation of and warning about the guerrilla tactics of de Certeau which Paterson finds ultimately a source of 'naïve and unrealistic claims' (Paterson, 2006: 158).

What Paterson notices is the way in which this apparent debate is situated in terms of familiar binary oppositions and the implications of this. Partly this is about defining youth and popular culture in opposition to traditional power and then about reinforcing this pattern in the dichotomy of cultural dupes (suckers) and cultural guerrillas (savvy). Paterson is concerned that the net result is of resistance with no discernible political direction since it is denied an appropriate context, a context which for us is obscured by a third and more damaging dichotomy, that between 'the media' and their consumers.

Paterson's point about 'an unsophisticated understanding of the economic and ideological model as monolithic or singular' could apply equally to that monstrous abstraction, 'the media', which obstructs our view of the diversity of cultural production (ibid.: 159). We cannot make progress until we begin to dismantle and disarticulate the specific discourses around 'the media' and address the false opposition of media and people. Even *We the Media* (2005), Dan Gillmor's book on 'Grassroots journalism by and for the people' remains very much in this false dichotomy. *We the Media* suggests a takeover, a semantic coup. But why not think in terms simply of 'We media'? 'The media' are fighting a rearguard action but only in our heads, as an antagonistic response to a shift in sensibilities. This is partly a classic case of what McLuhan called a rear-view mirror perspective; seeing the present through models of the past. In this way the unprecedented diversity of contemporary youth culture is seen as implicitly less authentic than its 'vintage' counterparts. And this is paradoxically to do with reading this diversity as homogeneity and always believing that the previous 'generation' of music/film/ television had more 'character' and distinction that the stuff available currently.

We, the Media: an interlude

> We tend to be bound by our past, even when we can imagine the future.
> *(Dan Gillmor, www.authorama.com/we-the-media-13.html,*
> *accessed on 12 December 2010)*

> By surpassing writing, we have regained our sensorial wholeness, not on a
> national or cultural plane, but on a cosmic plane. We have evoked a super-
> civilised, sub-primitive man.
>
> *(Marshall McLuhan, 1969: 16)*

It would be wrong to see Dan Gillmor as opportunistic. As one of the first to
see the potential of the blog as a journalistic tool, his timely intervention of 2005,
We, the Media, offers an intelligent overview of potential developments. However,
the former technology journalist is a man on a mission, with us as his potential
converts:

> I hope that I've helped you understand how this media shift – this explosion
> of conversations – is taking place and where it's headed. Most of all, I hope
> I've persuaded you to take up the challenge yourself.
>
> *(Gillmor, 2004: ch. 12)*

Gillmor's instinct is collaborative and his outlook principled. He explains that
'The ability of anyone to make the news will give new voice to people who've felt
voiceless – and whose words we need to hear.' He also backed these thoughts up
with actions. Not only did he post *We, the Media* on the internet as a series of drafts
so that his wider network community might have their say, when the book was
finished he offered the whole manuscript under a Creative Commons licence free
on the net simultaneously with the book hitting the stores.

However, the disappointment with Gillmor is that he does not quite deliver
what you think he is going to. Like McLuhan he offers energy, a breath of
evangelical zeal and strong one-liners And like McLuhan what he significantly
lacks is a political dimension. It may be true that 'the former audience has the most
important role in this new era: they must be active users of news, and not mere
consumers', and that Gillmor is sincere when he says that 'my readers know more
than I do, and that's a good thing'. Nevertheless while these may be part of a
'revolution in their heads', the call to action beyond blogging is minimal. Gillmor
is, in fact, though worried by what 'Big Media' will do in the future, keen to point
out that he does not nurse any antipathy towards his former employers:

> I've been in professional journalism for almost 25 years. I'm grateful for the
> opportunities I've had, and the position I hold. I respect and admire my
> colleagues, and believe that Big Media does a superb job in many cases.
>
> *(Gillmor, 2005: introduction)*

The grassroots journalism that Gillmor is promoting is somewhat idealised as a
super-efficient method of news collection; a collaboration in the service of truth.
It may be that, as Gillmor suggests, *We the Media* is a book about people. But what
is really being encouraged is participation in a liberal consensus, the liberation of
educated people who had not even realised they were in need of liberation. In the

same way McLuhan's claim that 'in all media the user is the content' merely compounded the struggle at the heart of *subject media* between 'the media' and 'the people. What Gillmor shares with McLuhan (and with Baudrillard) is a commitment to the idea of 'the media' as a useful and viable critical instrument. And frankly, a naivety:

> Your voice matters. Now, if you have something worth saying, you can be heard. You can make your own news. We all can. Let's get started.
>
> *(Gillmor, 2005: ch. 12)*

The analysis of culture (continued)

In such a context polarisation is just not a credible model. Finally media, culture and activity seem more useful than the media, consumer culture and text. Rather than being defined by what it is not, youth culture becomes potentially self-defining. We may still wish to offer strategic readings of Lady Gaga to exercise our theoretical perspectives but we surely cannot do so without questioning the value of these antagonistic critical interventions. When Angela McRobbie famously 'did' *Jackie* magazine in 1982 she admitted that 'until we have a clearer idea of just how girls 'read' Jackie and encounter its ideological force, our analysis remains one-sided' (1982: 283). Much one-sided work has gone on in media studies and much citing, like this one, of one-sided studies. Academics like anyone else have their 'greatest hits, and it is often work that has since been significantly 'revised'.

Paterson writes about 'the invention of the teenager', tracing this 'category' back to its coining in the 1940s by US market researchers, appropriate perhaps since this group has been largely defined by its consumption: lifestyle rather than workplace. He quotes from an 'astonishingly candid' report from 1966 which describes the youth market (14 to 25) as 'a well-defined consumer group, affluent and innocent, to be attracted and exploited and pandered to' (Paterson, 2006: 162). However, this 'myth of origin' is not the end of the story (or else we would all be etymologists rather than semiologists or post-structuralists). What 'teenager' is and who teenagers are has been and is constituted by all of us, is part of a patterning through which culture as 'the characteristic forms of a way of life' performs itself. Youth may indeed be wasted on the young, nevertheless it is theirs to waste. Of course they are complicit in the creation of youth cultures that may seem to the 'tolerant ironic eye' overcommodified but, in Geertz's terms, spinning webs of significance is a complicated business.

What easily gets lost in our anatomies and histories of 'the teenager' is the essence, Williamson's 'consuming passions', which she reminds us are 'not found in things but in ways of doing things'. Here is a force that requires a broader focus since 'like the wind, [it] is only revealed in forms' and which makes itself felt across all elements in a whole way of life. Williamson offers us a new dispensation if we choose to embrace it since she identifies not only much of our familiar territory 'in films, photographs, television' but also a broader compass: 'These forms … are a shared language, for the shapes of our consciousness run right through society, we inhabit the same spaces, use the same things, speak in the same words' (Williamson, 1986: 15).

Williamson herself, in *Consuming Passions*, is still concerned with ways in which 'the media' channel desire through representation to reinforce naturalisation, a world 'filled with obviousnesses, full of natural meanings which these media merely reflect'. However, she constructs an agenda which *subject media* has still largely ignored, though in our introduction we acknowledge it 'falsely believes it has been working with' it. The agenda is a cultural studies one since it is concerned centrally with the politics of culture: 'But we invest the world its significance, it doesn't have to be the way it is, or to mean what it does.' With this is an implicit call for a passionate response to contest the academic 'cool' with something hotter: 'But passion – passion is another story. It is to be written about but not with for the essence of all this academic work on desire is to stay cool' (Williamson, 1986: 12).

When she complains that 'it has never been fashionable to over-invest in any activity', her reproach is heart-felt and profoundly challenging. She is also binding us into the cultural studies project once again, and specifically the work of Williams, for whom culture idealises, documents and enacts human experience and potential so that descriptions of culture contain 'a genuine complexity, corresponding to real elements in experience'. The art-work, which for example might be a media text, is here 'as an activity, with the production, the trading, the politics, the raising of families'. This is categorically not 'texts in context', not, Williams insists, about relating art to the society, 'but of studying all of the activities and their interrelations without any concession of priority to any of them'. This is the sense in which Gauntlett chides media studies for being 'too much about the media' ('All forms of media … play a part in social life' – 2007: 192). Williams meanwhile rejects a 'bad method' which assumes social facts after which texts and theory can be adduced in favour of a more active engagement: 'we must study them actively, seeing all activities as particular and contemporary forms of human energy. If we take any of these activities, we can see how many of the others are reflected in it' (Williams, 2009: 35).

Williams defines his theory of culture as 'the study of relationships between elements in a whole way of life' with the critic charged with seeking potential patterns, both correspondences and discontinuities. For Williams each 'way of life' has a distinctive 'structure of feeling' which corresponds to its culture as a basis of community and communication and its selective tradition, the connection between culture lived and culture recorded, between practice and theory, almost in cultural terms *parole* and *langue*. Again activity is the key, and by comparison with the Frankfurt Marxists, the Marxist Williams is keen to keep the dialectic working. His 'long revolution' is realistic but certainly hopeful: 'Every element that we analyse will be in this sense active: that it will be seen in real relations, at many different levels. In describing these relations the real cultural work will begin' (Williams, 2009: 40).

And this applies just as much to critical methods and tools as it does to anything else. In a postscript to his monograph *Raymond Williams: Hope and Defeat in the Struggle for Socialism*, headed 'Positive criticism', Don Milligan lays out on the basis of Williams' writing a pragmatic approach to 'political criticism'. It begins by reinforcing a standard Marxist insistence on the conditions of production but moves on to an unwitting critique of much that's been passing for textual analysis in *subject media*:

> What is surely more important, in every case, is the attempt which must be made to derive the political and historical problems from the text or artwork under consideration, to approach the individual artwork (or particular body of work) as a distinct production, one concealing within it the appropriate means by which it may be read. Critics must not impose a critical context upon a work in advance of their reading and evaluation of it as a unique work of art.
>
> *(Milligan, nd)*

This means that the historical problems revealed or created by a text, its political register, its moral or philosophical implications, should be sought within the text – the critics' task is to determine during their encounter with a particular artwork the appropriate means of reading it. We should not measure and weigh works against ready-made critical contexts, offering a particular novel to post-colonial readings or another to a feminist account, and so on. In each case we should look within the artwork for the means by which it may be read most effectively (Milligan, 2007: 311). But performing an 'oppositional' reading of *Avatar* is light years away from dealing with that text as a site of contending meanings.

Six of one and half a dozen others

> I am not a number, I'm a free man.
>
> *(The Prisoner* [old and new]*)*

> A new Rousseau – like all copies, only a pale version of the old – he (McLuhan) preaches the gospel of the new primitive man who, naturally on a higher level, must return to prehistoric tribal existence in the 'global village'.
>
> *(Hans Magnus Enzensberger, 1986: 115)*

Nature, according to Aristotle, abhors a vacuum, which must give you pause for thought when you discover that a new version of the cult 1960s show *The Prisoner* was made in 2009. With US money insisting on an US star, Jim Caviezel, who had famously previously played an enigmatic rebel resisting autocratic authority (*The Passion of the Christ*, 2004), the six-parter, which screened first in the United States in 2009, promised to update the original. This relevance was also invoked in its claims that the ending would not only be as shocking as the original but would also reflect profoundly on our surveillance society. From the outset this did seem a little like putting the cart before the horse, the denouement before the development. Perhaps a brief exploration of this most impudent recent reproduction and its, in television terms, illustrious original will help to clarify the real political and ideological issues inherent in a particular kind of text analysis. By conceiving of a criticism capable of dealing with 'particular and contemporary forms of human energy' in context, we can hope to also forge inevitable links to the material focus of the next chapter: history. Here the dual historical context is most explicit, with both texts making claims to be 'of their age' in the face of a media studies 'randy' for the postmodernist perspective.

All this seems plausible enough, but it is worth remembering that co-creator and star Patrick McGoohan's original ending was precipitated by his failure to secure an extended run for his quirky zeitgeist piece. As a result he was forced almost to 'jam' the last episode, and the shock was the ease with which, after sixteen episodes, his captivity was so easily brought to a close: like Kafka's, the gate was always open. What followed, however, has much in common with the project of this chapter. Free of 'the Village', Number Six, who feels more and more now like McGoohan himself, slips out of character and back into the other reality: that 'global village', London in 1967. This 'village', which Conrad had labelled both 'the greatest town' and 'one of the dark places of the earth' 70 years earlier, this real 'heart of darkness', was where McGoohan was heading (Conrad, 1998: 135). Such an intensity was always going to be hard to reproduce to order.

As Number Six, now clearly McGoohan, hops from an iconic red London bus, he is returning us to the world in which we want experiences of texts to cohere. This is a positively Jacobean moment, an unspoken epilogue, delivered by one returning, like us to a different order of real, disrobing and unmasking, putting an end to 'the mystical'. In fact the final episode was viewed with horror and confusion, and it is reported that McGoohan had to leave for the country to escape the anger and frustration of bewildered fans, some of whom were literally beating on his door (with mallets) in frustration. Interviewed in 1977 by Warner Troyer, McGoohan reported: 'When they did finally see it, there was a near-riot and I was going to be lynched. And I had to go into hiding in the mountains for two weeks, until things calmed down. That's really true!'

The question we might ask ourselves is this. Given that this significant national television event, which produced, and still does, substantial fan response across more than four decades, has been remade for our times, what kind of media education might we need to address it? Politics, someone said, is the art of the possible, the interplay of contingencies and contexts. Judith Williamson offers a starting point when she reminds us that 'The original context of any product is that of its production' (1986: 13).

In the case of *The Prisoner* (1967 and 2009) this immediately puts clear blue water between them since the first provides something of a context for the second, both creatively and, perhaps more significantly, commercially. Interestingly *The*

Prisoner (2009) was summed up by its most positive US reviewer, Alessandra Stanley in the *New York Times*, in the following way:

> This version of *The Prisoner* is not a remake, it's a clever and engaging reinterpretation by Bill Gallagher, who shaped the script to contemporary tastes and sensibilities – notably, a postmodern fatigue with ideology and big thoughts.
>
> *(New York Times, 12 November 2009)*

As an image essentially without an original, Stanley is defining the show as a simulacrum, which only adds to both its postmodern sensibility and our sense of contrivance. It is as if intertextuality has become a thing in itself, a dominant discourse.

Stanley's review goes on to read the latecomer off the original, claiming that 'The 21st century adaptation pays only lip service to the human condition, and instead explores a power struggle between two human beings.' Certainly this reduction to personalities (the battle between numbers Two and Six) creates something entirely other than the original (parent might be more appropriate). This certainly pertains to the contexts of production, and particularly those media codes that constitute 'star'. From marketing to camera framing this project presents Ian McKellen (Two) versus Jim Caviezel (Six): Gandalf versus Christ. In this context the new tagline 'You only think you're free' is more homage than anchor. The profound controversy of the original is precisely that it eschews these oppositions, considering instead the abyss that, in Nietzsche's words 'gazes back into you' (*Apophthegms and Interludes*, in Nietzsche 1999: 146).

To find the 'vibe' of the original, we need a broader exploration of the contexts of production and reception. The mundanities and intensities of commercial production are essential to the story, as is the historical context, not least of the medium itself. When asked by Warner Troyer to 'explain' the state of the other villagers, McGoohan is remarkably explicit: 'Ah, the majority of them have been sort of brain-washed. Their souls have been brainwashed out of them. Watching too many commercials is what happened to them.'

These issues are just as important to the integrity of *The Prisoner* as the iconic costumes and setting, as the soundbites about numbers and free men. The problem with the 'not remake' is that the reimagining starts from the paraphernalia rather than the purpose, the shell rather than the lifeforce: Number Two rather than Number One! As such a better companion piece, and one that has met with far greater commercial and critical success, is Matthew Weiner's *Mad Men,* which taps the commercialised and mediatised world of the late 1950s and early 1960s at source through the knowing recreation of a Madison Avenue advertising agency. Not only does *Mad Men* offer what a future chapter might label a 'history of the present,' a Foucauldian genealogy of contemporary attitudes, but it does so through the conventions of television drama: through narrative, through characterisation, rather than from the paraphernalia. Thus although the implications of the ongoing drama may be as fashion (autumn 2010 marks the 'return' of the 1950s woman) rather than cult, the debate that has been engendered by *Mad Men* is genuine, organic and mature. The ideological issues of our contemporary situation are very clearly being addressed by way of the programme's tolerant ironic eye, postmodern without pastiche.

Entirely like the original *The Prisoner* there is a 'drawing' in *Mad Men* of myths in the Barthesian sense, myths eager to be symbols, involved organically in active negotiations. Don Draper (played by Jon Hamm) is a cipher, or more precisely becomes one, a 'cover' perfectly conceived for the world of advertising (our world). His recovered identity becomes the latent energy of the first season revelling in the aptness of a name designed to be 'donned' by an ideological 'draper'. All, as they say will be concealed (and revealed). Though not as heavy handedly perhaps as 'Number Six', the cipher 'Draper' is nevertheless exploring just as profoundly as McGoohan's character the limits of a world. The show's justly famous opening credits speak of a 'fallout' ultimately as painful as that endured by Number Six and his many followers. Appearance and reality is a fine old artistic contention, and it is here in both the end of episode blackouts and the understanding that when the time is right the end will come, that Draper like Number Six will leave, one way or another. This taps into a broader and deeper (but not more heightened or refined) discussion about the way reality might be 'made' and what may or may not be possible. However, our first thoughts might not be of the human condition but rather the specific positions occupied by men and women in their own social and economic circumstances. Where *The Prisoner* (2009) differs is in the fact that it starts with symbols forged elsewhere and relatively fixed in their meanings, then tries to renegotiate the terms of their signification. Though both principals put in good shifts they can be no other than they are: numbers Two and Six.

The construction of situations

> As the 'social truth' of power is permanent falsification, language is its permanent guarantee and the Dictionary its universal reference.
>
> *(Mustapha Khayati, Preface to a Situationist Dictionary)*

> In our time functionalism (an inevitable expression of technological advance) is attempting to entirely eliminate play.
>
> *(Guy Debord, in Knabb, 2006: 51)*

The Prisoner (2009) is fully aware of its postmodern sensibilities, playing with both the original and its apparent themes. Already by the second episode the scope and invention of Bill Gallagher's simulacrum is shown to be of a very different order with a different kind of focus on the relationship between Two and Six, where the former is more significantly (and therefore less disturbingly) an authoritarian personality and carries a threat that is explicit. His singularity is represented by his palatial mansion and his project by the tows and rows of identical chalet-like homes which constitute 'the (new) Village'. To some small degree this makes *The Prisoner* (2009) more like *Nineteen Eighty-Four* than its predecessor, with McKellen's Number Two in the role of O'Brien opposite Caviezel's Winston Smith.

For the record the original seventeen-episode UK television series had no fewer than seventeen 'versions' of Number Two, suggesting very much more a function than a personality, and more significantly a multiplicity which is key to the programme, its contexts and our discussions of a post-media media studies. To briefly consider the significant historical, cultural and institutional contexts in which *The Prisoner* was made and received will, we hope, further exemplify these issues and serve to remind us how little key postmodernist and post-structuralist ideas have influenced mainstream *subject media*.

If context is all, then *The Prisoner*'s context is extraordinary. First broadcast in the United Kingdom between 29 September 1967 and 1 February 1968, McGoohan's seemingly allegorical hybrid almost precisely bridged the gap between *Sergeant Pepper* and the student uprisings in Paris in May 1968. It sat, as it were, on the fault line of the countercultural revolution, and doing so felt the full force of the cultural implosion that this entailed. McGoohan's labour of love rarely escapes the epithet 'Kafkaesque' these days, and this is emblematic of an era where the boundaries of high and low culture were being redrawn or simply abandoned.

What needs to be added to this to fully appreciate the lesson this cult item has for our more general discussions about the political elements of media cultures is the institutional context that allowed McGoohan an almost unprecedented freedom. Patrick McGoohan had made himself a 1960s television star in the role of John Drake in the spy show *Danger Man* (aka *Secret Agent* in the United States), a role some would argue he reprised in *The Prisoner*. *Danger Man* was never described as 'Kafkaesque' but it did give McGoohan the leverage with ITV boss Lew Grade to pitch a new idea and demand artistic freedom, as McGoohan himself recalls:

> I'd made 54 of those and I thought that was an adequate amount. So I went to the gentleman, Lew Grade, who was the financier, and said that I'd like to cease making Secret Agent and do something else. So he didn't like that idea. He'd prefer that I'd gone on forever doing it. But anyway, I said I was going to quit.
> *(accessed on 28/6/2010: http://www.statemaster.com/encyclopedia/The-Prisoner)*

McGoohan developed the ideas for the new show with *Danger Man* script editor George Markstein, with the iconic location being provided by a location they had used to shoot 'Italy' in a couple of *Danger Man* episodes (Portmeirion in Wales). McGoohan continues:

> So I prepared it and went in to see Lew Grade. I had photographs of the Village ... So I talked for ten minutes and he stopped me and said, 'I don't understand one word you're talking about, but how much is it going to be?'

... I told him how much and he says, 'When can you start?' I said 'Monday, on scripts.' And he says, 'The money'll be in your company's account on Monday morning.'
(An interview with Patrick McGoohan, conducted by Warner Troyer, March 1977)

Sixteen episodes later and the idea is one way or another played out, though it has also been played for all its worth, not least by the technique that each episode follows either of two basic patterns: Number Six attempts escape or is 'pressed' (tortured/ tricked/ cajoled) for reasons for his resignation (that is, his presence in the Village). By this point McGoohan pretty much had complete artistic control, but for one reason or another (everything about this show is disputed) he needed to end the series. Cue one of the most extraordinary hours of UK television and McGoohan's subsequent flight from angry fans. This is also very much an exemplification of Benjamin's point in 'The work of art in the age of mechanical reproduction.' Where 'the criterion of authenticity ceases to be applicable ... the total function of art ... begins to be based on another practice – politics'. Also, Benjamin adds, 'today photography and film are the most serviceable exemplifications of this new function' (1997: 127).

What is certain about the finale of The Prisoner, entitled 'Fall out' to reinforce the point, is that it returns us all, actors, audience, even the text back to where we were (albeit altered by the subsequent experiences) in a manner which was earlier described as 'Jacobean'. In some ways this is just a matter of offering a final 'act' and then a kind of epilogue in which the participants disrobe (and in this case 'dismantle') and at some time reflect (and in this case the reflection is largely visual and, as a result, inconclusive, even oblique).

At the centre of this we get, ironically, a third resignation: McGoohan's as 'Number Six' and its author. How telling it is that in the period of The Prisoner's 'gestation', Barthes published, first in English then in French (1967/1968), his 'Death of the author', since this is certainly enacted in 'Fall out' and would also represent another kind of 'fallout' across the rest of McGoohan's career. Barthes explores what Wimsatt and Beardsley had much earlier (1954) called 'the intentional fallacy' (1954): the problematic relationship between what a writer consciously and explicitly intends and the meaning of her completed work, concluding that evidence of intention was inadmissible in the context of textual analysis. Thus, for example, the intertextual parallels between Clint Eastwood's last film as an actor, Gran Torino, and John Wayne's last, The Shootist (directed by Don Siegel) cannot be resolved (or proved) by asking Eastwood whether he consciously modelled the final showdown on Don Siegel's film.

Barthes reflects on the demise of the 'God-given' view in a manner that seems not unlike McGoohan's cruder, and blunter response:

We know that a text does not consist of a line of words, releasing a single 'theological' meaning (the 'message' of the Author-God), but is a space of many dimensions, in which are wedded and contested various kinds of writing, no one of which is original: the text is a tissue of citations, resulting from the thousand sources of culture.

(Barthes, 1988: 146)

It has been fairly well documented that McGoohan created 'Fall out' in a manic forty-eight hours, desperate to meet his production deadlines and give the piece a 'proper' ending. This in itself probably adds to its experimental qualities. The extreme and extended response to this hour of television tells us a lot about the dependent relationship between audiences of various kinds and critical models of meaning-making (see for example Gregory, 1997). The ritual horror of not having this seventeen-part experience explained gives way to anger that McGoohan, their hero, might have made 'Fall out' up as he went along, which finally leads to a reconciliation with 'the genius' McGoohan around the notion that, after all, the final episode is a proper puzzle with a proper explanation. McGoohan thus spends the rest of his life patiently avoiding the question while everybody else involved in the series sell their bit of the mystery, limb by severed limb.

All that McGoohan ever did imply is what is anyway obvious, and interestingly what is genuinely Kafkaesque. This is the notion that in effect Number Six has been symbolically standing before a door which only he can open for sixteen weeks. This is a situation not unlike T. S. Eliot's:

> I have heard the key
> Turn in the door once and turn once only
> We think of the key, each in his prison
> Thinking of the key, each confirms a prison.

(T. S. Eliot, The Waste Land)

And if this is true of Number Six it is presumably true of all of us *hypocrite lecteurs*. McGoohan's '*deus abscondus*' routine leaves us where we always were, having with luck been taught a useful lesson which it is easy to identify as post-structuralist since, as Christopher Horrocks confirms, 'the extreme post-structuralist position argues that the world is a text and that reality is a discursive construct' (in Appignanesi, 2003: 206). In *The Prisoner* (2009) this is merely a veneer, whereas the McGoohan version remained troubling, however flawed:

> In the multiplicity of writing, indeed, everything is to be distinguished, but nothing deciphered; structure can be followed, 'threaded' (like a stocking that has run) in all its recurrences and all its stages, but there is no underlying ground; the space of the writing is to be traversed, not penetrated: writing ceaselessly posits meaning but always in order to evaporate it: it proceeds to a systematic exemption of meaning. Thus literature (it would be better, henceforth, to say writing), by refusing to assign to the text (and to the world as text) a 'secret:' that is, an ultimate meaning, liberates an activity which we might call counter-theological, properly revolutionary, for to

refuse to arrest meaning is finally to refuse God and his hypostases, reason, science, the law.

(Barthes, 1988: 147)

These challenges are merely circulating in McGoohan's text. As we leave the Village we are taunted with textures, which have proved irresistible to *Prisoner* cultists (who like occultists believe there is an answer). We see for example the A20 trunk road, clearly signposted, a television room set on the back of a lorry and then London, that other village, temptingly hyper-real. And all the time this is unravelling, like a 'run' in a stocking: real life as the apotheosis of the surreal. This challenge to the very notion of representation has barely been raised or heard across the intervening years, though *subject media* would hardly exist without the counter-cultural movements of the 1960s.

It is part of our central critique of *subject media* that, predicated on *subject English*, it has clung to critical tenets long ago emptied of their productivity, like a number of El Cids strapped to a collection of mechanical hobby-horses. Outside of the Academy intention is one of these, dictating a series of largely limited activities (see Chapter 1) or constructing monstrous 'author' theories whereby the work of hundreds is given meaning only by the 'vision' of one. This, we have argued, has courted academic credibility (and not always successfully) through issues like aesthetic value, to the detriment of meaningful critical engagement with the rainy stony world. Thus opportunities have been missed and challenges, like Foucault's below, ignored:

It is absolutely insufficient to repeat empty slogans: the author has disappeared; God and man dies a common death. Rather, we should re-examine the empty space left by the author's disappearance; we should attentively observe, along its gaps and fault lines, its new demarcations, and the reapportionment of this void; we should await the fluid functions released by this disappearance.

(Foucault, 1991: 105)

We are not interested here in whether *The Prisoner* (1967) is any good: this is not a veiled aesthetic or even fan response. Rather we are exploring the critical and political potential of engaging with it and through it, prompted by its re-emergence via the sincerest form of flattery. When McGoohan (and Number Six) literally walked away from the show in February 1968, he was not only refusing the god role but also stemming a rising tide of support and affection for both himself and the character that had been building across the series. In a business that turns popularity into money (Debord said 'The spectacle is the flip side of money' – 2005: 24), this was at some level a big deal, and again lends the show an edge. There is a feeling that its very unevenness leaves it more able to respond to the zeitgeist.

In this context it becomes more and more appropriate to address *The Prisoner* (1967) in terms of the situationalist provocations of the periods as both a constructed situation and an exercise in psycho-geography. In so many ways McGoohan's experiment meets the expectations of Debord's Situationist International, the most significant ideologues of the subsequent student unrest. For Debord, 'the construction of situations begins beyond the ruins of the modern spectacle' in the way that *The Prisoner* (1967) looks back at the generic commercialism of *Danger Man*. Interesting too, is Debord's point that 'the most pertinent revolutionary experiments in culture have sought to break the spectator's psychological identification with the hero so as to draw them into activity' (1991a: 49). Here is the political intent: to lead to action in the world, even (or maybe especially) if that action leads people to form an angry mob in order to pursue their deceiver (as happened to McGoohan that February).

Seeing the 2009 simulation with its identical chalets also reminds us of the degree to which Sir Clough Williams-Ellis's eccentric architectural experiment is an essential part of the experience offered by McGoohan. In terms of response Debord says that 'the only progressive way out is to liberate the tendency toward play' (1991a: 51), which McGoohan does within and beyond the diegesis. Thought of in this way, *The Prisoner* (1967) reads very well as a constructed situation, 'an integrated use of artistic means to create an ambiance', 'an integrated ensemble of behaviour in time', 'a moment of life concretely and deliberately constructed by the collective organisation of a unitary ambiance and a game of events' (Debord, 1991a: 51).

Seen in this way, two situationist techniques are most apparent in the way in which *The Prisoner* (1967) performs. The first is the notion of the *dérive*, which Debord defines as 'a technique of rapid passage through varied ambiances' (Debord, 1991b: 62). However, this is not a journey in the classic sense since *dérives* 'involve playful-constructive behaviour and awareness of psycho-geographical effects'. It might be argued that McGoohan's extended *dérive* is not only through Portmeirion but also through the metaphorical psycho-geographical contours of the 1960s television series. Debord's text is wonderfully suggestive, speaking of 'psycho-geographical contours with constant currents, fixed points and vortexes which strongly discourage entry into or exit from certain zones' (ibid.). Foucault would clearly see these as discourses, as in their different ways would Six of One (the *Prisoner* Appreciation Society).

At the same time there is also something in the piece and in the wider cultural context of that plagiaristic technique *détournment*, 'the integration of present or past artistic productions into a superior construction of a milieu': a particular kind of bricolage. Such perhaps was Sir Clough Williams-Ellis's intention architecturally at Portmeirion, and certainly McGoohan's intention, if only at the level of making something 'good'. Again we are wandering consciously into a problematic area in even speculating about what was meant in terms of intention. This is a reading in context, a 'genealogy' of *The Prisoner* (1967) as a historically constructed text, an engagement with theory to effect 'action in the world'. It is not a search for the photographic evidence of McGoohan reading Debord's 'Theory of the dérive'. It hopefully has escaped the aesthetic ritual for the realm of politics that Benjamin so optimistically predicted would be the new domain of media 'art'.

Epilogue: commodification and culture

> Popular culture is not consumption, it is culture ... culture, however industrialised, can never be adequately described in terms of buying and selling.
>
> *(John Fiske, 1990: 21)*

For all kinds of reasons we are heading into a new era. The failure of neoliberalism and the free market seems as symbolic an event as the dismantling of the Berlin Wall. The economist David Harvey argues that capitalism is entering its final phase, during which the need for new markets will finally prevent its side-stepping of ever worsening crises. Enzensberger reflecting on the opportunism of McLuhan in another era of realignment suggested that 'this charlatan's most famous saying – "the medium is the message" – perhaps deserves more attention'. For the Marxist Enzensberger the message is silence, and the conviction that 'the bourgeoisie ... (despite having all possible means at its disposal)..has nothing more to say' (1986: 115).

More than thirty years on we stand in the teeth of a postmodernity Bryman characterises as 'the proliferation of signs, dedifferentiation of institutional spheres, depthlessness, cultural nostalgia and the problematisation of authenticity and reality' (in Paterson, 2007: 91). It is a context in which commodification continues unchecked, partly through what Featherstone (1991) calls the 'aestheticisation of everyday life', a further fetishisation of text and an increased tension between text and experience. In the absence of intention and an authorial identity, 'text' as a conceptual packaging becomes both predominant and disturbing, since it is the meaning of cultural practice that is also being 'pre-arranged'. All the more reason that we provide students with the critical means and the social awareness to be effective in this arena. Perhaps Storey, assessing the contribution of Volosinov, puts it best:

> Meaning, once it is problematized, must be the result, not of a functional reproduction of the world in language but of a social struggle – a struggle for mastery in discourse – over which kind of social accenting is to prevail and to win credibility.
>
> *(Storey, 2009: xvii)*

In this chapter we have argued for a 'new politics' for *subject media*, informed partly by a return to McLuhan and an expression of surprise that Baudrillard has been confined to the margins – units on postmodernism – rather than treated as a 'key thinker' for the whole pursuit. We are not interested in reforming a canon of Great Men, but rather argue that some less helpful theories have been privileged over these. Rather than dispensing with the concept of ideology, then, we suggest a reworking of how students might engage with it, ultimately arriving at the interplay of commodification and the politics of identity, to which we turn next.

5
IDENTITY AFTER THE MEDIA

A funny thing happened to us on the way to the future.

(Naughton, 2010: 8)

In so far as there could be a politics of media education, it would not be concerned with revealing truth (compared with the illusory nature of 'the media' – the shadows in Plato's cave). Nor would it be reduced to the development of skills related to work in the 'creative industries'. Both of these ideas impose a governance of the subject, again through the idea of 'the media' as external. Rather, the political act would create a space for a meta-language through/in which the subject (media student) can explore the conditions of their own subjectivity – to unravel the technology of their self (Foucault, 1988) and to think about how interactions with culture play a role in the flow of discourses that shape the way they think of themselves in relation to others.

The way that media education – in our experience in the United Kingdom at least – is arranged produces this kind of progression for those people who follow it through the various key stages. Primary media education will explore textuality and, especially with regard to the moving image, an extended range of literacy practices, with more or less use of information and communications technology (ICT) and an emphasis on the more protectionist version of 'being critical'. Through compulsory schooling media education will be very closely aligned to English, with lots more textual reading and the introduction of more 'factual' work on media industries – for example, how films are marketed – and some formally assessed production work, most commonly video and desktop published work. Post-compulsory media courses will divide into academic and vocational, and the concept of 'audience' will be important. But where identity is an element of these courses of study, before higher education it is unlikely that it will be considered as anything other than an aspect of the 'effects' of media. Within the frame of *subject media*, this seems logical and conventional – the more complex discussion of what identity might be, in relation to more difficult questions about what kind of role, if any, media might play in how we form our identities, will be for more mature, academic students. And yet looked at another way, we can argue that by the time students are introduced to these 'more complex' questions, they will always-already view them as an alternative to an orthodoxy. The same thing happens with the teaching of post-structuralism – a chronological imposition of a normative set of reference points frames the 'more complex' as an optional extension activity – a different (but less legitimate, intentionally or not) way of seeing.

In this chapter the concept of identity will be discussed in three ways – first, a review of the contested nature of the term and its usage in media education; second, a deconstruction of the identity of media studies itself – the stories it tells to itself; and third, a proposal for 'doing identity' after the media, informed by Zizek's take on media and ideology in dialogue with Butler's performative identity. The disjuncture between these two will be played out as a kind of Lyotardian 'differend'.

Identity: a site of conflict

The dissemination by Gauntlett (2007) of research methods utilised with the objective of creating such space for participants to reflect on identity, and the response of Buckingham (2010b) among others to such approaches, will inform the version of identity we want to work with here. This will lead us to an analysis of media education through the lens of Foucault's ways of seeing discourse and identity. We will finally suggest a number of ways in which media students might 'do identity' without recourse to the idea of 'the media' in the early part of the twenty-first century. Identity will be understood here as an event – practised, active, dispersed – a process. Identity is, then, a performance, and we will directly pose the question of how to teach and study it as a journey. 'When we dismiss media as meaningless, what we are really expressing is confusion over where to place their significance' (Ruddock, 2007: 70).

Ruddock discusses the importance of the disposable nature of media events in understanding how we attribute meaning to them. It seems to us that *subject media* has rather missed this point, opting instead to overstate the 'effect' of media in bolder, more 'macro' terms. We want to imagine a media studies which takes the 'throwaway event' seriously – for academic reasons – but on its own terms, not through recourse to another language game borrowed from sociology or English literature – in which the 'role of media in our lives' is offered as legitimation. Identity, performed and fluid, will 'pick and mix' disposable 'bits' of media culture in a process of becoming. What it will not do is stop too long to be 'affected' by a singular cultural product to buy us time to produce a unit of work that equates such engagements to 'close reading' of eighteenth-century novels.

Gauntlett's work is political in the sense that he wants to depart from what he sees as a patronising sociological model employed by the likes of Bourdieu, and to some extent Giddens (and, we will argue, Buckingham), in which social class is privileged in the analysis of taste and self-awareness:

> On the one hand, Bourdieu's analysis effectively shows how cultural value is both socially constructed, and is a manifestation of inequality. At the same time, though, his approach presents the working class as basically ignorant (especially when contrasted with the high-culture privileges and agency which Bourdieu himself enjoys), and permanently stuck at the bottom of the heap with no particular story to tell, or cultural contribution to make.
>
> *(Gauntlett, 2007: 69)*

There is more complexity here, of course, than Gauntlett concedes since Bourdieu is attempting a critical reading of taste and could fairly be invoked to argue that the observations he makes are of what he finds – that taste is connected to degrees of cultural capital and that there is, in 'Distinction' no agenda to relate taste to perception or critical thinking.

It is important, then, for students to consider the relationship between 'trivial' engagements with media culture and structural patterns that may be shared with others – which Ruddock calls 'structured idiosyncracy', but not in such a way that the latter are understood to determine the former. This is tricky. Our entire project here is concerned with thinking around and outside of the discursive arrangements that put structural determinants before subjective agency – not because such forces do not exercise power, but because their privileged status in media education has obscured the more complex ways in which we 'do identity'. Another theme which we return to is the importance in realising that 'new media' have not in themselves facilitated any great advancement in reflective identity construction – they merely offer an archive, a repository for cultural exchange which was in many cases already in operation, but not in binary code. While we recognise that not all media students are 'young people', the majority are, and so we are interested in the rather conservative practices of *subject media* to date – see our reading of the 'wrong way around' development of the subject in the aftermath of the Birmingham Centre for Contemporary Cultural Studies' focus on 'the media' and ideology. These practices have served, intentionally or not, to produce a normative technology through which media studies imposes a set of discursive frames for peoples' reflective scrutiny of their media practices in everyday life. What attention has *subject media* paid to the developmental nature of its work in the lifeworlds of its participants, to the extent to which its intervention is dialectic?

> A focus on identity requires us to play close attention to the diverse ways in which media and technologies are used in everyday life, and their consequences both for individuals and for social groups. It entails viewing young people as significant social actors in their own right, as 'beings' and not simply 'becomings', who should be judged in terms of their projected futures. The needs of young people are not best served either by the

superficial celebration or the exaggerated moral panics that often characterize this field. Understanding the role of digital media in the formation of youthful identities requires an approach that is clear sighted, unsentimental, and constructively critical.

(Buckingham, 2008: 19)

If one effect of the proliferation of media culture has been to increase the prevalence of a 'sense of identity' in the way we think about everyday existence, then the study of the exchange and reception of cultural products must be concerned with this interplay – this constant sense of being – between the embedding of identity in everyday life and the way that media material connects more or less to other parts of the lifeworld. When Gauntlett, reporting on his Lego research in which participants engaged in a series of metaphorical model-building activities to represent their identities, reports that 'the clearest finding is that, when asked to consider influences upon their identities, the participants did not usually think of media products' (2007: 194), what do we do with this? Is it just that his research subjects are so 'duped' by the media that they do not recognise its influence? Or is it that identity need not be an important factor in media studies – given that it does not appear to be much of an issue either way on this evidence? The answer, again, is to go further than Gauntlett and start from somewhere else – removing the notion of 'the media' from the question, to focus instead on how identity negotiation does work, and then to think about how 'mediation' might be a factor in such performance. Clearly, Gauntlett's Lego models – analysed as evidence of people's desire to belong to a collective (he comments on the lack of fragmentation and suggests this might be a riposte to postmodern ideas about how we see ourselves) – are performances, just as a gamer blogging about their experiences in *Grand Theft Auto* is a retelling of identity-work, for an audience (more or less imagined, more or less 'real'). And so our work as media educators ought to be in the province of such performance – we cannot begin to know 'identity' any more than it makes any sense to study 'the media', but we can find ways to articulate the nature of performed identity as a significant factor in media reception. Judith Butler's work is important in this regard, and we shall turn to it shortly.

Buckingham's responses to two different (but related) interventions from Gauntlett provide a helpful context for what we want to suggest about identity after the media. These responses are concerned with the idea of 'media education 2.0' and the celebration of visual and creative research methods respectively, Gauntlett relating the latter to the former as one aspect of a new approach to media education. While (rightly) resisting the parodic version of 'Media 2.0' and its construction of an unhelpful binary opposition between old and new media and old and new ways of teaching, Buckingham accepts some potentially radical shifts in the study of culture:

Enthusiasts for new media typically claim that they entail a distinctively different orientation towards information, a different phenomenology of use, a different politics of knowledge and a different mode of learning. If this is the case, it has potentially far-reaching implications for pedagogy – not just for what we teach but also for how we teach.

(Buckingham, 2010b: 2)

This is a starting point for our project: we believe in these 'far-reaching implications', and yet we start from a different place from both Gauntlett and Buckingham, preferring to question the idea of 'the media' as opposed to a view of a shift in how 'they' operate in relation to people. Buckingham is sceptical about the version of the democratisation thesis that he calls the 'Californian ideology', with its exaggerated claims for emancipation (we would accuse the entire *subject media* project of this). He reminds us that 'digital divides' mirror broader structural inequalities and that participation online may often reproduce patterns of activity offline or in 'old media' spaces:

> To a large extent, the most active participants in the creative world of web 2.0 are the 'usual suspects'. Indeed, if online participation is as socially, culturally and politically important as the enthusiasts suggest, it seems likely that, far from liquidating social inequality, it might actually accentuate it.
>
> *(Buckingham, 2010b: 6)*

Although we are not sure that Gauntlett believes anything differently – other than to suggest that web 2.0 might be a starting point for change as there are tools and affordances which clearly provide the impetus for people to create and communicate – Buckingham favourably compares Henry Jenkins' work with the 'Media 2.0' argument as he interprets it. We can, it seems, all agree that there has been an elitist thrust to the discourse of 'critique' at work in media studies. We extend this to the entire approach which sees teachers tell students how to look at 'the media' differently, but Jenkins' notion of the 'participation gap' is privileged over what Buckingham sees as a complacent 'digital natives' thesis. The latter is in danger of ignoring the differences between young people and the conditions of possibility for them to be creative or participative/political. Is it not the case, though, that the separating of 'the media' from those young people has constructed a binary opposition of its own, and that any sustained erosion of the participation gap will need to start by reimagining the relationship between media and culture in a way that avoids lumping together all forms of private and public sphere cultural exchange in this way? Moving on to the 'naïve empiricism' at work in recent discussions about research methods, Buckingham accuses Gauntlett of ignoring the socio-cultural context of research in favour of an idealist psychological view of identity:

> I would challenge the repeated claim that visual or 'creative' methods are in themselves any more 'empowering' than other methods, or that they are uniquely placed to give participants a 'voice'. All research creates positions

from which it is possible for participants to speak, to perform or to represent themselves. The political and ethical dimensions of that process do not derive simply from the methods that are employed, but are a function of the wider social contexts in which research is conducted, distributed and used.

(Buckingham, 2010b: 648)

This is important to use since we will later, as part of our proposal for a 'pedagogy of the inexpert', favour a kind of ethnography as a learning context for students looking at media culture. With regard to identity, we strongly suggest that students give time to working with people in situated reception and consumption of culture, as opposed to framing our work by either abstracted 'critical' readings of texts or production work within a vocational employment modality. But in so doing we are vulnerable to the kind of naivety Buckingham warns against here. How can an A level or an undergraduate student construct research which gives sufficient time for people to express aspects of their identity but which at the same time is sensitive to these wider social contexts? Is it possible in this light to rethink our view of what we want to know about identity in relation to media?

Performing identity

There are three aspects of Judith Butler's work that inform our approach to identity. First, she develops the idea of performativity from the Derridean 'take' on Kafka's parable of the man from the country before the Law. With regard to gender, Butler suggests that it is the elusive disclosure of the law that manifests itself in our performance of the (endlessly deferred) meaning of gender so that in this sense identity 'operates as an interior essence that might be disclosed, an expectation that ends up producing the very phenomenon that it anticipates' (Butler, 1999: xv). Second, she resists (as we do) the notion of a pre-existing identity for the subject that can then take political action in response to discourses that it seeks to resist. Instead, the self and its actions are reciprocal due to the 'discursively variable construction of each in and through the other' (1999: 195). Third, Butler poses the question 'to what extent is "identity" a normative ideal rather than a descriptive feature of experience'(1999: 23) and 'identity is formally constituted by the very 'expressions' that are said to be its results (1999: 34). In our account we want to consider the interplay between identity and 'the media' as normative ideals and – equally – the determining reciprocity between the two – for example, the role of 'the media' in constructing identity as another regulatory ideal which cultural analysis ought to scrutinise.

Subject identity

'Doing Foucault' on education is relatively straightforward in contemporary contexts, as the practices of educational institutions, from primary schools to universities, in the early twenty-first century are neatly 'panoptical' and the affordances of virtual learning amplify the surveillance culture yet further in this respect. The media educator, though, is relatively likely to see herself as a counter-agent. After all, media education is the object of a discourse of derision and it constructs its own identity as other to the classic nineteenth-century curriculum in terms of its shiny technology, emancipatory critical analysis and 'fit for purpose' employability. The genealogy of the media educator, then, will be an account of radical, 'edupunk' pedagogy. And yet, looked at through a Foucauldian lens, it is more realistic to say that we would find a deeply conservative, normative and regulatory grain running through much of contemporary media education. In Ball's 'application' of Foucault to education, he points to discourse as the theoretical idea that most clearly serves the exploration:

> We are concerned here with educational sites as generators of an historically specific (modern) discourse, that is, as sites in which certain modern validations of, and exclusions from, the 'right to speak' are generated. Educational sites are subject to discourse but are also centrally involved in the propagation and selective dissemination of discourses, the 'social appropriation' of discourses. Educational institutions control the access of individuals to various kinds of discourse.
>
> *(Ball, 1990: 3)*

In its desire to reach out into the lifeworld and require students to adopt a 'critical language' to rearticulate the personal domain – their own 'media culture', *subject media* is a hegemonic imposition. In the discursive formulation of the analysis of identity, we can trace this most clearly. Here we are concerned with the attachment of subject positions to 'identities' that inform us about how the subject occupies the differentiated social field of education and in its ontological conditions, or 'dasein' (Heidegger, 1962).

In previous work (McDougall, 2006), we have traced the dialectical nature of the relations between the self-identity of the subject – media studies – and its social identity as reflected through its contexts of operation, in this case the assessment of production work for the A level in the subject. This is the cultural politics of subject identity – in other words how the subject occupies specific spaces and distributes power/knowledge through its pedagogic determinations (Bernstein, 1990). To review the question of the genealogy of media studies in relation to its institutional being is to explore how media studies makes a claim to enter the educational field in relation to the (assumed to be) pre-existing identities of its participants. How does this account of the relationship between the 'spirit' of subject identity and its classification and framing play out through assessment procedures? The reading of examiner discourse we deal with here is located in the different positions offered by Habermas (1993) and Lyotard (1988) in response to the future (anterior?) of the project of modernity. Habermas's desire to retain a 'theoretical perspective' is refuted by Lyotard as a clinging to meta-narratives.

Abandoning such an approach is, for Habermas, a postmodern relativism shot through with neoconservativism. Habermas' modernist anthropology calls for consensus as the object of politics, and the 'ideal speech situation' is where we must turn for a return to the project of modernity. In this conception, human subjects in completely equal communicative interaction are unable to legitimate inegalitarian distributions of power. For Lyotard, the postmodern condition presents opportunities for micropolitics, mobilised by subjects creating new rules in language games.

In previous research we provided a forensic critical discourse analysis of A-level Media Studies examiners 'standardising' the marking of practical coursework (McDougall, 2004, 2006). Nine hours of examiners' meetings were recorded, with ethical clearance and permission from a major awarding body, transcribed and grouped into discursive categories. Every statement made about the work in hand (paralinguistic material was excluded) was counted as a separate utterance. Statements about process, those that articulated concerns, doubts or anxieties about 'doing the job', or rather the responsibility that comes with examining or moderating (the latter is more sensitive since it involves judging fellow teachers), accounted for 22 per cent of the recordings. Roughly the same amount of time (23 per cent) was the sum of statements about the tensions between teacher and examiner/moderator and moments of uncertainty about how to apply the criteria. Together, then, discussion about the process rather than assertions of judgement accounted for 45 per cent, with the remaining 55 per cent devoted to expressions of value (clear judgements of the work under scrutiny in relation to mark schemes to be applied).

Through the prism offered by Bernstein's ideas about modalities and discourses, we can trace some patterns in these statements. For Bernstein, pedagogic practice is fundamentally a social process through which cultural reproduction takes place. We are urged by his work to consider education, and particularly schooling, not simply as a carrier of power relations external to itself. Pedagogic discourse is itself a power distributor – determining identities: of responses (good/bad, simplistic/sophisticated), of particular instances of subject expression (an 'A' grade answer/an 'E' grade answer), of subjects (strong student/weak student). Strong classifications of discourse maintain strict distinctions between forms of knowledge, and weaker classifications offer a bringing together. Communication is thus framed in pedagogical relations through codes and their modalities (Bernstein, 1990).

The 'crux' of the matter is the claim of media studies to be potentially a dislocator of traditional pedagogic power relations, or an antidote to the unequal distribution of cultural capital (Bourdieu and Passeron, 1990). A teacher, as indicated, is principally an agent of control. Media studies teachers and examiners, however, are unlikely to represent themselves as agents of control in the field of cultural consumption. Nevertheless, in the codes identified for our transcriptions we can deconstruct the attempts to form classification, to create a coherent pedagogical practice, which in its very intent mobilises an unequal 'keeping apart' of things. There is a powerful contradiction between the need to make the discourse of *subject media* hierarchical to secure its status and academic authenticity, and the desire to 'liberally' recognise and celebrate the honest endeavour, and to recognise positively the idiom of the student. This tension might be gleaned from these examples:

> As someone who has seen a lot more media than my students and comparing that with my knowledge of media professionally, how far do I think they are along that scale?

> We cannot presume to provide a context for the candidates' work which the candidate is unable to provide for themselves.

> At first I was hit by all these technical terms, which is why I read some of the other question 1 answers to see if the kids generally do and some of them do, but they don't hit all these kinds of technical terms and I thought after a term's teaching this probably deserves to edge into the competent because they had obviously been listening and learned, but I wanted the Why?

These statements reveal what we might refer to as a 'logocentric' need to compensate for a lack of mastery over standards with a confessional discourse about desire, personal agenda and a collaborative sense of a 'mission' (Derrida, 1976). In other words, in Bernstein's terms we can see these examiners striving for rules of combination by which to judge students, the 'meaning potential' of their work – the potential of their discursive performances to be 'pedagogised' and the extent that the work presented for examination accords with the realisation rules of the subject.

Tensions and needs for justification in these recordings seem to be arising from anxiety over the vertigo of just having to decide whether a video piece is 'any good' or not. We might say that the examiners are operating a recontextualising principle, and even that their discussions reveal as much about their own identities and values as about the students' work, which would account for the time spent (almost half) on talking about process. Viewed another way, this group of 'experts' are working through the basis on which they are going to decide which students have acquired the legitimate (pedagogised) code and which have not. This framing activity needs to be given time because without it the subject lacks the strong classification that would solidify criteria for judgement. The openness of subject identity does not preclude the need to standardise; rather, it changes the modality of making judgements. Power is not eradicated or reduced; power works through different principles. The recontextualising shift is an interplay between understanding 'a good video' from an audience point of view versus assessing a video text as demonstrative of various forms of theoretical or conceptual understanding. The language game which might provide the idioms for such an approach is unstable, hence we might witness in the standardisation process a series of gaming moves, as Lyotard would have it, rather than an egalitarian communicative consensus, from Habermas.

Returning to our notion of the 'project' of media studies, we might suggest that, its very potential to be radical lies in its lack of strong classification. Thus the standardisation process offers distributive rules that reduce any potential for progressive learning to the logic of the same. So statements made by examiners such as 'I get the impression they were given the brief and they thought Right! What do we like? We like this and we like this, so let's do it' reveal a predictable but significant desire to articulate and reduce the uncertainty that arises from media study that is arranged more as a horizontal discourse, that 'has its origins in the life world' (Bernstein, 1996: 207). By trying to imagine the students' intent, and judge the extent to which it is justified (presumably against a more measured or considered set of objectives for the work), they are attempting to frame the standards vertically. Inevitably this will occur as a public 'awarding' institution frames such discussions within discourses about standards and grades. We can see that the context of the meeting gives rise to an energising of a symbolically controlled pedagogy:

> Pedagogic modalities are crucial realisations of symbolic control, and thus of the process of cultural production and reproduction. Symbolic control, through its pedagogic modalities, attempts to shape and distribute forms of consciousness, identity and desire. Here, one can distinguish between official pedagogical modalities and local pedagogical modalities. The former are official symbolic controls and give rise to macro/micro regulation of contexts: practices, evaluations and acquisitions at institutional levels. The latter, local pedagogic modalities, are familial: peer and 'community' regulations.
>
> *(Bernstein, 1996: 201)*

Bernstein is struck by the potential of local modalities for 'colonisation'. It may well be the case that the tension uttered throughout our recorded discussions can be understood as an attempt to 'colonise' or to 'delocalise' the horizontal range of media studies learning and replace it with a vertical, symbolic framing that matches it with other academic discourses. Thus the personalising of much of the discussions ('I was thinking ...', 'I suppose I want to ...', 'I think what was in my head was....') is a public playing out, in the relative safety of the examiners' council, of a discomfort with the duality of being at once a 'carrier' of a local modality and a paid expert charged with setting the standard of its institutional form, the official pedagogical modality of *subject media*. Within the framework of a discourse, such as media studies, that claims to be inclusive, liberal and free from the cultural prejudices of other adjacent cultural discourses, this tension will be particularly uncomfortable.

One of the key elements at stake in these relations of difference is the identity of the examiner and of the student. In a sense here we are considering a theorisation of accounts of media pleasure and cultural appropriation offered previously by sociology (Willis, 1990). Foucault's notion of a 'mark' is useful in extending our understanding of how assessment practices operate in relation to identities:

> For a Foucaultian understanding of culture, the most important thing to note is that the examination and the mark, the production of a new sort of knowledge about the child through a specific means of capturing the child in an inscription, is not the operation of a negative power .... The intention is not to deny children access to the truth about themselves, but to produce them as functioning, maximised citizens, to produce the truth about themselves.
>
> *(Kendall and Wickham, 1999: 137–8)*

In this sense, the educational institution is to be viewed primarily as a regime for a special form of historically specific, normative culture management. The 'mark' of assessment has an intent within a logic of diagnosis and improvement. Pedagogic practice occurs in relation to the co-existence of a variety of social identities expressed in practices (or discourses from the life-world, in Bernstein's terms) that come within the ambit of the institution. The student's culture is brought into an arena that will make both explicit and implicit judgments about the student's identity and seek to address these in performances within the frameworks of knowledge furnished by the curriculum. In this process, in the 'outcome' of media student's production activities, however ludic, the culture of the student is brought into a domain of judgement and correction (Hunter, 1988). Sifting the recordings, we find statements such as: 'one thing that strikes you immediately when students are beginning to understand video ...'; 'I suspect that these students have really enjoyed working on this production'; and 'unfortunately, given it's clearly a good candidate, it just doesn't meet the criteria'. These sound like sensitive attempts on the part of senior examiners to personalise/humanise a cold, impersonal process, and indeed clearly – in their reference to a subjective context behind the object of assessment – they are attempts to provide a 'warmer' context for judgements. However, when considered in the context of Foucault's concept of 'the examination', we might consider these utterances as diagnostic operations serving to impose a mark on the 'amplification of capabilities' of these students. The management of culture operates here by asserting a range of qualities/ intentions for students, for which there is no evidence. After all, the life-world of students (see Bernstein, 1995) is likely to be very different from that of their teachers, and of examiners. Why is 'enjoyment' of a production relevant? How is it clear that students are 'beginning to understand' video (and is this a coherent development to assess)? Why is one candidate 'clearly good' even though s/he has not performed to a high standard in this exam? These 'para-judgements' can be read as indicators of examiners' scrutiny of students' production of 'self-truth' in each case. According to an application of Foucault's concepts of discipline and governmentality to education, the crux of the approach is to understand the importance of allusions to the visibility of a 'self' that is being accorded due recognition while judgments are being made about the realisation of that self in a strictly coded performance.

Education, then, is an extended arrangement of symbolic space as well as a literal, physical entity; is an arena, above all else, of the mediation of subjectivity. The relative autonomy of the teacher (despite the apparent increase in centralised control of education under recent governments) arises from the acquisition of some teaching and learning methods (and the rejection of others), belonging to certain communities of practice. The teacher becomes one of a network of interventions into a student's life, an agent in the management of culture. However, any autonomy is relative, and as such teacher identity is constructed in relation to the cultural regularities that control ideas, preferences and practices within the institution. The prize of legitimacy for media studies sets up a transliteral conflict of competing discourses. The media studies examiner, herself a teacher, will be subject to the same regularities, again as an agent in an uneasy co-existence of practices and identities (teacher, academic, media consumer, examiner, parent). Take this statement:

> I had a problem with this one; it says a lot but I didn't like the English used which is quite clumsy and I can see people coming down quite hard on this, and I can see people saying you can't give this kid a high level because the English is so poor.

This is highly revealing as the speaker appears to be using a series of disclaimers to frame a statement about the student's lack in relation to standard English. At the same time, this examiner is distancing his self from 'the other' – the conservative examiner who would want to (unfairly?) penalise the student for expressing themselves in their own language. This tension is introduced as a personal dilemma – 'I had a problem' – the examiner is unsure how to make the mark. What is articulated here is the co-existence of a number of different discursive positions in which the speaker is entangled. The tension encapsulates the condition of *subject media* as would-be liberal, inclusive and alternative to culturally exclusive curriculum domains and the requirement to introduce systematic socio-cultural distinctions into what are frequently expressions of cultural identity.

Bernstein seems to echo Foucault when suggesting that discourses cast a gaze (for example Foucault's 1977 work on the medical discourse casting an objectifying gaze on the body). The recontextualising principle carries the gaze in the context of the institution. The would-be 'new' subject can only enter the institution in so far as it becomes 'academic' – and partakes of a vertical discourse that introduces a hierarchical structure.

> Looking through the set of languages and their fractured realities, forever facing yesterday rather than a distanced tomorrow, is rather like visiting a gallery where paintings are in a continuous motion, some being taken down,

others replacing and all in an unfinished state. The invisible energy activating this movement is changes in the landscape already taken place or taking place, some disfiguring, some eroding, some opening new prospects.

(Bernstein, 1996: 171)

Pedagogic discourse, crucially, may be perceived as a transit for something 'external' to it. In the traditional 'hidden curriculum' account, this external is social, economic relations in the world outside. For Bernstein (and the account which we offer here), pedagogic practice is itself the fundamental social context through which cultural reproduction takes place. It is the inner workings of the discourse structure itself that must be considered, as it is the principles of the communication itself within pedagogic relations that will regulate knowledge and power. The relationships between categories of knowing is vital. Since the Enlightenment, certain discourses have found the space to acquire unique places as subjects, as categories, with knowledge increasingly 'singularised'. A discourse with a weak classification will arrange pedagogic encounters around a spread of specialisms, or sub-categories, whereas a stronger classification will allow a discourse to operate in a more linear fashion:

> Strong classification of discourses is likely to lead empirically to a dislocation in the transmission of knowledge, because, with strong classification the progression will be from concrete local knowledge, to the mastery of simple operations, to more abstract general principles, which will only be available later in the transmission. Thus there is an internal classification and distribution of forms of knowledge. When children fail at school, drop out, repeat, they are likely to be positioned in a factual world tied to simple operations, where knowledge is impermeable. The successful have access to the general principle, and some of these – a small number who are going to produce the discourse – will become aware that the mystery of discourse is not order, but disorder, incoherence, the possibility of the unthinkable. But the long socialisation into the pedagogic code can remove the danger of the unthinkable, and of alternative realities.
>
> *(Bernstein, 1996: 11)*

So it would appear that an application of Bernstein's ideas about pedagogic discourse would suggest that the dynamics of space, framing, assessment and coding perpetuate the very traditions – both symbolic and empirical – that media teaching seems to want to challenge. *Subject media*, its practitioners and agents, including teachers, students and luminaries are equally and necessarily unable to determine the conditions of their own being, a state which makes the attempts to create self-identity and organise a free space for practice impossible.

Doing new media studies

> Relationships between identity and everyday technologies are material as well as imaginary. An awareness of computers may offer ways of thinking about the self, but users, programmers and players are changing, working with their subjectivity in learning to manipulate the hardware and software. Taste and preference, self-presentation and performance in popular technoculture are inseparable from the embodied nature of technical expertise and dexterity.
>
> *(Lister et al, 2009: 276)*

We are not, for this project, adopting a 'new media' approach as we are resistant to the idea that *subject media* stands at a crossroads which is determined by a temporal, technological shift. Instead, we are intrigued by the ways in which new digital media allow us to 'see clearly now' what should always have been our concern – what was under our noses all the time, as it were. Amongst new media scholars and academics engaged in ethnographic research with and into gaming cultures, in particular, theories have emerged to deal with the apparently altered states of identity and subjectivity – shifts in the relationship between public and private, real and virtual, life and media and ultimately human/machine relations (see Lister et al, 2009). These ideas, often developed in the field of 'cybercultural studies', look at the way that our sense of self may be altered and how this allows us to consider further the always-already 'mutable' state of the human subject. There is disagreement, or at least there are nuanced distinctions, over the extent to which this is determined by technical operations:

> The notion that there are important shifts in the nature of identity or subjectivity attendant on the advent of digital media is evident across the diverse conceptual frameworks of new media studies. There is little agreement over the precise nature of these shifts, their historical and technological location, and their epochal import, but each – in different ways – makes claims for the importance of these shifts in understanding everyday life in a digital technoculture.
>
> *(Lister et al, 2009: 285–6)*

To assert the epochal equation lets *subject media* off the hook. If 'taste, preference and performance' are seen as central to an understanding of the reception and circulation of media in culture, and media studies has largely ignored this in favour of looking at 'mass media' with a range of analytical tools pulled together from sociology and literary theory, followed by a move to 'creative production and evaluation' which left this way of seeing media intact despite appearances, then to view web 2.0 as the determining factor for a new approach masks the fact that we should have had our eyes open to this anyway. Indeed, as we traced in the early chapters, cultural studies had these intentions in the first place 'before the media'. For example, the work of Paul Willis has rarely been cited in A-level Media Studies work, and now that students are directed there in relation to online symbolic negotiations – young people connecting with bricolage, mash-up and remixing of 'real media' – it is a mistake to somehow imagine that the ideas of Willis, or Baudrillard for that matter, have simply been 'brought to life' by the internet.

However, 'Media 2.0' does open up some new debates, for sure. Lister et al (2009) rightly explore the complexity of dealing with identity as we want to – informed by Foucault and Butler – in relation to social media, where an interplay of fluid, decentred subjectivity is contested by the normalising 'essential self'.

Flecks of identity

Clearly if we are arguing that the visible and archived nature of online exchange is only new in its accessible 'being there' for us to discuss, it is much more difficult to suggest that the panoptical opportunities for surveillance of identity are only new in this same sense. Rather the temporal shift is one aspect of the former but defines the latter. Fuller describes 'flecks of identity' that identify the bearer in particular relations and network us in far less emancipatory ways:

> According to the script, we live in a culture that sees things in individual terms: we construct oppositions of modifications to surveillance on the Enlightenment concepts of rights to privacy and to property. But control lives off the memetic part objects that are the flecks of identity in a sorting system … control has no need of individuals per se, only as referents: as scalar nodes in the flow of cash, commodity and behaviour.
>
> *(Fuller, 2007: 154)*

Fuller offers a sobering antidote to Wesch's 'digital ethnography' work, in which he advocates young people's participation in online expression and new forms of political engagement. Wesch (2009) describes the flow of webcam exchange and comment as 'humanity without fear or anxiety', whereas Fuller (who also deals with affordances) is concerned with abuse and surveillance – the other side of the 'processing' coin. So for the study of culture, we are once again returned to the inevitable, if remixed, choice between attention to structure or to agency. The distinction between the way that Fuller and Wesch are responding to essentially the same data illustrates our obligation to avoid the well-trodden path of assumption on our terms about how people 'do' media. By far the most inconvenient 'truth' for us to apply to the constrained and highly pressurised context of the social practice of contemporary pedagogy is the realisation that ethnographic work will help students with this kind of work more than any teacher-led activity. This has too often been a missing link – where students take empirical audience work seriously, it has usually been the transmission and recall of work in the field. While *subject media* has responded to the affordances of digital creativity, it has inconsistently facilitated student research with real live people.

Doing ethnography

Ethnography does not fit with unit or module boundaries because of its compulsion to spend time with the everyday. But is it the best we can do in *subject media* to make our students familiar with ethnographic work conducted by professional researchers, rather than expecting them to produce their own? Like so many elements of radical or progressive pedagogy, a broader 'deschooling' may be required before the individual teacher can respond. Examples to 'pass on' in this way ought to include Stald's work on 'mobile identity' and Stern on online authoring. In our view the following observation from the latter speaks volumes for the blind alley that *subject media* has followed for so long:

> At least part of the general bewilderment about youth online expression stems from the fact that public attention is disproportionately paid to what teens disclose and produce online, such as the words, text, images and sounds that can be observed on the screen. Yet little consideration is typically given to understanding why young people express themselves in these ways or how their authorial experiences are meaningful to them.
>
> *(Stern, 2008: 95)*

This view is critical of the conservative practice of teaching young people to apply 'critical reading' of their culture through the imposition of a middle-class, adult-language game. And so the antidote must clearly be to facilitate ethnography for students, beginning with small-scale design and then the implementation of method and the acquisition of fragments of autoethnographic and ethnographic data from student research work. While it is taken for granted now that students learn by making, the making of texts is still privileged over the making of data.

Identity after the media

Butler's departure from conceptions of identity as more or less related to such defining characteristics as sexual difference was to remove that equation entirely:

> Here, for the first time, gender and sexuality were fully liberated from any stable notion of intrinsic, sexed identity, feminine or masculine, except as performatively monitored, incited, named and marked in discourse.
>
> *(Segal, 2009: 39)*

Crucially, we want to take Butler's view of how gender identity works as applicable to all questions of how we manage identity. This is not a new idea, as Storey demonstrates:

> What Judith Butler (1999: 33) argues with regard to gender identities also, I think, applies to identities in general; that is, 'an identity is performatively

constituted by the very 'expressions' that are said to be its results.' In this way, the performance of identity is the accumulation of what is outside (in culture) as if it were inside (in nature). Popular culture is a fundamental part of this process.

(Storey, 2003: 91 – cited in Hills, 2005: 141)

Here, then, is a way of thinking about identity that lets us assess media culture but does not restrict us to looking at the 'internal' properties of texts as objects of study or to taking a reductive view of reception by 'audiences'. Instead, we can support students in thinking about the part media play in identity performance, so the disconnection between 'the media' and people in life is removed:

> Pop culture can be viewed less as an inherently democratizing or commercially imposed cultural force which we must choose to be for or against, and more as a system of classifications – a discursive field – through which constructions of pleasure are made meaningful. Rather than magically producing an ineffable and untheorisable pleasure, on this account popular culture can be viewed as the cultural site par excellence where self-consciously cultural pleasures can be publicly ascribed to the self or to imagined Others, and where cultural performances of pleasure (and/or their evaluation) can be carried out. By virtue of its near-ubiquitous presence, popular culture provides a common ground and a set of systematic differences through which consumers can, as textualised agents, define aspects of their cultural identities.
>
> *(Hills, 2005: 140–1)*

So could this 'textualised agency' replace 'the media' as the thing to be looked at – in the academic discourse – and played with – in the vocational modality? How would this work in practice, in the classroom? Can we imagine an alternative pedagogy in 'real terms'? In the UK system, GCSE is the default qualification for 16-year-olds and the GCSE in Media Studies accounts for a large percentage of formally accredited media learning. A GCSE specification for Media Studies offers this choice of work:

RADIO

Analyse the opening five minutes of a specific talk-based radio show paying particular attention to codes and conventions. How does the show try to appeal to its audience?

Prepare a script for a radio show aimed at a specific audience. This could include references to idents, inserts, bedding music and any other appropriate features.

MOVING IMAGE

Analyse the opening five minutes of a specific film or television programme. How does the film or programme attract the interest of its audience?

Present ideas for the opening of a film or television programme in the same genre. You can submit ideas in the form of a script for the opening or most dramatic scenes; as a storyboard using drawings, writing or photographs to represent what is seen on screen.

ADVERTISING AND MARKETING

Analyse two television or print or viral advertisements. How effective are they in selling their products?

Design your own advertisement for a product targeted at a specific audience. You can submit ideas in script form, as a storyboard (using drawings, writing or photographs to represent what is seen on screen) for TV or viral advertisement. For a print advertisement you should design the advertisement itself.

PRINT

Analyse the cover pages of two popular magazines or the front pages of two popular newspapers.

How do the covers/pages appeal to their audiences?

Design the cover for one edition of a magazine or the front page of a newspaper aimed at a specific audience.

WEB-BASED MEDIA

Analyse the home pages of two popular entertainment websites. How does each site appeal to its target audience?

Design a home page for an entertainment website targeted at a specific audience.

PACKAGING OF DVDS

Analyse the covers of two film or television programme DVDs. How does each cover appeal to its target audience?

Design a DVD cover for a film or television programme targeted at a specific audience.

PROMOTION OF MUSIC

Analyse a music video. How does it appeal to its target audience?

Present your own ideas for a music video for a song aimed at a specific audience. Ideas should be presented in storyboard form using drawings, writing or photographs to represent what is seen on screen.

CHILDREN'S COMICS

Analyse the front pages of two children's comics. How do they appeal to their respective target audiences?

Design the front cover for one edition of a children's comic aimed at a specific audience.

(http://store.aqa.org.uk/qual/newgcse/pdf/AQA-4810-W-SP-10.PDF – accessed 10 June 2010)

Thinking, then making

The eight options provided in the box above for GCSE Media Studies follow a pedagogic orthodoxy which is well established – students study a kind of media and then demonstrate their understanding by imitating the format. In each case students analyse and then reproduce in a linear order, and the formative critical 'reading' influences the creative act. In every case there is the compulsion to identify a 'specific' or 'target' audience for the kind of media product being analysed/constructed. In Chapter 7 we will deal thoroughly with these assumptions, but here we are concerned with the privileged status of the 'text-type'. Partly the specification is merely old-fashioned, with its separation of one media from another, in which case we could apply 'new media studies' to fix this. And partly it is a question of something more long-standing in *subject media* – the avoidance of people. There is no requirement for students to question the idea that DVD covers, magazines, comics, websites and viral adverts straightforwardly appeal to their 'target audiences' with any consideration beyond the internal properties of each text. The subsequent production activity in every case follows through with the compulsion to target a specific audience. The ways in which such an audience might come to exist – through the complicated elements of identity which we have dealt with in this chapter – are ignored, but surely that is of more interest in the study of culture than the detail of the colour of the font on a DVD cover and a set of assumptions about how that 'appeals'? Hills paraphrases the collective sense of this problem here:

> Cultural theory – studies appears to all too often respect specific demarcations of the text, where industry-given and institutionally or communally

constructed-constituted constructions of bounded and discrete texts (within art worlds) are typically replayed, and where attempts at studying how boundaries between texts might be eroded nevertheless rely on notions of intertextuality that construct sets of bounded and discrete or identifiable texts which can then be said to interact... This absence in cultural theory is hardly accidental: it has occurred as a result of the way that cultural studies/ theory has treated texts as naturally bounded and discrete objects of study, tracking audience 'readings' of specific films, TV shows and books, or providing scholarly (post-) structuralist readings of the same things.....Under these contemporary conditions of media culture it has arguably become impossible to clearly isolate out what the meaning of a single, specific, bounded text would be.

(Hills, 2005: 26)

Once again, we would play down the idea that there is any contemporary – or new – climate which forces this issue. Instead, we suggest that this text-bound approach has always been a strange and unhelpful – but relatively quick and easy – way of 'doing culture' in education. The alternative, to look at performing and networked selves making decisions about culture and everyday life, is much harder to pin down and 'look at' in a classroom or lecture theatre – or even a virtual learning environment (VLE). What new media does is complicate so much the idea of the singular text – Naughton (2010: 10) just plainly states that 'Even if you don't accept the ecological metaphor, there's no doubt that our emerging information environment is more complex – in terms of numbers of participants, the density of interactions between them, and the pace of change – than anything that has gone before' – and merely act as a catalyst for a paradigm shift that ought to have happened anyway.

So can we rework this to privilege a concern for performative identity above the more straightforward (assumed) transmission of text to audience? Can we bring together some connected ideas from Foucault, Hills and Butler to this – but without annexing the approach to an extension task for the more able in school or an optional critical theory module at university? In other words, could young people as routinely do cultural studies – as it was intended before 'the media' as they routinely do textual analysis currently? If the connecting point is a working consensus on the technology of self, then we want students to explore ways in which people produce a range of modes of identity which may be self-regulatory and normalising (Foucault) and also will be performed (Butler), textualised (Hills) and to a greater or lesser extent 'networked' (Lister et al). So we want students to think about the way that cultural products work to connect with people's construction of their selves; play a part in performance of identity – perhaps through fandom or other affiliations that signify within language games and foster the connecting of people to one another – on or offline. How people attribute meaning to cultural material, along with how they attribute meaning to themselves.

Zizek

Although we were able to cherry-pick some neatly fitting elements of Zizek's work when dealing with representation, at first glance it looks much harder to do this more broadly, as Zizek more than any other contemporary writer is very clear about the existence of – and ideological impact on our daily lives of – *the media*. Most of this book will be, for Zizek, part of the liberal problem of social taboo – we are so busy navel-gazing about our discipline that we are complicit with the ongoing capitalist media technology. In other words, we are more comfortable with the Lacanian Zizek – who helps us tackle the concept of media representation – than the Marxist, with whom we might agree politically – we want to fight inequality – but will collide theoretically, at first glance. But looking again, it is clear that Zizek wants to make explicit the media's political ideology by resisting fashionable leftist theoretical work such as ours which, he argues, allows the media to continue unfettered. We will not pay much attention to the idea of 'the media' as an understandable technology within broader capitalist structure but only because, and precisely because, Zizek is, in our view, complicit in undermining his own project when he allows recourse to the very idea from which he calls us to 'look awry':

> Zizek uses his short circuit juxtapositions of mass culture with philosophical and psychoanalytically-fuelled insights to create his ongoing project of looking awry and adopting a parallax view – a mode of critical thought that offers at least a glimpse of a way out of the self-referential, closed circuits of capitalist media.
>
> *(Taylor, 2010)*

But will the mode of critical thought not be undermined by the idea of looking awry from the very ideal object that exercises power through our perception of it as powerful? If Zizek's 'call to arms' is predicated on beginning to think differently – thinking again, then the othering of, and disdain for 'the media' is surely a manifestation of the dominant liberal hegemony he wants to undermine. Zizek wants us to ask the right questions. Some such might be these. What, in the early twentieth century, is capitalist media? How do we work with ideas of convergence culture, Media 2.0, creativity at the same time as dealing with power expressed in culture if we return to this outdated notion of a collective, abstracted force – the media – rather than looking (awry) at the micropolitics of specific forms of cultural exchange – but each on their own terms? As we stand, *subject media* is a cog in the wheel of self-regarding circularity – of the 'universal category of the mediated spectacle'. As is Zizek.

Pedagogy of the differend: Butler versus Zizek

As the GCSE example demonstrates, magazines have always occupied a central space in media studies in schools and colleges, and this is clearly an outcome of the academic backgrounds of media teachers, who are English graduates and are more comfortable

– or 'expert' – with film and print media. Later we will argue for a 'pedagogy of the inexpert' to dispense with such notions of comfort, but for now we will explore the orthodoxy around 'doing magazines'. Students are commonly introduced to questions of gender representation and ideology and might, alongside the work of Althusser and Winship, read such 'popular' responses as Laura Barton here:

> These days, the insinuation that all gents are satisfied by 29 cans of Stella and a slightly stained copy of Razzle is as quaintly outmoded as the suggestion that the lady loves Milk Tray. Nevertheless, Zoo and its brethren seem to act like some elaborate cultural muck-spreader, coating everything in an impermeable layer of tits and ass and porn and fighting. And the intimation is that any bird who can't handle that can feck off and take her scented candles with her.
>
> *(Barton, 2004)*

And so, understandably (and, politically, quite rightly), students explore the view that gender-based magazines do some damage, and that there is a correlation between the representation of gender in their pages, the readers' acceptance of them and problems in society. A different view comes from Gauntlett's 'pick and mix' reader who selects in more or less regular ways how s/he forms identities in relation to them:

> I have argued against the view that men's lifestyle magazines represent a reassertion of old-fashioned masculine values, or a 'back-lash' against feminism. Whilst certain pieces in the magazines might support such an argument, this is not their primary purpose or selling point. Instead, their existence and popularity shows men rather insecurely trying to find their place in the modern world, seeking help regarding how to behave in their relationships and advice on how to earn the attention, love and respect of women and the friendship of other men. In post-traditional cultures, where identities are not 'given' but need to be constructed and negotiated, and where an individual has to establish their personal ethics and mode of living, the magazines offer some reassurance to men who are wondering 'Is this right?' and 'Am I doing this OK?', enabling a more confident management of the narrative of the self.
>
> *(Gauntlett, 2002: 180)*

Kendall (2002) researched young people's reading habits and, predictably, magazines featured heavily. Kendall was concerned with students' ideas of themselves as particular kinds of readers. She found that male readers adopted a less critical stance than their female counterparts:

> The magazines functioned, as for female readers, to offer prompts and possibilities for representing self through negotiation of symbolic codes.

However, the male readers were characteristically less critical and more acquiescent to the identities inscribed through the modalities of their 'hobby' magazines.

(Kendall, 2002)

Why this would be so is open to debate, and students might – depending on the teacher – get to speak to this. The GCSE example does not explicitly compel any interest in these broader questions of identity, coming instead from a simpler idea that there are audiences out there for media products and they have interests that can be catered for:

Analyse the cover pages of two popular magazines or the front pages of two popular newspapers.

How do the covers/pages appeal to their audiences?

Design the cover for one edition of a magazine or the front page of a newspaper aimed at a specific audience.

This is something like two 'lesson plans' for GCSE students that start from a different place:

DEVASTATED DANNY DYER

In 2010 the 'infamous' actor Danny Dyer committed an 'error of judgement' by releasing into the public domain an email in which he 'joked', in response to a problem shared on his 'agony uncle' blog, that a contributor might deface ('cut her face', in his words) his partner in order to prevent her from finding another suitor. This relates to the material that can be found on: www.guardian.co.uk/media/2010/may/07/danny-dyer-zoo-magazine1

This is a simple exercise but it is important – for it to work – that students stick to the 'role play' brief they are given, because it is all about understanding competing discourses.

You need ten groups or pairs.

Give each group/pair a large sheet of flipchart paper.

Group 1 is at one end of the continuum in this debate – they believe that Danny Dyer was just 'having a laugh' and no harm done. Group 10 is at the other end, believe that Danny Dyer should be prosecuted for a hate crime or at least incitement. The other eight groups are positioned between these two poles, with group 5 being undecided about whether such an event has any impact on society whatsoever.

Then you give them three aspects of the issue to respond to with a statement, which they write on the flipchart paper. Then these are pinned up around the room and for the next half hour, students circulate the room responding to the statements on the paper with their own statement but always in precise role (for example, group 7 will be more of the view that Dyer's actions represent a harmful view of women – with real world effects on people, but less fulsome in that view than group 8, and group 3 will be relaxed about the importance of his statement but less so than group 4).

At the end of the activity, each sheet of paper should have the full debate recorded. The final stage is to ask the students to give themselves a number to represent their own view.

Then you can keep returning to this whenever you have such a discussion on *any* issue relating to disagreements between people about identity and culture – what number are you, between 1 and 10?

GEEZERS AND BIRDS

Distribute a range of birthday cards for mum and for dad and gendered new baby cards (ideally ask students to bring these in at the end of the previous session).

Spend some time on structured small group discussions on nature/nurture (each group has chair, scribe and presenter), followed by the presenters sharing the group views as a whole and describing any disagreement without using names. The way in to this big area is to ask some groups to simply describe the differences they can see reinforced by the cards, and ask other groups to consider the extent to which the cards just represent the 'Venus and Mars' thing or whether such images actually create ideas of difference in our heads as we grow up.

Next play 'Geezers need excitement' by The Streets (from the 2002 album *Original Pirate Material*). The narrative of this song follows its central character, Mike Skinner, on a night out which involves drugs, clubbing, fast food, moral dilemmas about infidelity (and double standards in that area) and the ever-present undercurrent of violence. Play the song once without any context and clarify the narrative in case the lyrics are unclear (it is best to offer a printed transcript at the end of the exercise).

For the main activity, play the song three more times but ask each student to cross-gender by taking on the role of female (if they are male) and vice versa. Then they note down every reference to their gender during the song.

After they have listened three times, pair the students (male/female) to share their responses and facilitate a discussion about the representation of gender in the song. At this stage avoid all critique, the task is simply to describe how each gender is portrayed. Manage this process by first grouping the pairs into teams of four, then asking for the group's overall outcomes in each case. You may wish to ask for visual representation of this also. It is important here that you pick different presenters from the first exercise so that you increase the scope of verbal participation.

It is not the function of this book to provide teaching resources – we offer this elsewhere for media teachers (McDougall and Potamitis, 2010). But these two examples allow us to start thinking through – in this case within the specific context of GCSE Media Studies (we do not claim this as universally applicable) – a pedagogy of the *differend* through the simple shift to starting with the more complicated discussion of disagreement over identity, as opposed to the 'metaphysics of the same' with which we might accuse *subject media* of complicity. It does not matter that the two examples here are highly specific in context – shot through with the nuances of class and gender performance against a contemporary UK backdrop – the process and the emphasis is key, not the subject matter. Replacing 'how do the magazines appeal to their audiences?' with an exploration of the different possible responses to Danny Dyer's 'lapse' and the way that gender is performed in a song (interpreted through the displacement of adopting the other gender) we start with the idea that gender and power are negotiated and challenged in everyday life. We would want these GCSE students to explore the idea of a magazine – the conditions of possibility for a magazine to exist. The magazine itself is of little concern – merely an artefact, disposable and lacking any coherent objective state of meaning to analyse or imitate. Subjectivity and, in Butler's terms, the category of women in discourse is the focus of the learning. Signification is the object of study:

> If identity is asserted through a process of signification, if identity is always already signified, and yet continues to signify as it circulates through various interlocking discourses, then the question of agency is not to be answered through recourse to an 'I' that pre-exists signification. In other words, the enabling conditions for an assertion of 'I' are provided by the structure of signification, the rules that regulate the legitimate and illegitimate invocation of that pronoun.
>
> *(Butler, 1990: 196)*

What, next, would students *make*? The specification follows the orthodox linear compulsion to analyse, then create within the idioms of what has been 'understood'. This means that students make a magazine that looks and reads like a magazine. There is nothing here that disrupts the workings of *subject English* with its imitative framing of 'creative writing', and in this sense 'media literacy' is constructed along the same lines of more traditional forms of literacy – there are techniques to be understood, internalised and practised. Merely reversing the order of things only goes so far – students might make a magazine first and then work back from that to theorise their attempts to make meaning within conventional and discursive templates. But we will still preserve the binary between us and 'the media', just as English sets up literature as the other to everyday discourse. But just as literary values can only ever be a product of certain ideas about reading practices, so too is the very idea of how a magazine appeals to 'an audience' always-already predicated on a set of ideas about what an audience might be, which are discursive and exercise power, and this ought to be the 'material reality' of the GCSE. Students, then, need to make things that help them explore the idea of the audience – this need not necessarily be 'alternative'. Masterman (1985) posited the political argument that media students should demonstrate their theoretical understanding of the ideological practices of 'the media' by making media which subverted conventions of the form they were working within/against. This approach merely reinforces the idea of 'the media' and is thus unwittingly conservative. Whether students make magazines that challenge or imitate whatever they come to think are 'the conventions' of the medium is neither here nor there, as both responses will be parodic and it is here that we can 'do Butler at GCSE' most easily: 'There is a subversive laughter in the pastiche-effect of parodic practices in which the original, the authentic and the real are themselves constituted as effects' (Butler, 1990: 200).

Peim set up media studies as a 'radical cousin' of sorts (our term) based on his idea that the limiting (and alienating) pedagogy of *subject English* is at least partly a result of its devaluing of popular culture. In his discussion of oral English, Peim suggests students make a documentary about language and power. In the contextual discussion around this, the kinds of activities that media students might be seen to be routinely engaged in – analysing soap operas, news and popular music – are cited as 'other' to what English is about, and thus the documentary task is understood to be borrowing something from the more progressive discipline. In reality, what the GCSE example typifies is an approach which simplifies textual practices to the idea of types of media products meeting 'needs' (with Maslow regularly cited), and for this reason we would say that Peim's suggestion would be just as defamiliarising for many media teachers in 2011 as it was intended to be for English practitioners almost twenty years ago:

> English, at the heart of state education, is fundamentally anti-democratic in its values and practical application of them. To begin to attempt to understand how different literacies may be organised within communities might mean to begin to operate against the systematic discrimination which, in the name of English, officially denigrates what it doesn't recognise as identical within itself.
>
> *(Peim, 1993: 192)*

And here we refute the assumption that *subject media* does *anything* towards this more democratic pedagogy. Returning to Butler, in dialogic space with Zizek, we would ask our GCSE students to produce a magazine about their own engagement in 'paratextual' (Gray, 2010) work, and most importantly the conventions and idioms of magazines should be used as the 'mode of address' for a presentation of the 'parodic' moments in their paratextual work – where they perform elements of identity through the appropriation of the 'symbolic capital' of bits of media. This does not mean that students at GCSE level will use these words or even hear them. We are simply asserting that a set of assumptions about students as textualised agents replace assumptions about students as 'members of audience groups'. Next – or alternatively – they would make a media product looking at magazine reading, and in comparing and contrasting both outcomes (or either), pretty soon the question would arise of how much magazines 'matter' in students' lives and, if they do, on what terms in relation to other media and the (larger) rest of everyday life. Now, Zizek would presumably view such a 'turn to Butler' as exemplifying the liberal complacency that prevents us 'looking awry' at the power of the capitalist media. By retaining a link from Marx to Lacan he is able to set up 'the media' as a 'Big Other', and to lose sight of the abstracted power of media (in its disguise in the abstract – in everyday life) will be our political undoing:

> There is a certain fundamental belief – a belief in the Other's basic consistency – that belongs to language as such. By the mere act of speaking, we suppose the existence of the big Other as guarantor of our meaning. The only subject ... whose relation to the big Other of the symbolic order is characterized by a fundamental disbelief, is the psychotic, a paranoiac, for example, who sees in the symbolic network of meaning around him a plot staged by some evil persecutor.
>
> *(Zizek, 1992: 153)*

The problem with the GCSE specification as it stands is that it does not do anything. It neither gets to grips with the Big Other nor does it look at the mediated performance of identity. Lacan converges Butler and Zizek, and Jenkins most carefully describes hybridity and the networked nature of contemporary media, with Gray providing an explicit account of the 'paratextual' realm. Gray (in conversation with Jenkins) talks about the ways in which the material surrounding the text – in so much as it can be centred – are 'picked and mixed' in the assemblage of a unique version of the textual experience, thus adding to the notion that 'textual poaching' and fandom offer us visible 'reimaginings' of textualised identity:

> I wanted to focus on how one can use paratexts to cut one's groove through a text in a way that isn't necessarily working against the producer's version, but that is personalised nonetheless. Many relationship and character study fanvids, for example, don't necessarily repurpose a character, but they do ask us to stop and think about that character and his or her history in ways that the official text, in its breathless progression, may not have time to do. I don't mean to suggest that this is either the dominant form of fan use of paratexts, or even one that's necessarily changed in a more obviously

convergent media era. But it might help cultural studies to back away from some of the desires for an orcs v hobbits style bad-and-good battle between The Industry and The Fans, and to focus on smaller, humbler moments of repurposing.

(Gray, 2010)

Jenkins himself has offered something towards an 'application' of the ideas of convergence culture to pedagogy in seven principles of 'transmedia education'. Here, he argues for the expression of learning through various dispersed modes of performance. At its most simple, this is a process of adaptation – students translate material across different media. This is what our GCSE 'scheme' is designed to facilitate – the continued act of dispersal and displacement, whereby students make a magazine about their paratextual performed identities and then a documentary about magazine reading, thus 'endlessly deferring' the insulation of any one form which would undermine the affordances of transmedia learning (which will be, in this case, about transmedia meaning and identity).

We do not wish to privilege only Butler, or Jenkins or even Zizek, but we do want to inject all of these ideas into *subject media* as the foundation, the premise, not as an annexe or suite of options. To this end, through the requirement for our GCSE cohort to make things which bring to the surface their own sense-making of the symbolic network of meaning – *psychotic* or otherwise – we engage with both Butler and Zizek, develop a pedagogy that 'applies' the idea of converged transmedia culture, and thus we can at least begin to 'do identity' after the media.

In this chapter we have tried to make the differend a practical resource for pedagogy, once again not as exception in the margins but as the rule at the heart of things. If identity is the stuff of dispersal and performance, then it can only be under critical scrutiny if the mode of learning is in keeping with the experiential nature of the 'thing in question'. Next, with history, we look outside of the developing vertical discourse to explore the relative merits and tensions arising from 'doing history' in (and to) *subject media*.

6

HISTORY AFTER THE MEDIA

Those who cannot remember the past are condemned to repeat it.

(George Santayana)

In an era of stress and anxiety, when the present seems unstable and the future unlikely, the natural response is to retreat and withdraw from reality, taking recourse either in fantasies of the future or in modified versions of a half-imagined past.

(Adrian Veidt [aka Ozymandias] in Alan Moore's Watchmen)

Preamble

It might seem at first glance odd to contemplate history as a key element of a reconstituted media studies, or even to think that 'the media' as a concept might be an obstacle to historical understanding. The debate about historical knowledge and understanding in the broader curriculum is well established, so what particular relevance does it have to us as people interested in media education, save that it functions as a potentially limiting context?

This chapter hopes to address these concerns by systematically indicting *subject media* for both its essential unwillingness by design to embrace a consideration of historical contexts and for its championing of an uncritical and ahistorical postmodernism to perpetuate this failing in a 'post-media' context. This results in the creation of a series of hyper-realities which become subjected to critical but uncontextualised analysis in which the past has become merely an emotional construction, a literal nostalgia: the ache to return 'home'.

A country without a memory

> Human history becomes more and more a race between education and
> catastrophe.
>
> *(H. G. Wells, Outline of History, 1920)*

How can we reconcile two decades in which history has become once again, in all its forms, a staple of mass media entertainment with a widely held opinion that our young people in particular are lacking a historical context? The answers lie not in our suspicions about contemporary education or our moral panics about 'kids these days' but in a return to first principles.

Among other things this means asking the fundamental question 'what is history?' and then taking the time to consider the essential part any answer might play in a configuration of theoretical and practical work which is moving beyond that totalising concept 'the media'. What media studies is sometimes thought to lack is historical context – both by way of itself academically and with regard to contexts for specific texts. One suspicion is that this 'flaw' is also a design feature and that the subject's willingness to embrace certain kinds of deconstructive theory amounts to an unwillingness to put in the intellectual 'work'. That 'work', it might be argued, is knowledge of 'cultural stuff', which includes 'cultural historical stuff'. This 'stuff' is entirely that cultural capital on display in *subject English*, and most especially in works of high modernism, from T. S. Eliot to Joyce and Woolf.

As it was principally configured as a study of popular culture, such history has been considered by some as that 'nightmare' which media studies was designed to avoid. Attacks on the discipline have in fact been attacks on the 'discipline', on a rigour that is predicated on a model of 'inaccessibility' as practised by high cultural forms. The 'relevance' of media studies is sometimes seen as largely predicated on the myth that anyone can do it and that no prior knowledge (of anything) is required. Students comparing the films *Gladiator* (2000) and *Spartacus* (1960) are expected to have knowledge of neither Roman history nor the socio-historical contexts of 'the 1960s' and 'the 1990s'. Their responses to the texts are thus often clinical structuralist and poststructuralist readings, coldly technical versions of the 'personal responses' so central to *subject English*. History it seems is another game, another language, in L. P. Hartley's words, 'another country' where they do things differently.

This unfamiliarity with ideas of and about the past creates much anxiety for teachers and students alike. Some might argue that this significant lack of contexts blights both the analytical and practical work, and reinforces a superficially postmodernist view which merely dismisses 'history' as a grand narrative. The focus of practical work then fast becomes 'form' and issues which are properly contemporary like celebrity. The argument is that students lack a sense of history and that media studies cannot be expected to provide it: in the practical context all that is needed is a bit of old-fashioned 'research'. There are all kinds of reasons anyway to think that traditional history (as a curriculum subject) is in decline as a sort of defunct ally of modernism. Many surveys have been done which confirm that unsuspecting English and American university students are vague even on the dates of their respective civil wars (1642–45, 1860–65). Accept it, 'history' is over.

What this chapter attempts to do is to uncover the reasons why significant opportunities to engage with ideas about the past have been neglected, and to articulate a method that will re-engage media students with these discourses. To do this we will need to patiently document the sometimes wilful misreadings of both the project of modernism and those deconstructive theoretical approaches (post- and super-) that problematised it. It will also unpick the deficit model which argues that we (and more particularly our students) do not have the historical knowledge we once had as essentially nostalgic and misplaced. If nostalgia has, as Baudrillard suggests, in postmodernity 'assumed its full meaning' (1998: 354), then why does this critique not include the history which it is apparently and alarmingly usurping? If what our students lack is an uncritical master narrative, then perhaps they are better off without it.

This should lead us to a proper appreciation of the potential to work historically with critical tools provided by Nietzsche and Foucault, among others. These methods will hopefully stimulate a more productive attitude to both analytical and creative work.

Misplaced modernism

It may be that the dichotomy which exists in the public imagination between media studies and apparently serious areas of study like literature is partly exemplified in the ways in which the project of modernism has been rejected and appropriated by each discipline respectively. As a result of some 'bad' history which needs cause and effect more than it wants to examine propositions, media studies has been seen to site itself, in almost every sense, including psychologically, as that study which is non-, post- or even un-modernist. This creates a set of potential oppositions which say much about the state and status of media studies some fifty years or so after its formal conception. These are all contentions, but also baseline assumptions:

Media studies	Modernism
Mass	Individual
Popular	Elite
Relative	Absolute
Social	Aesthetic
Accessible	Allusive
Transparent	Opaque
Easy	Difficult
Ideological	Idiosyncratic
Stereotypical	Archetypal
Continuous	Discrete
Context	Content
Kitsch	Art

Media studies	Modernism
Experience	Knowledge
Low culture	High culture
Challenged	Challenging
Meaningless	Meaningful
Suspect	Valued

This is not of course a definitive list but it has a kind of face validity. It is perhaps less about what media studies thinks it is, and more about what it thinks it is not. Partly these meanings are assigned by others; much is our fault, though. Jean Starobinski characterised modernity and the modernism that attempted to express it as the presence of the past in a present that supersedes it but still lays claim to it. Starobinski writes of 'a bass line that ... marked the position that used to be (and could still be) occupied there by ancient ritual' (Auge, 2008: 61). One of the 'bass lines' in this book is our contention that the project of modernism is not rejected wholesale by those theorists of post- and super-modernity, nor necessarily by the project of cultural studies. Lyotard, as we have seen in the introduction, is very much interested in extending the project, going beyond it collaboratively by offering analysis not annihilation, appropriation rather than assassination. His is a *coup d'état* rather than a *coup de grâce*.

Storey offers a better balanced view of the ultimate crisis of modernism as very much a running out of steam:

> Instead of outraging from the margins of bourgeois society the work of Bertolt Brecht, T. S. Eliot, James Joyce, Virginia Woolf, Pablo Picasso, Igor Stravinsky and others had not only lost its ability to shock and disturb, it had become central, classical, the canon.
>
> *(Storey, 2009: 405)*

This is the other appropriation that theorists like Lyotard are working to encounter and resist. It is partly ideological, a cultural rerooting of deviant energies to serve social and political needs: Foucault reminds us that even 'the concept of liberty (e.g. artistic freedom) is an invention of the ruling classes' (1991: 78). It is also though partly an organic process in which artistic rebellion will, like 'Pop', ultimately eat itself.

Modernism was a response not so much to industrialisation as to its consequences and implications: the different range of horrors visited on the modern consciousness by Einstein's relativity, Freud's psychoanalysis, Nietzsche's blasphemies and the mechanical brutalities of modern warfare. Its aesthetic experimentations seemed inevitable if this strange modernity was to be expressed, its motivations both personal and political. At the centre of this diverse movement was a common feeling that the other project 'the glorious progress of Western civilisation' had met its apocalypse on the battlefields of the First World War, a feeling expressed best by Ezra Pound:

There died a myriad,
And of the best, among them,
For an old bitch gone in the teeth,
For a botched civilization,
Charm, smiling at the good mouth,
Quick eyes gone under earth's lid,

For two gross of broken statues,
For a few thousand battered books.

(from 'Hugh Selwyn Mauberly', 1920)

The rejection of this 'botched civilisation' is so often missed out in the appropriation by a kind of high-cultural elitism. Modernism came tragically to be associated with refinement and allusion, with a series of cryptic puzzles. It was cultural criticism (literary and otherwise) that privileged cultural knowledge, whereas the work depends on personal cultural experience offering 'the possibility of a polyphony' which would provoke 'the virtually infinite interlacing of destinies, actions, thoughts and reminiscences'. The great works of modernism, far from being 'refined', are in fact imperfect, unfinished, revealing of the process of their own construction.

They have much in common with Foucault's models of genealogy: addressing problems in the present by seeking contingencies rather than causes. Picasso's *Guernica*, for example, or Eliot's *The Waste Land*, bear all the marks of their own creation, and offer journeys through landscapes which offer all manner of difficulties, none of which can be solved by chasing the references or translating the Sanskrit. 'Art does not reproduce the visible,' wrote Paul Klee, 'rather, it makes visible', and that's all (1920: 162).

Post-onanism

Nostalgia is the opium of the age. Our place in history is as clock watchers, old timers, window shoppers.
(Billy Bragg, 'The home front', from the album Victim of Geography, 1993)

When the real is no longer what it used to be, nostalgia assumes its full meaning.
(Baudrillard, 1998: 354)

This section should perhaps begin with a disclaimer. It is not an attempt to discredit critical approaches or undermine the application of theoretical models in media studies, or to belittle or condemn those of us who have laboured on them and with them. It does however, represent a mild confession that some work has proved to be more productive than other work, and a conviction that the singular proposition that 'the media is an ideological state apparatus' has ultimately served us worst. This is not to attack Althusser's critical analysis of 'the state of the ruling class' but rather to cite this as an example of where the totalising concept 'the media' has put paid to the subtle productive potential of a critical tool. And this argument belongs here entirely because these critical 'suspensions of disbelief' are so often abandonments of specific context, suspension of the dialectic, oases of ahistorical judgements.

All of these approaches, be they semiological, deconstructive or vaguely problematising, offer a more significantly active role to readers, and with this significant responsibilities. Textual analysis is fine but it has its limitations. There is a danger of it becoming virtuosity for its own sake, aping the worst excesses of literary criticism, the equivalent of hypothesising angels on pinheads. Take Barthes's *Mythologies* (1957),[1] which constitutes a critical approach that is at the same time systematic and plural: a spontaneous engagement with the myths that surround us all in our daily lives. In its compilation of specific responses to the contemporary concerns of postwar France and in particular issues surrounding mass culture, it demonstrates its thesis rather than merely expounding it.

In fact the theorising comes (appropriately) last: a reflection among other things on the importance of a sense of historical context at a time when such a notion is everywhere under threat, rearticulated by the glib innocence of myth. It is dubbed 'myth today' (*le mythe aujourd'hui*) to date it, to establish its transitory quality, to prevent it from being 'the theory' underpinning (and overwhelming) the fifty-four helpings of practice. However, this suggestive collection of speculations and dynamite one-liners has often proved impossible to leave alone, the particular longing to be universal. Barthes set out to analyse those assumptions that just 'go without saying' in a culture and then to reflect on what he discovered in analysis.

Terry Hawkes sums up Barthes's understanding of myth in a social context as 'the complex system of images and beliefs which a society constructs in order to sustain and authenticate its sense of its own being: i.e. the very fabric of its system of meaning' (1977: 131). Barthes's concerns about this complex system return time and again to its ahistorical character: 'myth is constituted by the loss of the historical quality of things in it'. Put simply myth naturalises: 'What the world supplies to myth is an historical reality .... And what myth gives in return is a natural image of this reality' (Barthes, 1972: 142). This cannot be an end point. Barthes is addressing those of us who wish 'to connect a mythical schema to a general history', 'the reader of myths himself who must reveal their essential function' when he calls for an answer to a specific question: 'How does he receive this particular myth *today*?' These are Barthes's italics, and they leave little room

---

1 There are fifty-four 'readings' in the original French version with an additional, and important, theoretical essay 'Myth today' written out of and after the active readings and thus serving them rather than being served by them. This priority of engagement over theoretical speculation is key to Barthes's model and our response to it. The English translation of 1973 only has twenty-eight of the readings.

for misunderstanding: 'today' is a particular place in time, a context which is specifically historical, not a fragile platform for fanciful intellectual speculation. 'Myth today' must be renewed.

Barthes introduces his work on mythologies with the following:

> The starting point of these reflections was usually a feeling of impatience at the sight of the 'naturalness' with which newspapers, and common sense curiously dress up reality which, even though it is the one we live in, is undoubtedly determined by history .... I resented seeing Nature and History confused at every turn,
>
> *(Barthes, 1972: 11)*

The same is true of the draining of the historical which accompanies the 'loss of the awareness of the reality itself' in the postmodernist Baudrillard's recasting of the biblical term 'simulacrum' to imply a baseless image, what Storey describes as 'an identical copy without an original' (1998: 347). This is a central concept of postmodernism which pitches simulation as a replacement for representation. Baudrillard argues that this is a transition from 'signs that dissimulate something to signs which dissimulate that there is nothing' (1998: 354). One of the casualties of this hyper-reality is cause and effect, and more seriously any genuinely historical sense or context. This 'draining of history' may be seen to be constituted by Baudrillard's precession of the simulacra:

- 'It is the reflection of a basic reality
- It masks and perverts a basic reality
- It masks the absence of a basic reality
- It bears no relation to any reality whatsoever: it is its own pure simulacrum.'

(Baudrillard, 1998: 353–4)

In some ways the above 'model' is a model of a process of alienation from a productive relationship with historical reality. What stands in the place of this loss of historical context is nostalgia: history as masquerade. As Baudrillard (1998: 354) suggests, 'when the real is no longer what it used to be, nostalgia assumes its full meaning'. Looking at film and television schedules 'retro' is full flow, as it is in all other media, from fashion to home furnishings. Here is a desire to rediscover the 'real' acted out in yet further simulations whose watchwords are 'real', 'authentic', and 'objective'. The most significant is the hopefully named 'reality television' phenomenon, spearheaded by a show in which thirty-seven cameras attempt to find (and film) a reality. This lived and observed experience has proved ultimately unconvincing, and *Big Brother*'s manipulation of the format has failed also to whet jaded appetites. All that remains, living and breathing, is a celebrity franchise which further blurs the boundaries between the 'real' and 'imaginary'.

Here we have arrived at a postmodernist sensibility, a culture in which, Frederick Jameson claimed, real history is displaced by nostalgia. Jameson also accuses the postmodern world of 'pastiche, depthless intertexuality and schizophrenia', and of the creation of a 'discontinuous flow of perpetual presents' (Storey, 1998: 347). These are powerful claims in the current climate, wherein 'retro' and 'vintage' are consistent themes and where nothing is safe from the threat of remake: cartoons, computer games, even classic films frame for frame. Storey sums up Jameson's critique as follows: 'history is always effaced by historicism, the "random cannibalisation" of past filmic styles and past experiences of viewing'. However, the more important point is that merely confirming the hypothesis does not get us where we need to go or constitute a productive response to Baudrilliard's critique. In a piece entitled 'Fashion and postmodernism', Elizabeth Wilson takes up the critical cudgel with a little more intent. While praising Jameson's 'brilliant' work she deftly argues that although 'fashion fits so well into Jameson's postmodern dystopia' it also reveals that Jameson's focus on 'a sensibility in which all sense of development and history are lost' seems in itself both schizophrenic and nostalgic. Ironically what the postmodernists are most significantly asking for is an new engagement with the historical. Andreas Huyssen sets out both the problem and the implicit necessity for action:

> [Postmodernism] operates in a field of tension between tradition and innovation, conservation and renewal, mass culture and high art, in which the second terms are no longer automatically privileged over the first; a field of tensions which can no longer be grasped in categories such as progress vs. reaction, Left vs. Right, present vs. past, modernism vs. realism, abstraction vs. representation, avant garde vs. Kitsch.
>
> *(Wilson, 2009: 451)*

This is a failure of the old dispensation of binary oppositions, of history as a set of appropriations masquerading as 'immobile forms', as things as they really are. It is the end of essentialism, of the search for essences, truths, origins because it is these impulses which are essentially nostalgic:

> When the real is no longer what it used to be, nostalgia assumes its full meaning. There is a proliferation of myths of origin and signs of reality; of second-hand truth, objectivity and authenticity.
>
> *(Baudrillard, 1998: 354)*

This is a call to action, not a wringing of hands: a wish for an effective historical sense to restore complexity, disorder and contention in a world that potentially wants none of it. In such a context, wallowing in the mire of popular cultural excess is simply not an option:

> In passing from history to nature: myth acts economically: it abolishes the complexity of human acts .... it organises a world which is without contradictions because it is without depth, a world wide open and wallowing

in the evident, it establishes a blissful clarity: things appear to mean something by themselves.

(Barthes, 1972: 143)

Towards a genealogy of history: contingencies not causes

do not look for progress or meaning in history; do not see the history of a given activity, of any segment of culture, as the development of rationality or of freedom; do not use any philosophical vocabulary to characterize the essence of such activity or the goal it serves; do not assume that the way this activity is presently conducted gives any clue to the goals it served in the past.

(Rorty, 1986: 47)

The human being, that is to say, is a kind of creature whose ontology is historical.

(Nikolas Rose, 1986: 129)

In his classic thinking through of the historian's role, *What is History?* E. H. Carr describes a process very much more amenable to the work of media students than that which merely suggests their ignorance. Attempting to answer the question his title sets, necessarily, he suggests, 'reflects our position in time and forms part of the answer to the broader question "what view do we take of the society in which we live"' (Carr, 1990: 8). In other words history is about who, where and (significantly) when you are: it is both political and tellingly 'historical'. Reflecting on the work of Sir George Clark, Carr respectfully points out that Clark's suggestion that history consists of a 'hard core of facts' and then (regrettably) the 'surrounding pulp of disputable interpretations' neglects to follow through its metaphor', 'forgetting perhaps that the pulpy part of the fruit is more rewarding than the hard core'. Carr tentatively offers a contrary provocation, that history is rather 'a hard core of interpretation surrounded by a pulp of disputable facts' (Carr, 1990: 8–9).

This perhaps evokes Nietzsche's famous dictum, 'There are no facts, only interpretations', but whether as cause or effect becomes another question about what might be said to have happened. Carr unequivocally dismisses the 'show it as it really was' approach, popularised by the German historian Ranke in the 1830s: 'It used to be said that facts speak for themselves. This is, of course untrue' (Carr, 1990: 8).

By contrast the whole project of history is a process of preselection and predetermination long before our critical faculties get to work on the 'facts':

Our picture (of the past) has been preselected and predetermined for us, not so much by accident as by people who were consciously or unconsciously imbued with a particular view and thought the facts which supported that view were worth preserving.

(Carr, 1990: 13)

This is fairly easy to evidence from media texts as diverse as, say, *Birth of a Nation* (1915) and *Roots* (1977), both historical dramas but also, in Carr's terms, historical documents, revealing as much of their own time as that they were particularly addressing. When Leni Riefenstahl was invited to film the Nazi Party congress at Nuremberg in 1934 she made four days into 104 minutes of 'evidence' of the facts that supported her view. Carr (1990: 22) also offers us Oakeshott: 'to write history is the only way of making it' which will likely provoke a significant debate if juxtaposed to the opening of Riefenstahl's film *Triumph of the Will* (1934):

Am 5ten September 1934
[*On 5 September 1934*]
20 Jahre nach dem Ausbruch des Weltkriegs
[*20 years after the outbreak of the* **World War**]
16 Jahre nach dem Beginn unseres Leidens
[*16 years after the beginning of* **our suffering**]
19 Monate nach dem Beginn der Deutschen Wiedergeburt
[*19 months after the* **beginning of the German renaissance**]
Adolf Hitler flog wieder nach Nürnberg um die Massen seiner treuen
Gefolgschaften zu überprüfen.
[*Adolf Hitler flew again to Nuremberg to review the columns of his faithful followers.*]

(FilmEducation.Org)

Where, it is fair to ask, and to what extent is history being made here, and how much knowledge does any of us need? Carr also insists that 'this element of interpretation enters into every fact of history', and even more directly, 'History means interpretation.' Carr also quotes the American historian Carl Becker's provocative claim that 'the facts of history do not exist for any historian until he creates them' (Carr, 1990: 21). It is good to ponder this openness with images of Hitler's 'Volk/Reich/Fuhrer' stuff fresh in our minds. Becker is not being disingenuous for, as Carr points out, we need to explain why Caesar crossing the Rubicon is a historical fact and the fact that many millions of others have crossed that river (many at the same point) is not.

Equally interesting, and perhaps more concerning, are the echoes of 'Team Hitler' (Leni, Adolf, Heinrich and the rest) in something like J. R. R. Tolkien's *The Lord of the Rings*. This event, an attempt to write the oral epic British culture never had, is hardly postmodern, nor is it superficially nostalgic. In director Peter Jackson's hands, it may unwittingly become 'The triumph of the West'.

What is needed is not a focus on 'subject history' and historical knowledge but rather a focus on historical process and understanding. Moreover what is needed is a plan of action and not an abdication. Foucault provides both in his seminal

1991 essay 'Nietzsche, genealogy, history'. Drawing on Nietzschean notions of 'effective' history (*wirkliche Historie*), Foucault offers a *modus operandi* for problematising 'the historian's history' and liberating our own. What he principally borrows from Nietzsche is the notion and metaphor of the genealogy, which becomes both an analytical tool and a creative framework.

Foucault's 'genealogy of history' is non-teleological; it is not a search for origins or essence. It does not believe that history is going somewhere or indeed has come from anywhere. Like the true genealogist Nietzsche, Foucault does not presume 'the existence of immobile forms that precede the external world of accident and succession': that he addresses as traditional or the historian's history. His genealogy 'does not oppose itself to history …. It opposes itself to the search for "origins"' (Foucault, 1991: 77).

Whereas traditional history works to unmask 'that which was already there' and pursues an 'exact essence', the genealogist rejects the master narrative of progress in favour of 'a number of contingent and altogether less refined and dignified practices' (Rose, 1996: 129).

As Kendall and Wickham point out, 'Foucaultians are not setting out to find out how the present has emerged from the past … the point is to use history as a way of "diagnosing" the present'. Foucault himself wrote that we should seek to 'use, to deform it, to make it groan and protest' prompting Kendall and Wickham to add that 'History should be used not to make ourselves comfortable but rather to disturb the taken for granted' (1999: 4). This 'taken for granted' is the history that persuades us that there is a story, and that we should know it or else be culturally defective and excluded. For Foucault, when the genealogist 'listens to history he finds that there is something altogether different behind things … the secret that they have no essence' (1991: 78) This is reinforced by a comment Carr 'selects': 'The historian belongs not to the past but the present.'

Foucault focuses on differences. Therefore, as a historical method, he refuses to examine statements outside of their historical context: the discursive formation. The meaning of a statement depends on the general rules that characterise the discursive formation to which it belongs. The genealogist works knowingly on 'a vast accumulation of source material', and attempts to uncover what the discourses of historical knowledge hide from themselves. The genealogist works with what is available as a kind of meticulous bricoleur, seeking to redistribute and demystify. Paul Thompson argues that 'All history depends on its social purpose' (2000: 1). For Foucault this lies not in narrative but in effect, in action in changing the ways we conceive things. As E. H. Carr says, 'All history is the history of thought', though we may prefer the more continuous (and contingent) 'thinking' (1990: 22).

Making History

It is not the literal past, the 'facts' of history, that shape us, but images of the past embodied in language.

(Brian Friel, 1989)

> Some nations have prophecy and some have not; but of all mankind, there
> is no tribe so rude that it has not attempted History.
>
> *(Thomas Carlisle)*

In Brian Friel's 1989 play *Making History* such a genealogy is attempted. Friel is
concerned to understand and 'diagnose' the present, which in his case is the
divided Ireland of the 1980s. Rather than seeing the present as the culmination of
events that occurred in the past, Friel follows Foucault in contemplating the
present as simply one of many events in a process that continues into the future.
Of course, the present 'emerged' from the past, but not in a fixed, frozen form.
The genealogist attempts to leave the forces of history in motion. Those forces are
'the hazardous play of dominations'. The centre of Friel's genealogy is a crude
two-hander between the Irish Catholic rebel O'Neill (apparently a history maker)
and his biographer Peter Lombard, an archbishop and historian. Lombard has the
task of writing 'The history of Hugh O'Neill'; however, as O'Neill accuses him,
it becomes the history of the person writing it. As Lombard says, there is no such
thing as a single history based on truth:

> I don't believe that a period of history – a given space of time – my life –
> your life – that it contains within it one 'true' interpretation just waiting to
> be mined. But I do believe that it may contain within it several possible
> narratives: the life of Hugh O'Neill can be told in many ways. And those
> ways are determined by the needs and demands and the expectations of
> different people and different eras.
>
> *(Friel, 1989: 15–16)*

Here Friel concerns himself with what Nikolas Rose describes as 'disreputable
origins and unpalatable functions' (the inevitable outcome of any 'family tree').
The limitations of stage drama mean that the 'systems of subjection' (interactions
of power and interest) are crudely drawn, but contemporary audiences in Derry
would have well understood Foucault's contention that 'These developments may
appear as a culmination, but they are merely the current episodes in a series of
subjugations' (1991: 83). This is not abstract: 'History is the concrete body of a
development.' As Kendall and Wickham confirm, 'it involves histories that never
stop'.

This is very much the same set of issues, though handled more diversely on a
broader canvas, addressed by Andrew Dominik in his genealogy of celebrity *The
Assassination of Jesse James by the Coward Robert Ford* (2007). Dominik's film moves
through and beyond its stated focus, 'the laying of poor Jesse in his grave', to address
contemporary problems of celebrity: the accompanying documentary, *Death of an
Outlaw,* explicitly claims that James returned to 'outlawing' because he missed the
notoriety rather than needed the money. The film is 'epic' in the Brechtian sense, a
series of self-contained episodes meticulously captured as tableaux against the pitiless
beauty of the natural world, cycling through its seasonal rejuvenation.

Of course one element of this performance is generic: this is a tale of the West, adventure capitalism with six guns and saloons. Jesse is a more ambivalent character than Liberty Valance (an outlaw in John Ford's 1962 film, *The Man Who Shot Liberty Valance*), but freedom and licence (and Jesse's borderline psychosis is about treading such a line) is very much in the play of truth and falsehood, as is the more contrived implied stuff about printing the legend at the cost of imagining you can tell the legend from the facts. Dominik's script and direction mean that this is a work of narratology as much as it is a discrete historical narrative: we are aware of the suturing, of the notion of 'textus', something woven.

Its use of a knowing, if not omniscient, voiceover and documentary-style freeze frame offers a kind of tarot reading of 'his-story', though we are always aware that *la mort* has been dealt and is waiting to engage. Foucault's notion of heritage as 'an unstable assemblage of faults, fissures and heterogeneous layers' (1991: 82) suits this project well since it is also a proper heritage 'trail': Jesse is billed as both 'the nation's most notorious criminal' and 'the land's greatest hero, lauded as Robin Hood by the public'. Robert Ford on the other hand is 'a nobody'. Enter Hollywood A-lister Brad Pitt and a Hollywood actor turned director's kid brother and the blood lines are extended, albeit haphazardly.

Alexander Kluge talks of the three cameras (2007: 214) which frame any film: the technical equipment, the eye of the director and the mind of the spectator. Pitt and Casey Affleck feature perhaps most significantly in the last of these, even if subliminally. These 'heterogeneous layers' contribute greatly to the overall effect; a recognition of historical vicissitude. Think of the way in which Francis Ford Coppola augments *Apocalypse Now* (1978) by giving the next generation of Hollywood male acting talent (among them Martin Sheen and Harrison Ford) the task of bringing in Brando.

When the actor formerly known as Achilles (perhaps the first celebrity) finally stands up on his chair to meet his maker(s) it is as staged as the version that Robert Ford and his increasingly embittered older brother Charley (and by implication Ben?) apparently toured in the immediate aftermath of the assassination/ mercy killing/murder/act of patriotism★ (★ delete as appropriate). However, in many ways the film's key moment is when the Bowery saloon singer (Nick Cave both in and out of character) gives the 'dirty little coward' line to a tipsy Robert Ford, which receives the tragically defiant 'I'm Robert Ford' – surely an echo of the equally defiant 'It is I, Hamlet the Dane'. And neither has long to be anything.

Friel's insistence on a complexity of identity for his 'historical' O'Neill as a play of ambiguities reinforces the complexity of the issues. There are no easy answers here. Foucault begins 'Nietzsche, genealogy, history' with the following: 'Genealogy is gray, meticulous and patiently documentary. It operates on a field of entangled and confused parchments, on documents that have been scratched over and recopied many times' (1991: 76).

Such an act of patient documentary is central to a whole host of engaging media products. One remembers classics of early television like John Berger's *Ways of Seeing* (1972), which embody this critical attitude, 'an almost unfettered eclecticism' (Kendall and Wickham, 1999: 17). Moreover, the profound influence of something like Ken Burns's mighty discourse on the American Civil War derives entirely from its insistence on treating the Civil War as a historical problem impacting on America's idea of itself in the present and continuing into the future, and not merely a period or historical narrative. What we get is a genealogical descent which seeks, in Foucault's terms, 'to maintain passing events in their proper dispersion ... to discover that truth or being does not lie at the root of what we know and what we are, but the exteriority of accidents' (Foucault, 1991: 81).

Burns's achievement with his documentary film *The Civil War* (1990) is to understand that 'the predicament of the historian is a reflexion of the nature of man' and to share this with us in every compassionate frame (Carr, 1990: 29). He knows, as Nikolas Rose does, that 'the ways in which humans "give meaning to experience" have their own history', and therefore he is working 'at the intersection of a range of distinct histories' (Rose, 1996: 129). Burns's history (rather than the facts) 'speaks' for itself and is unapologetically disparate, involved, contentious and ambiguous. His is primarily an oral history embodying historian Paul Thompson's account of the role of history (the telling not the events) in everyday life: 'In such diverse ways through history ordinary people seek to understand the upheavals and changes which they experience in their own lives' (Thompson, 2000: 2).

Rejecting traditional master narratives of the war (even the phallocentricity of war is 'assuaged' by an erudite plurality) which 'pretend to base its judgments on apocalyptic objectivity', he rises instead to Foucault's challenge for history (as genealogy), 'to become a curative science' (Foucault, 1991: 90). Burns's conclusion included these lines:

> It was the most horrible, necessary, intimate, acrimonious, mean-spirited, and heroic conflict the nation has ever known'.
>
> Inevitably, we grasp the war through such hyperbole. In so doing, we tend to blur the fact that real people lived through it and were changed by the event. One hundred and eighty-five thousand black Americans fought to free their people. Fishermen and storekeepers from Deer Isle, Maine, served bravely and died miserably in strange places like Baton Rouge, Louisiana, and Fredericksburg, Virginia. There was scarcely a family in the South that did not lose a son or brother or father.
>
> Between 1861 and 1865, Americans made war on each other and killed each other in great numbers – if only to become the kind of country that could no longer conceive of how that was possible.
>
> *(http://www.pbs.org/civilwar/war/)*

The only alternative to this process of meticulous patience is the acceptance of a truth that by the very nature of the enterprise is merely 'error that cannot be refuted because it was hardened into an unalterable form in the long baking process of history' (Foucault, 1991: 79). This truth is no more or less than Barthes's second order, meaning 'myth', meaning determined by collective (and long-term) consent in a journey from history to nature. In doing so, Barthes claims, 'myth acts economically: it abolishes the complexity of human acts … it organises a world which is without contradictions because it is without depth'. Moreover it is, by its nature, without history, as Mark Paterson explains: 'a crucial property of myths is that they have no historical character, they lose the memory that they were once manufactured' (Patterson, 2006: 33).

Look for contingencies instead of causes

> We are dealing with judgements that are not regulated by categories. I judge. But if I am asked by what criteria do I judge, I will have no answer to give.
> *(Lyotard, 1985: 14)*

The work we are proposing here, both analytical and creative, is a challenge to such conceits. Freed from a prescriptive history which is predicated on predetermined truths and particular kinds of largely patriarchal authority, both media analysis and media production will, it is hoped, be able to reacquaint themselves with the 'historical' as a no longer dying mutual friend. When Foucault insists that his genealogies will never confuse themselves with quests for their origins, he also promises that a genealogy 'will never neglect as inaccessible the vicissitudes of history' (1991: 80). Partly this is an appeal for us all in the discipline formerly (and largely still) known as media studies to keep this faith, along with its rejoinder, 'to cultivate the details and accidents that accompany every beginning'. This is not an escape from the 'discipline' of history (whatever the problems involved in this), but rather 'to' history as an essential component.

Kendall and Wickham offer pragmatic advice on how we might use history according to Foucauldian principles. They offer two important premises and then two 'effective techniques'. The first premise is that 'when we use history … we do not allow this history to stop, do not allow it to settle on a patch of sensibleness in the field of strangeness. Thus we address problems not periods. Secondly we must understand that 'Foucault's historical methods are crucially about problematization' (Kendall and Wickham, 1999: 22). Foucault himself defined problematization as follows:

> Problematization is not the representation of a pre-existing object, or the creation through discourse of an object that does not exist. It is the totality of discursive and non-discursive practices that brings something into the play of truth and falsehood and sets it up as an object for the mind.
> *(Foucault, quoted in Castel, 1994: 237–8)*

Here is a manifesto for real work, for genuine explorations: 'not the anticipatory power of meaning but the hazardous play of dominations' (Foucault, in Rabinow, 1984: 83). The 'play of truth and falsehood' seems particularly important since the notion of 'historical sense' which Foucault has got from Nietzsche is 'explicit in its perspective and acknowledges its system of injustice' (Foucault, 1984: 90). This is also about a scepticism which does not allow an easy retreat through gates of ivory or horn, to either superiority or self-pity. As Kendall and Wickham argue, 'Treating seriously the proposition that we cannot know even that we cannot know means accepting all intellectual influences with the same sceptical acceptance of how things are' (1999: 17).

Notions of cause and effect model a vertical model of history as an unbroken continuity whereas, as we have shown, a genealogy is 'put together somewhat contingently and haphazardly' to emphasise a multiplicity of possibilities. In simple terms, 'When we describe a historical event as contingent, what we mean is that the emergence of that event was not necessary, but was one possible result of a whole series of complex relations between other event' (Kendall and Wickham, 1999: 5). The work James Burke did for the BBC on the history of science, which sold around the world, was a good example of this contingency model: he called his work *Connections*.

Or take *Life on Mars*, a drama now running indirectly into its fifth season. Detective Sam Tyler is transported via a coma back thirty years to a Manchester which is part historical reconstruction and part reflection on the police series. While there are clearly positions to take up on this, which offer, for example, readings which are feminist or Marxist or perhaps most obviously postmodernist, our stated approach is to hold off these second-order judgements (which will always be there when we get back!). Rather than impose our interpretations on this creative data, we need to listen to it and account for its 'appearance': to its forms of thought, speech and action, to its techniques of regulation, to its problems of organisation. Nikolas Rose writes about seeking 'to unpick', and what is unpicked is what is first described and considered. In this particular case this means problematising the assumptions on which the text works, for example considering the narrative and psychological premises of the piece: that trauma is best addressed and 'gone through', and that there is a little Gene Hunt (the unreconstructed 1970s copper) in all of us, hence his mythic status.

Or take Alan Moore's ur-graphic novel *Watchman*, filmed in 2009, which in itself provides a genealogy of 'superheroism' while exploring a significant range of contemporary US history. Starting with ideas about discourses of power based on accounts of the interactions between Nite-owl, Rorschach and Dr Manhattan may be more fruitful that jumping straight into intertextuality and postmodern irony. Jameson may argue that nostalgia is replacing history, the simulation usurping the reality but the 'critical' paraphernalia that Moore provides in the original graphic novel does so much more than merely 'play'. In the addendum to Chapter IV (a discourse by Professor Milton Glass entitled 'Dr Manhattan: Super-Powers and the Superpowers'), Moore brings notions of moral panic in the postwar United States to a somewhat pointed conclusion: 'We are all of us living in the shadow of Manhattan.' Here a superhero, a skyscrapered New York island and the development of the atom bomb collide, and something is brought 'into the play of truth and falsehood' and set up 'as an object for the mind'.

Ultimately *Watchmen* earns the qualifier 'postmodern', and in doing so redeems the terms from those who would disconnect it entirely from the project of modernism and untemper its critical edge. Here intertextuality is no 'turn', but rather a genealogical inevitability. Here bricolage is not about playful juxtaposition but rather about a visceral suturing of ill-fitting parts. Here depthlessness is an issue not an end, and nostalgia is a perfume selling briskly in an age of anxiety, like the ache of an old wound. All chapters (originally issues) apart from the last have their own attendant paraphernalia: police reports, extracts from autobiography, learned articles, letters, drawings, advertisements. Chapter 5 has (what else but) Chapter 5 from a supposed history of comic books featuring the *Tales of the Black Freighter* comic which has featured heavily in this issue. This includes examples from this imaginary classic drawn by 'classic' comic artist Joe Orlando, who is pictured in the article (circa 1953) and who turns out to be 'v-p creative director' on the *Watchmen* project. Many acres of cyberspace are devoted to these and other 'leads', but do not be fooled into thinking that this is mere cleverness. Moore is locking us into an intense experience which seeks to confront us with the implications of our cultural practices and products, and in particular to give us a feeling for the multiplicity of contexts: historical, cultural, intellectual as well as generic.

His is a loving anatomy of the superhero: an extended deconstruction of a disreputable genre that with a proper forceful irony makes it finally reputable: *Watchmen* was the only graphic novel to feature in *Time*'s 100 Greatest Novels poll in 2005. Here the marginalia is essential to Moore's rolling us all towards an overwhelming question as we look back through this multi-accented text, this grand design. Moore himself has been dismayed at what this dark masterpiece has unleashed:

> to some degree there has been, in the 15 years since *Watchmen*, an awful lot of the comics field devoted to these grim, pessimistic, nasty, violent stories which kind of use *Watchmen* to validate what are, in effect, often just some very nasty stories that don't have a lot to recommend them.
>
> *(interview with Tasha Robinson accessed at*
> *http://www.avclub.com/articles/alan-moore,13821/)*

This 'validation' has often been under the banner of a 'postmodernism' reduced to an ideology of 'anything goes'. Moore's deconstruction and destruction, on the other hand, offers a more profound critique based on actions and implications. He may, like his hero Brecht, call for 'Feast first, morals later', but the consequences must and do arrive. The final chapter returns full circle to the 'bloodied' badge but also to two final statements, one an overwhelming question; two reflections on all that has gone before. The first is from John Cale, from his song 'Sanities': 'It would be a stronger world, a stronger loving world to die in.' Then the Roman satirist Juvenal folds the whole text into his most famous epigraph, now subtly altered: '*Quis custodiet ipsos custodes?*' (Who watches the watchmen?)

And as the critical, so the creative. In an unprecedented way the archive is open to us, 'a vast accumulation of source material', scope for 'relentless erudition' and patient documentary. And with this an invitation to pursue our own historical sense with a proper sense of its existence as a point-of-view, that 'its perception is slanted, being a deliberate appraisal, affirmation or negation' (Foucault, 1984: 90). The understanding that interpretation is an active ingredient in creative media work is vital. It destroys the artificial delineation between documentary and narrative, and exposes the naivety of those who think it is the job of the documentary film maker to present 'his subject matter as if the equipment and the technical processes were not there'.

William Stott's definition of 'documentary' might be more useful: 'the presentation of actual facts in a way that makes them credible and telling to people at that time'. Stott is quoted in a very interesting essay on documentary realism by Trinh T Minha-ha entitled 'The totalising quest for meaning'. She is even more 'flexible', suggesting that 'Truth has to be made vivid, interesting; it has to be dramatised if it is to convince the audience of the evidence, whose confidence in it allows truth to take shape'. She also quotes extensively from French documentary film-maker Georges Franju: 'You must re-create reality because reality runs away; reality denies reality. You must first interpret it, or re-create it …. When I make a documentary, I try to give the realism an artificial aspect' (Franju quoted by Minha-ha in Bennett, 2007: 214).

This almost returns to Kluge's call to 'represent reality as the historical fiction it is', though from the opposite direction. All of these encourage us to investigate and explore and to make sense to the degree that this makes sense. Of course our individual and cultural identities will be central to knowing what to do, since they themselves are still subject to historical contextualisation: to some a proper study in a proper context. The last words are Stuart Hall's:

> Though they seem to invoke an origin in a historical past with which they continue to correspond, actually identities are about questions of using the resources of history, language and culture in the process of becoming rather than being: not 'who we are' or 'where we came from' so much as what we might become, how we have been represented and how that bears on how we represent ourselves.
>
> *(Hall, 1996: 4)*

Arriving at another unexpected outcome, we have in this chapter moved outside of *subject media* only to provide our most explicitly textual reading – of the idea of history. Perhaps it will be our most controversial gambit – that the absence of history from media studies, despite appearances, does more to extend its conservative reach into the lifeworlds of students, than its reliance on the assumptions of English teaching. Next, we consider the status of what some have referred to as 'the concept formally known as the audience'.

7

AUDIENCE AFTER THE MEDIA

Rorty observes that:

> anything that Habermas will count as retaining a 'theoretical perspective' will be counted by an incredulous Lyotard as a 'metanarrative'. Anything that abandons such an approach will be counted by Habermas as 'neoconservative'. French critics of Habermas are ready to abandon liberal politics in order to avoid universalistic philosophy, and Habermas (is) trying to hang on to a universalistic philosophy, with all its problems, in order to support liberal politics.
>
> *(Rorty, 1991: 162)*

And Usher and Edwards comment, with – we suggest – direct relevance for a study of contemporary media education:

> Some have attempted to reintroduce the modern grand narrative of emancipation in a modified form, as localised networks become the basis for resistant and emancipatory practices previously impossible under the state's tutelage of the social totality.
>
> *(Usher and Edwards, 1994: 167)*

Much of the debate around the respective falling apart and together of the more or less 'fragmented' audience for media products can be understood as speaking to the idioms of the above 'differend', and as such, much of this discussion will relate to modernity/postmodernity and how media studies may pay lip service to the latter but operate institutionally in the logics of the former – and what the implications of this might be for our students. 'Technologies of the self' exercise power. Learning about 'the media' and demonstrating that one understands them for assessment are practices embedded within such technologies. Crucially, we cannot claim to be attempting some kind of overarching definitive account of these things, but claim rather to locate and examine particular events within the workings of *subject media* and to suggest some alternative practices which may amount to a resistance of sorts.

Such an 'application' has been attempted by Hunter (1988), thinking through culture and schooling in the context of discourses of individuality and the use of time and space through architecture and administration to distribute and order citizen-subjects. A set of principles for education were mobilised in statements from the nineteenth century onwards that have been taken up by Marxist writers such as Bourdieu, Bowles and Gintis, and Apple. Hunter argues that discourses about contemporary education emerged from specific historical concerns about control, and that culture can best be understood not as an entity or an acquisition but as a set of practices aimed at producing a particular kind of citizen. In this reading culture is the exercising of power. Citizen-subjects are products of schooling – they do not exist prior to it. Hunter views literary education as an exemplary form of governance, of moral supervision. This is, of course, counter to the self-identity constructed by the English teacher with her belief in the emancipatory function of literature. Hunter deploys a genealogy, from Foucault (a shift, the formation of new ways of thinking about literature and the citizen), to explore a wider dynamic, that of the understanding and 'use of culture' in modern society. Hunter traces the ways in which literary education can be understood as part of the machinery of popular education providing 'social welfare' through moral supervision. Hunter views English education as a panoptical supervision of the self, with the goal of ensuring the formation of desirable and functional forms of citizenry. And so for Hunter, literary education emerged not as a merging of aesthetic culture and society, but as a technology for normalising, as a technique for moral observation. There is in this analysis a resonance with Usher and Edwards' (1994) Lyotardian (1992) reading of contemporary experiential learning, in that it has the double-face of increased self-expression and increased self-regulation. Literature becomes a part of the apparatus of governance essentially and necessarily because of its (perceived) proximity to lived experience. The 'appreciation' of literature, previously a minority aesthetic experience, became a part of the supervised freedom of modern education.

Culture, media, 'the media'

Elsewhere, we have deconstructed the ways in which, in the United Kingdom, the *Richard & Judy Book Club*, in its provision of prompts for reading group discussion of its listed novels, operates in a hybrid space between opening up reading to an audience connected by a daytime television show and maintaining schooled literature appreciation discourses. In this example, the imposition of the idea of 'thematic significance' is discussed:

> Readers are interpellated into the act of discussing something that is assumed to exist – thematic significance. This is presented as objective, such a theme

can only be significant if it exists and can be looked at and known as such, outside of the thinking of the reader. There is no space for the reader to think that the phrase is not thematically significant, or that themes are questionable or that the idea of lines from a novel echoing other lines is subjective.

(Kendall and McDougall, 2010: 18)

Just as this 'reaching out' by the Richard and Judy group on behalf of, and by the idioms of, *subject English* is a deeply conservative practice, so too can *subject media* – and its more recent manifestation in 'media literacy' – be viewed as an intervention which appears more progressive than it has proven to be in its more normative and regulatory impact. Hunter, with Foucault, suggests that normalisation operates as self-regulation *through* self-expression. In Hunter's genealogy of literary education we can trace the same relationship between freedom and regulation as we can in Foucault's account of discipline and punishment and Usher and Edwards' discussion (via Lyotard) of performative self-assessment in the contemporary educational climate. There is no hidden agenda, as the 'hidden curriculum' thesis has it, or a radical alternative to be achieved through reform or revolution. As Kendall and Wickham explain:

> The school is a factory-laboratory where children are manufactured out of educational experiments. The intention is not to deny children access to the truth about themselves, but to produce them as functioning and maximised citizens, to produce the truth about themselves. Culture actively works by producing citizens by management – it is not simply a repository of meanings.
>
> *(Kendall and Wickham, 1999: 138)*

Peim links Foucault to Derrida in tracing the genealogy of the transition from sovereign power to governmental power (from Foucault) in the 'binary logic' of pastoral discipline:

> Foucault's later development of the idea of power and of the history of the self goes beyond the fixity perhaps implied in the 'panopticonic' account of capillary power in the condition of governmentality. But it is Derrida's rethinking of the very idea of structure and the alternative account that may be derived from it – of the idea of culture, the self and of a politics of practice. The 'grammar' of the school, its habitual semantics and syntax, will be – like all grammars – provisional and partial. In the light of Derrida's approach to language, the grammar of the school will have mobility and difference written into itself. Evidence of this mobility and difference can be drawn from the tensions between normative practices and the counter-practices they give rise to.
>
> *(Peim, 2001: 12)*

For a 'grammatology' of the educational encounter, then, we need to consider, taking a lead from Foucault and Derrida, the key social practices in which the self is negotiated through reformation. The notion of 'the audience' as a key concept in media studies can be read as a normative and regulatory principle for the production of subjects.

> Arguably, audience research has always revolved around issues of power. Either we want to know what the media do to people, what people do to media, or perhaps, what people do to themselves and others *with* media.
>
> *(Ruddock, 2007: 25)*

The history of the present of media studies is the genealogy of a discourse – the idea of 'the media' as an object that qualifies for an educational response. As we have explored in detail earlier, the departure of cultural studies from its starting point is bound up with the notion of 'the media', and so what we are dealing with is the uneasy relationship between popular culture as a category, understandable only in its insulation from art, literature, theatre and classical music, which were already 'catered for' in the curriculum, and 'the media' as an idea. What is different about media studies is that it has never been coherently defined by practices or any vertical discourse of such, so the identity of a media student set against an artist or actor has been much less clearly defined – for teachers, students and the public. At the same time, the consensus in popular discourse that 'the media' are powerful, and as such it is worth educating people to protect them from the media (through critical thinking) and prepare them for employment in the sector, has been used in confusion, with advocates of the subject oscillating between these two positions in the quest for legitimation. In the inaugural edition of the *Media Education Research Journal*, Berger and McDougall offer a detailed account of this 'history' (see also Buckingham, 2003), with this extract dealing with the 1980s as a formative decade:

> The 1980s and 1990s, not only saw an entrenchment of media studies at GCSE and A-Level, but the attacks on the subject were at its height. John Major's Education Secretary, John Patten, called media studies 'cultural Disneyland' and 'pseudo-religion' just as his government established the first 'heritage' – later 'culture' – minister, David Mellor. Media – or *medium* – studies were generally the preserve of the polytechnics, but the creation of the new post-1992 universities added further impetus; the study of media was OK if it was in a poly, but not in a university, seemed to be the view.
>
> *(Berger and McDougall, 2010: 9)*

Desperately reading the audience

Once again we return to the speculation that media studies might have got closer to its idea of its own identity had it avoided an instrumental and ultimately alienating set of oppositions between producer and audience and between 'target audiences' themselves. One way in which media education looks very different from *subject English* is in its focus on 'the audience' (English has never had much time for the reader). But looking awry, it is generally the case that reading practices and what people do when they give meaning to media are obscured by a short-circuit to questions of needs, targeting and appeal, with an over-emphasis on an unproven 'feedback loop' model, very often predicated on assumptions about genre. The GCSE assessment mode we spent time with in Chapter 5 is demonstrative of this.

What has been lacking, despite good intentions, is any kind of strategic approach to the aspiration for media education that is more difficult to achieve – supporting students in audience research, and a coherent method for the dialogic work of connecting reflection on their own media use with the 'prepared earlier' models derived from experts' research. As we have stated throughout this book, *subject media* does not describe the academic perspectives of educators, and it does not represent every aspect of media education as social practice. Rather, it describes the institutionalised configuration of the study of media as experienced by the largest number of people, and as such we are interested in the broadest impact of media in the curriculum in terms of social reproduction. At the same time, while readers in 'the academy' are more likely to refute our observations in relation to their own practice, we would resist setting up higher education as generally other to this discourse, as it is clear that the orthodoxy we critique here as *subject media* – and that Merrin and Gauntlett challenge in a different way in their 'Media 2.0' polemic – does run through a great deal of media studies across sectors and in international contexts. Students may escape it through options, or through encounters with particular courses or lecturers, but at the core the conceptual premise is, we argue, restrictive in its belief in the metaphysics of the idea of 'the media'.

> 'Media Studies 2.0' is interested in the every-day participatory and creative possibilities of media, as compared to the focus of traditional media studies on professional media consumed by audiences who had to take what they were given …. 'Media Studies 2.0' also emphasises a sociological focus on the media as it is in the world, and as people experience it – and therefore is (happily, but less crucially) associated with a welcome end to the armchair ramblings of 'textual analysis'.
>
> *(Gauntlett, 2009: 3)*

After the media, audience research has to deal with two linked confrontations. If whatever version of 'Media 2.0' we can accept does transgress, to some extent at least, orthodox ways of dealing with audiences, then this will make a difference to the reception of media. At the very least we can think of this as a continuum with at one end the 'prosumer' who sees herself as a producer as much as a member of any audience, and at the other, the lingering dynamics of power and value that keep the idea of a more or less shared audience reading in place. At the same time, a greater or lesser shift to 'making and connecting' makes the role of the media in the formation of identity less significant and, for the academic and her student, this makes the practice of generating (or passing on, from others' work) any empirical evidence of the 'tapestry' of influences of media in everyday life a lot more complicated.

Put simply, the majority of what is produced by students as an outcome of engagement with *subject media* pays only lip service to even the basic idea of the 'diffused audience', less attention to imagined community and scant regard to textual poaching. This is not to say that media teachers are disengaged from the contemporary discussion of audience (or the concept formally known as that), but that there is a systematic disconnect between these theories and their basis in research with people – situated audiences – and the requirements of 'the subject' to privilege that which can be objectified in the text as serving or appealing to an imagined other – 'the audience'.

Ethnography

Monaco (2010) very clearly describes (although this is our interpretation and application) the awkward space between the academic culture and its undermining itself in transmission to students, in her discussion of autoethnography and fan ethnography. Citing the ways in which Couldry, Jenkins and Hills navigate the terrain of their own fan-scholar hybridity in their research, she brings us to the central issue, which will be how to facilitate the same reflective approach in students: 'It is through empirical work with audiences that media fan studies can further pursue the question of power relations by examining how this dual scholar-fan identity is actually negotiated during the research process' (Monaco, 2010).

While not all media students are fans in this sense, they are all people living in culture of which media plays a part. So the fan-scholar method is transferable to their experiences of learning. Wardle considers the seemingly odd and unhelpful distinction made between fandom and learning in this way:

> Perhaps some of the emerging strategies and practices developed by television drama to elicit fan engagement are equally as pertinent to education institutions seeking to improve the learning experience. Since 1988, when Henry Jenkins published Textual Poachers, being a fan has been reconceptualised into something more positive. Drawing on the work of Michel de Certeau, Jenkins describes fans as 'active producers and manipulators of meanings'. This positive conceptualisation of fandom has much in common with notions of deep learning.
>
> *(Wardle, 2010)*

Wardle goes on to apply the same principles of contemporary theory about 'deep learning' as 'they seem equally true of being a fan as being a learner'. In his

2003 'state of the subject', Buckingham describes the study of media audiences as involving targeting; mode of address; circulation; uses, making sense, pleasures and social differences (2003: 60). In the more recent fifth edition of their commonly used undergraduate textbook *The Media Student's Book*, Branston and Stafford begin the section on audience with an overview of academic representations of audiences, then move from effects to uses and gratifications, and on to 'cultural approaches' and hybridity. Sensibly, students are encouraged to steer between the uncritical celebration of the prosumer and the lingering idea of the single audience. Despite the range of ways to 'do audience' in both of these influential texts, though, the annexing of the 'cultural' element, often a result of the simple phasing of the scheme of work (where sender – message – receiver comes first) remains a problem in *subject media*. If Wardle is right in suggesting that fandom and learning offer rich connections for pedagogy, and we are supportive of Monaco's recent audience work and how she puts the dialogics of audience–fan–analyst at the heart of cultural study, then we ought to dispense altogether with the notion of audience as a part of production, and start from the interpretive communities in which our students are dispersed and more or less connected.

Audience research within, around and in between media and cultural studies has been the subject of much debate 'at the crossroads' for many years. The question of what to do with digital media exchange is merely the latest instalment. The University of Westminster holds 'Transforming Audiences' conferences, some contributors talk of 'the concept formally known as the audience', and the journal *Participations* (edited by Martin Barker) invites papers that speak to the contested nature of contemporary audience research. Livingstone (2010), an academic long associated with empirical audience research, sums up some of the current challenges:

> In the face of an unholy alliance between political economists and popular prejudice, audience researchers sought to defend television viewers against the attack that they were mindless and unthinking, lacking in the reflexivity or critical literacies exemplified by scholars and critics. Informed by a particular mix of semiotic, cultural and reception theories, this hermeneutic turn was motivated by a commitment to recognise the value of ordinary experience, to hear from marginalised voices, especially women's, and to inquire into rather than presume about the processes by which social realities are constructed and reproduced. This research paid off: audiences were shown to confound the authority of supposed textual givens by creating distinctive and multiple interpretations unanticipated by producers but meaningful within their lifeworlds, even enacting individual or collective resistance under the radar through routine acts of tactical evasion. One might say, how much easier to make this case today, when our respondents no longer sit still and silent, demanding all our efforts to interpret their apparently blank gaze as thoughtful and engaged. Now they click and type, moving around and adding to the text on the screen in a way that we can record – their thoughts and engagement are clearly evident. And yes, we

should seek to capture and interpret this, as before. But today I suggest we face a different but equally unholy alliance – still involving popular prejudice but now linked not to mass society critics but to network society's optimists, cheered on by technologists, futurologists, controlling states and commercial imperatives.

(Livingstone, 2010: 6)

At the heart of what Livingstone observes as a paradox is surely, once again, the modernist stability of an unhelpful opposition between audience and text or audience and medium/the media. Whereas television viewers were effectively defended by academics from the 'cultural dupes' thesis, and media studies unwittingly maintained the discourse by arguing so strongly against it – not just watching television but critically reading it – now, she argues, 'the active reader' and the rebranded prosumer are commodified, and the assumptions about their audience behaviour are spun the other way – they are a rich market of digital natives who can be co-opted for all kinds of new modes of commercial practice, including educational activity.

Returning to *Participations* and also for a moment to 'Media Studies 2.0' – although we do not intend to further that discussion here – one of Gauntlett's examples of the latter, in his development of Merrin's theme (or meme?) was the title of the journal. He celebrates it as being a journal on audience studies that 'manages to avoid calling them audiences', but goes on to lament the addition of a subtitle, which continues the paradigmatic framing that we should be 'getting away from'. This is less trivial than it may appear, and the same view informs much of what we mean by 'after the media'. *Participations* discusses a broad range of cultural activity that researchers can observe and analyse, but without the obligation to return to the idea of audience – a term only meaningful in relation to assumptions about text/cultural product and producer. So just as Gauntlett and Barker wish us to continue researching what people do with and around media, Gauntlett more explicitly sees a liberation in removing the idea of groups of people in audiences altogether. We see this as part of a broader project. To listen to people in culture, we need to dismantle the idea of the tripartite dynamic between producer, text and audience, and to do so we have to dispense with the idea of 'the media', as it is this at once empty and full discourse – empty in its lack of any substance and full in the power that such lack exercises by escaping definition and precision – which situates text and audience as 'big others' to one another.

Of course, the whole Media 2.0 argument is bound with conflicts over the audience for audience research. Just as the chapter on identity needed to discuss the identity of media studies (or rather, the various versions of identities at play), so too does a consideration of audience need to engage with the readers of journals, set against the users of more 'quick and dirty' web 2.0 knowledge transfer. And so part of the argument expressed by Merrin and Gauntlett is that peer-reviewed journal articles are an outmoded medium for the dissemination of ideas. Clearly there is a vested interest in the critical responses to such arguments, coming as they do mainly from published journal authors and their editors. Hermes captures this here:

> The moment audiences are producers and co-creators, as a 2.0 perspective suggests, they hardly need the mediating voice of research to tell them how what they are doing has meaning. In point of fact, Media Studies 2.0 could be taken to suggest that audience research has only ever been in the business of explaining audiences to interested parties that rarely include audience members themselves. After all, who reads our work? To whom do we sell research and reports?
>
> *(Hermes, 2010: 112)*

Hermes discusses the ways in which 'audiencehood' develops over time and is contingent rather than linear or tautological. Seemingly in keeping with our approach, she argues that distinctions between fans and other audience members, or audiences and the rest of the public, are unhelpful as web 2.0 allows for more fragmented and organic media exchange which undermines these unifying concepts. To return to our central claim, the difference here is that Hermes identifies web 2.0 as a temporal determinant in this shift, whereas we will assert (and reassert) the idea that all web 2.0 does is let us see more clearly how we went about things the wrong way in the first place – these 'unifying concepts' were always-already obscure and obstructive to our work. But where Hermes' suggestions are of direct practical use to our pedagogic project is in her call for a compromised form of ethnography that she calls 'temporary co-travelling' with people and their media and the affordances of feedback:

> In a webbed world, feedback could be the answer of the audience researcher against her imminent desire as translator of knowledges and literacies that are, today, arguably more widely shared than ever before. To combine such literacy with the power of strong ethnographic work could make for fascinating and challenging analysis, and theorisation of identity and cultural practice.
>
> *(Hermes, 2010: 120)*

Paralogy: rules and exceptions, exceptions or rules

To make sense of this and suggest a way of working in educational spaces, we want to first confirm our view of the shifting discourses around audience as political, and propose a strategy for pedagogic practice informed by Lyotard's call for paralogy. Media and cultural studies, then, have operated in and between three conflicting desires concerning what to do with 'the audience'. They move from everyday life and identity to 'the media' and its influences on identity and representation, to an empowerment discourse seeking to liberate the 'active reader' from derision, and ironically, back to a more sceptical, hierarchical, and for some protectionist, agenda in response to audiences providing their own evidence of active engagement – especially those awarded approval by the burgeoning field of fandom. In many cases, media audience research has spoken for its respondents – even the advocates of 'Media 2.0' tend to conclude their studies with expert readings and generalised arguments about the outcomes. The challenge is to work with students in auto-ethnographic contexts in such a way that they can at once be the expert researcher and agent of critical reflection in shaping their own media literacies: 'In moving forward and reinventing media studies, the balance needs to be made up: what might audiences "need" us for, and what do we need the audience for? Older idealism and new pragmatism can rebuild the discipline' (Hermes, 2009: 124).

Take away the idea of 'the audience' and the us and them binary, and this call to arms suits us well for 'after the media'. The older idealism addresses our desire to take cultural studies back to its aspirations, looking at people in life without the distraction of the mass media as the big agent in identity. And the new pragmatism is the space we want to occupy with paralogy, and we can achieve this by turning around the orthodox equation of rule and exception. For example, when teachers 'use' McMillan's work on hybrid identities with students, this research material is generally 'packaged' as an interesting, but exceptional case study in post-colonial audience research:

> Hybrid programming is considered a symbolic representation of transnationalism, and hybrid television programming is upheld as an indication of the market's attention to local needs and wants. Yet such a focus on micro choices and cultural experiences distracts from its very limited trajectory in relation to a capitalist structure which plays a significant role in defining autonomous needs and wants.
>
> *(McMillin, 2007: 126)*

Another 'exceptional' example is Durham's research (2004) into teenage girls of Hindu cultural heritage living in Florida, who were using the media partly to construct a 'hybrid' identity. Durham discovered, through the ethnographic endeavour (spending time, observing from the location), that the girls were using *Friends* alongside Hindi film songs to switch and combine the two poles of their identities, as paraphrased here by Ruddock:

> Both of these experiences were meaningless on an explicitly textual level; Friends was just 'stupid', where Hindu musicals probably mean something, but the girls did not know what. But on a cultural level, both resources helped the girls mediate the different worlds they inhabited; Friends accessed a high school (language) where musicals contained a sense of Indianness shared with parents. The girls found themselves being Indian in Florida due to forces beyond their control. They had to figure out what this means, partly by using media products made by multinational systems of production

and delivery. But it was up to them to make these power dynamics real by embodying them in specific ways.

(Ruddock, 2007: 71)

When we call these 'exceptional', we are just drawing attention to their situated status within *subject media* which is at the margins of the orthodox 'mainstream' attention paid to 'classic' mass-media audience models – and we include 'Media 2.0' in that. Hybridity is set up as 'other' – something for us to bear witness to, but as an alternative to more 'straightforward' models for audience reception. Could we, instead, begin with hybridity as the norm – as the orthodoxy for how we think about people using media to partly negotiate identity and to construct all sorts of representations? Alongside this, could the construction of the 'meaningless' be a starting point instead of an interesting aside, perhaps for the 'more able' only? Fandom is only one part of the equation – attributing a lack of meaning to media is equally important in how we tell stories about being human.

McMillin, in mapping audience research traditions in a global context, talks of the ways in which its agents have failed to ground media theory adequately in contexts of global culture and variations in class, gender, religion and language – the things that 'texture subjectivity' (McMillin, 2007: 135). If we are to respond to her findings, then working with students on media courses will be problematic as long as such programmes of study remain self-regarding. How can a student understand the nature of their own textured subjectivity in the context of global culture, hybridity and diaspora if they only study media? This takes us to our boldest claim – that media studies must be connected to the study of culture more broadly. Politics, economics, history, philosophy – media theory cannot be insulated from these other categories. Students need ideas to make films about. They need an understanding of how their use of media exchange is connected to the broader social and geopolitical landscape. Perhaps ironically, then, as 'the media' disappear from view and people come sharply into focus, as texts give ways to events and reception is no longer separated from production, then so too do these other areas of social science become important.

There may be an immediate rebuke to this with recourse to Ang's exploration of how humanities and social science differ, but we would argue that ethnography must draw on both in connecting the private to the public. We are not arguing for cultural study after the media to favour Lyotard's event over Habermas's public sphere, but for the subject to embrace the way in which its every operation is situated between these discourses. Studying culture will always be an act of becoming. Crucially we return again to the importance of what McMillin describes as 'putting the media in their place in the social lives of their consumers' (2007: 192), and the simple, but essential act of starting from the premise that media use is always-already a part of something else, and thus there is no purchase on 'the media' as distinct from rituals in the broader lifeworld. Where we depart from the research methods described by McMillin is that we want to move away from explorations that merely measure the relationship between what 'the media' communicate and the existing communicative contexts of audiences. Instead, we concur with Couldry who sees life as media related but not media centred, and suggest that the main reason for the longevity of the idea of 'the media' in academic work and teaching can be attributed to how difficult it is to deal with the alternative within the constraints of teaching and learning as configured institutionally. Hills (2005) writes about scholarship in relation to faith discourses, and the peer review process is certainly akin to a theological dispute in many cases. We are not exempt from this by any means – our obsession with dismantling the constructed idea of 'the media' is clearly as much a matter of faith as the belief in such a 'big other' in the first place.

Ethnomethodology – the act of bearing witness to the interpretive work of the researcher – requires students to reflect critically on the construction of meaning not only 'in the world' – between people and with use of media – but also by the student-researcher. If this work is collaborative, then the process of reflexive co-creation of interpretive knowledge is stronger. Students look for patterns in and between fandom, 'audiencehood' – attachment to media in more or less understood power structures (Grossberg, Nelson and Treichler, 1992) – and the forms of cultural exchange described in 'convergence culture' (Jenkins, 2006), and out of these unforeseen findings from the lifeworld, start to theorise identity and representation. In so doing the 'mainstream' of media study will 'theorise audiencehood as a layered palette of activities, attachments and investments, widely differing in intensity and importance, especially paying attention to how audiencehood is caught up in everyday social relations' (Hermes, 2009: 116).

Nationwide: the remix

Taking season 4 of the US drama *The Wire* (which deals with schools), we have explored (McDougall, 2010) – through research – how it might be possible to 'remix' Morley's *Nationwide* study for the post-broadcast era (which we take to be a debatable term). In so doing we were unpacking much of the 'Media 2.0' thesis to challenge the part of that intervention which might assume too much about the end of the hierarchical nature of media production and reception, at the same time as wanting to 'try out' the move from 'doing media' to 'doing people'. So we arrive at something like a 'back to the future' for audience research – bringing a classic cultural studies approach (from *Nationwide*) into dialogue with a television drama consumed by large groups (and hence very much a 'mass media' text) but in fragmented contexts – box sets, downloads – and with a heavy dose of what we will call 'secondary encoding'.

Morley maintained Hall's distinctions between encoding, encoded and decoding, and observed how such processes would be manifested in the reception of a popular current affairs programme by different groups of people in socio-economic sets, defined largely by occupation.

Our concern in the *Nationwide* research project was to connect the theoretical question of the maintenance of hegemony with the empirical question of how a particular programme acts to 'prefer' one set of meanings or definitions of events.

(*Morley, 1992: 91*)

In this study, the act of decoding was privileged above others, and as a result the 'preferred reading' was assumed to be encoded and ideologically 'fixed' within the text. Morley's objective, then, was merely to measure the degree to which this reading was accepted, negotiated or opposed, in contrast to an attempt to acquire proof of how it might be constructed, in between and across these domains. It was, as such, itself 'preferred', and thus a dubious claim to objectivity was made:

The concept of the preferred reading makes clear the central point that encoding/decoding programmatically established, namely that there was no necessary correspondence between the two moments of encoding and decoding. There was no guarantee that the ideological message encoded in the television programme would be 'bought' by all those who viewed it.

(*Scannell, 2007: 213*)

Audience research of this kind will look at the interplay of the internal discursive hierarchy of the text (in which a 'preferred reading' reveals itself) and the likelihood of this reading being accepted or challenged (or 'negotiated') in relation to the socio-cultural locations and 'back stories' of audience groups and in the context of everyday life. The 'preferred reading' is thus realised through semiotic analysis of the encoding of the programme, an assumption later challenged by the author himself:

Is the preferred reading a property of the text per se? Or is it something that can be generated from the text (by a skilled reading) via certain specifiable procedures? Or is the preferred reading that reading which the analyst is predicting that most members of the audience will produce from the text? In short, is the preferred reading a property of the text, the analyst or the audience?

(*Morley, 1992: 122*)

In the research on *The Wire*, we pay more attention to how a preferred reading about the authenticity of the drama circulates (largely online) and informs (by way of a secondary encoding) reception.

In relation to 'Media 2.0', this research into reception of *The Wire* was dialectic – at once challenging and unpacking elements of the thesis in a frame of complex hybridity. *The Wire* is a media product that, despite its relatively new modes of distribution, is arranged through very orthodox storytelling conventions, not to mention the channelling of authoritative praise for the series through traditional structures – reviews, discussion on television shows and academic responses. And yet at the same time the consideration of *The Wire* 'as it is in the world' and the subsequent 'remix' of Morley turns on the shift to the notion of the 'preferred reading' as being viral and experiential – from within the text to paratextual and dialogic. Again, whilst studies of fandom identified audiences as creative and participatory a long time ago, the argument here seems to be that these layers of interpretation, homage and negotiation of meaning are now more visible. What is happening here, we suggest, is a kind of 'after the media' reimagining of the culture which is, in fact, not temporal, similar to Lyotard's version of postmodernity (1992) as being less 'after the modern' and more concerned with a refutation of grand narratives. Second, Gauntlett's suggestions (2007: 126) for research methods aimed at making sense of everyday creativity and visual representations of identities (discussed at length in the chapter on identity) were teased out through a 'mash up' of methods aimed at resisting any parodic othering.

Five audience groups participated – trainee teachers, youth workers, media lecturers, drama lecturers and online fan-critics (some famous, some 'prosumers'). In an extension of Gauntlett's 'visual research' approach – and bearing in mind Buckingham's critique of it, discussed in the chapter on identity – each group was given a different data acquisition context – blog postings, visual responses, film-making, paired interviews, focus groups. The intention here was, through multi-modal research intervention, to tease out further some of the assumptions made about particular research methods, especially where there may be some convenient othering of alternatives, by deliberately comparing the effect of each on the data within the same study.

The five groups, almost without any exception, adopted immediately the dominant discourse – that 'the game' depicted in the show is really being played in social reality – and that the producers of *The Wire* are offering a window to this world, and that the show has things to teach us. From Charlie Brooker to the youth workers, this motif was repeated. Each group gave a different context for this – the media teachers provide an intertextual 'metalanguage' coded as a semiotic chain of meaning (or a 'taxonomy' in their words), with their own identities woven in. They assume that the proximal relations of *The Wire, Do the Right Thing* (the 1989 Spike Lee film) and Public Enemy (the rap group) – and the meanings attributed to such by white professionals (as several choose to identify themselves – an important detail since ethnicity is not a 'marker' for this study) will be understood. The drama lecturers were alike in their eagerness to discuss *The Wire* as a text, but more comfortable with a discourse of 'cultural value', and more distant from the form – television. Though their acquisition of cultural capital was close to their media counterparts, their 'mapping' of the text to their lifeworlds came less instinctively. The youth workers appeared to have the most at stake, contrasting greatly with both the media teachers (for whom the reality depicted is mediated through other media references) and the drama teachers, who confess to having little direct experience of such aspects of social reality. For the youth workers the preferred reading was apparently articulated through lived experience, either in the present or projected into the future ('it's gonna come down on us'). And subsequently there was less interest in the text, the craft or its objectives. For the education students a great deal was also at stake – their life experience and proximity to the social reality represented was closer to the youth workers, but their optimism for change marked their responses as different from all the other groups – including the online critic-fans.

Here, a media teacher offers some reflection and intertextual mapping:

> The 'hood' fires off connections. I was something of a b-boy wannabe as a teen in the 80s, so the whole blackstreet culture reminds me of that dalliance: Public Enemy, NWA, Beat Street etc. The truth is that, although it's engaging as a drama, it's all too far removed from where I am in my life: growing veg, watching my daughter grow up etc. The liberal in me reels at the injustice and the squalor that they appear to live in but in some respects representations like this being to lose their impact.

Responding to a question about *The Wire* as teaching resource, another media educator suggests:

> Could be used to illustrate cause and effect in story and representations of 'heroes' and 'villains'. The emphasis on enigmas could be used as an entry point into Barthesian codes – esp. hermeneutic. Could also be used in a comparative exercise with the 19th century novel – let's see if there really is a 'Dickensian aspect'! Or how about *The Wire* vs. *Middlemarch*? All exercises encourage a critical distance from the text – a focus on construction rather than allowing suspension of disbelief to be indulged.

A youth worker 'maps' the drama to everyday life:

> The moral of *The Wire* for me is this, communities with a large diverse range of cultures and so on, need more powers amongst themselves to make positive changes in their own communities. For example, more non-white teachers, police, politicians, business directors etc. This would then allow ethnic minorities to feel empowered and part of society, rather than feel as though crime is the only accepting and rewarding path for them. Hegemony plays a big role here. I also feel that this has a lot to do with social control and modern day slavery but that is another topic …

Drama lecturers were more ready to articulate an appreciation of the 'craft' of the programme's construction:

> The characters, I think, above all. The characters are sympathetically drawn and it doesn't feel artificial at all. And the way the storylines are woven, they manage

to pull you in, so you are waiting to go back into that classroom or waiting to go back to that street corner to see what's going on. It's addictively written.

The trainee teachers related the show directly to their own career aspirations:

It puts it into perspective. You go into teaching and you might just think its about teaching but then you've got to realise that things happen behind closed doors to children and they are gonna bring it into the classroom. You have to think about the social side of it. I did mentoring at school and we got trained about this, how to approach things like drugs and parents being in jail and I can see things in the programme that we got told about, but not had experience of.

However, these extracts are not representative of the data since written and spoken words accounted for less than half of 'what came back'. Returning to our discussion of audience research 'after the media', what this study revealed about *The Wire* is far less interesting than how the research methods allowed for some more experimental and reflexive work with people. The mode of response and professional context of the participants could not be extracted from one another in the telling. The distinctions in data were not only a product of identity but of research method. The higher level of reflection and intertextual connecting on the part of media teachers might be a product of what Gauntlett calls 'giving time' and an unstated and internalised expectation of a more creative outcome. The discourse of emancipation and optimism expressed by trainee teachers may have been the result of their being interviewed in a group and having signed up to a course shot through with the rhetoric of 'Every Child Matters'. Had this group been presented with the opportunity to produce visual outcomes over a longer period, might they have told a different, more cynical story? And to what extent were the youth workers, collaborating on their films, performing?

Rather than undermining the outcomes of this research, these more visible inflections by method simply serve to reveal what is always already at stake in research – the context of living in culture is always subjective. Indeed, by adopting a range of different methods and contexts for the acquisition of data, the researcher is able to make more sense of what comes back. Perhaps a problem with Gauntlett's 'othering' of language-based research data is that his work only offers the alternative and as such there is a danger of constructing a 'parodic' representation of audience research. In this paper another strategy has been attempted – a 'mash up' of methods with the deliberate intention of exploring (and exploiting) the difference this additional set of determinants (in addition to the cultural map) makes to the outcomes.

(McDougall, 2010: 98)

Student research might, then, adopt this 'mash-up ethnography', which differs from ethnography in its deliberate multi-modality in method and, crucially, the representation of data, in order to move away from the text (and the 'armchair') to explore, in new ways, how people in culture attribute meaning to media. Crucially, we are not offering the 'Nationwide Remix' as anything radically or progressively different from the cultural studies research that media studies ought to spend more time. Rather we understand it as part of that tradition and are merely arguing that it takes us 'back to the future' in that sense. More ideas for so doing conclude this chapter.

Postmodernism and (media) education

Lyotard moves us from the text to the event and from generalised principles for the legitimation of knowledge (truth, justice) to local, micro narratives with the intention of giving voice to the margins and to local differences. Resistance to any guiding principles is key here, and for our project we see both 'audience' and 'the media' as such. Paralogy, then, will consist of invention without recourse to these regulatory ideals. For this there will be no explicit goal – such as 'critical media literacy' or its great other – 'employability'. Instead, the project of cultural study after the media will be a paradox – it will be liberating in its very resistance to the orthodox modernist assumptions of the grand narrative of *subject media*. In their work on postmodernism and education, Usher and Edwards cite both cultural studies and media studies as 'new territories' in the academy, as examples of the breaking down of enlightenment configurations of the knowledge that 'counts'. And yet both have become part of the modern in their situating themselves in a proximal relation to 'the media', and – as we have argued in our interpretation of Hunter and Peim's work – through the adoption of the same surveillance techniques as reside in the teaching of literature. At the same time we will not accept the charge that this reimaging of media and cultural studies is profoundly relativist or neo-conservative, as Usher and Edwards view it here. This approach more squarely faces up to the contested and dialogic nature of media learning, described as: 'the dialogue between feminists, critical pedagogues and postmodern writers such as Lyotard – a dialogue on the relative strengths and weaknesses of contributions to the ongoing questioning, understanding and, in certain cases, purposive changing of the contemporary world' (Usher and Edwards, 1994: 185).

From text to event

The problem with *subject media* is that it adheres to the regulatory principle of the media to make judgements about texts. As such its desire to bear witness to multiplicity – of reception and, increasingly of parody and audience reworking – can only ever be an extension, an exception to this normative principle – as in the idea of Media 2.0 with its reliance on the internet as an epochal determinant. Lyotard's ontology of singularity – of the event – can get us out of this cul-de-sac.

If culture is a flow of unique events, these could still be understood as texts but paratext and appropriation would be always-already a part of the chain of events – no universal concept can be offered to take account of all events, of all media.

Lyotard's alternative – paralogy – provides a performative justice with no recourse to meta-narratives. Plurality is privileged over consensus and, as we have seen in the Rorty statement that begins this chapter, such a turn away from the logic of general principles is resisted by many for its potential to undermine democracy and liberation. Our thinking 'after the media', as we have stated, is Lyotardian (or postmodern) in so much as we view the study of 'the media' as a metanarrative which excludes and undermines difference and marginalises more than it includes or emancipates. An alternative must be found – a performative way of bearing witness to lifeworld media exchanges as singular events – these might be textual but will not be read as sealed texts with producers and audiences divided by time and space. As such the quest for new answers to questions of identity, representation and culture will be 'paralogical'. Chaos theory and other 'micro' areas that start from difference and the 'long tail' of micro effects have influenced Lyotard and, in keeping, we want to formulate an escape from *subject media* through a new kind of media education which situates plurality and difference as its object of study and its unit of resource for assessment.

We are not, in this book, suggesting that we do away with the 'big concepts' (including audience) but that we view them as metanarratives in need of experimental 'gaming'. This will be the legitimising principle for doing culture after the media. Will audience research then need to work without rules in order to formulate 'the rules of what will have been done'? Or will we fall into the Lyotardian trap whereby working without rules becomes a dogma, just as the collapse of the meta-narratives becomes one? Equally, where the idea of the 'media text' comes into focus as part of the social practice at stake, the text will have the status of event, in Lyotard's view it will 'come too late' for its producer. This is crucial for us because in the institutionalised practices of *subject media* 'the audience' is reduced to the more or less active destination, distributor of deferrer of meaning in relation to the idea of a text with encoding qualities, more or less directly shaped by producers. Of course this is not the way media academics view things from/in the academy, but we are not dealing in this book with their scholarly affiliations or publications, but with the daily practice of teaching as experienced by students in all institutionalised socio-cultural framings of media studies. There is a disconnect between the two things. If we view the media event as always-already formulating the rules for its own existence – always too late for any model of producer-reception – then we must reformulate pedagogy to account for this. This will be a political move, not before time:

> If it is true to say that much of Lyotard's most vital thinking is carried out in some sense against Marxism, his pretension has never been that of refuting Marxism, but of showing that it is one way of thinking (genre of discourse), and that its pretension to be the way of thinking (the way that reality thinks

itself) must be illegitimate. This general orientation may help to make some sense of the idea that Lyotard is fundamentally a political thinker, to the precise extent that he contests the totalisations fundamental to most ideas of politics.

(Bennington, 1988: 9)

And so we co-opt Lyotard to speak to our dilemma – that we support the politics of *subject media* in so much as it intends to give voice to people in the face of a perceived oppression, but we attack the legitimacy of its pretensions which work, undoubtedly, against its premise.

'Doing people' after the media – pedagogy and dialectics

Unexpected dialogue between ideas here ought to mirror the open-ended dialogic practice of media learning. To this end we conclude this chapter with an imagined conversation between John Henry Newman, Lave and Wenger, activity theorists and Brookfield, a discussion that concerns emancipation, participation, truth and knowledge – with students as the audience for education.

John Henry Newman is often cited as an intellectual whose 'idea of a university' can be returned to as a foundation for the kind of personalised, student-centred experience the contemporary educational institution is generally unable to provide. However, his discourse of knowledge as an end in itself relies entirely upon an Enlightenment view of darkness and light, ignorance and truth, and so it is, we would argue, often an awkward alliance that is formed between liberal academics and Newman's doctrine – his mandate *ex umbris et imaginibus in vertitatem!* (from shadows and symbols into the truth!). And yet in his discussion of the distinction between the vocational modality and this more spiritual, liberating ideal – currently set as a differend against the employability discourse – another view of social advancement is framed by entirely separate logic, Newman articulates a view of the learning process which resonates with the more current and certainly more fashionable (if less formative in practice) work of Lave and Wenger (1991) on 'communities of practice'. What the many recent considerations of contemporary higher education and particularly 'widening participation' in the 'light' of Newman's rhetoric and vision of expansion observe is that the spirit of the enterprise has been undermined by the institutional discourses – of the student as customer, of 'quality control' and of input–output measurement of learning against targets. So we might suggest that the work Peim undertakes against *subject English*, which we extend to *subject media*, might also be applied to the (post)modern university – that there is a differend between 'spirit' and socio-cultural framing. Further, we can see in Newman's construction of knowledge and of truth a similar recourse to an ideal (constructed in theological language, of course) as we find in the idea of 'the media'. So just as *subject media* cannot realise itself in relation to either the big other of the media or with a temporal flight to 'Media 2.0', neither can the contemporary university resist the discourse of employability by recourse to Newman's truth:

An assemblage of learned men, zealous for their own sciences, and rivals of each others, are brought, by familiar intercourse and for the sake of intellectual peace, to adjust together the claims and relations of their respective subjects of investigation. They learn to respect, to consult, to aid each other. Thus is created a pure and clear atmosphere of thought, which the student also breathes, though in his own case he only pursues a few sciences out of the multitude. He profits by an intellectual tradition, which is independent of particular teachers, which guides him in his choice of subjects, and duly interprets for him those which he chooses. He apprehends the great outlines of knowledge, the principles on which it rests, the scale of its parts, its lights and its shades, its great points and its little, as he otherwise cannot apprehend them. Hence it is that education is called 'Liberal.' A habit of mind is formed which lasts through life, of which the attributes are, freedom, equitableness, calmness, moderation, and wisdom; or what in a former Discourse I have ventured to call a philosophical habit. This then I would assign as the special fruit of the education furnished at a University, as contrasted with other places of teaching or modes of teaching. This is the main purpose of a University in its treatment of its students.

(Newman, 1996: 77)

However, Lave and Wenger's notion of a collaborative, participative conception of learning as social *has* been largely accepted in the discourses of teacher education and research. There is less evidence of applied pedagogy that coherently engages with such a view of social practice at the level of curriculum and the point of assessment. We see two opportunities to move forward by conceiving of students as being connected within networks of audiences for media exchange and for media learning. So 'doing audience' after the media amounts to rethinking and resisting the assumed boundaries between learners, the media and audiences, and replacing this model of insulation with a view of students as being textual agents across these domains. In Wenger's terms, the domain (requiring some kind of formal membership or affiliation) is media education, the community (the less formally defined network) is both the domain and the concept formally known as 'the audience', and the practice is the lesser or greater convergence of resources produced in the lifeworld – from fandom to less tangible forms of reception – and in the systemworld, both formative and summative outcomes of learning – this repository of material and experience is accumulated collectively in practice, making students *practitioners* – producers of media and of learning.

Clearly, then, attention moves from the content – transmission – of 'knowledge' – the question of what 'counts' in epistemological terms – to the conditions of possibility for learning as praxis, a question of pedagogy and of social context. *Participation* becomes a key word, and fits neatly for our ends because it is the descriptor favoured by Lave and Wenger and also by the journal we have discussed as being indicative of an 'after the media' approach to people in culture. Such participation:

refers not just to local events of engagement in certain activities with certain people, but to a more encompassing process of being active participants in the practices of social communities and constructing identities in relation to these communities.

(Lave and Wenger, 1999: 4)

Lave and Wenger observe the process by which individuals make the move from peripheral participation in social 'apprenticeships' to full participation. With this analogy we can develop a model of social learning by which students, through their participation in social media education, progress from being peripheral to full practitioners in media 'audiences'. So we are no longer looking at the audience as an object of study or at our own audience behaviour as reflection. Instead we are conceiving of full participation in culture as the key learning outcome. This full participation – *situatedness* in Lave and Wenger's terms – leads to the making of meaning and the articulation of identity, as we have considered in another chapter. This involves learning *to* articulate in culture, through and with media, as opposed to learning from the articulations of others – whether elite producers, canonized texts or legitimated fans. Once again, it is the construct of 'the media' which has denied us this opportunity: as a 'big other' it imposes a distributive model of social capital whereby this currency is always-already and can only be acquired in relation to its normative gaze – social capital achieved through the academic modality – being critical about 'the media', or through the vocational modality – working within its idioms to gain access. The 'in between' space will be a community of practice in which texts, events and exchanges are produced in the practice but 'the media' are ignored.

Again, there are plentiful 'applications' of Lave and Wengers's ideas that seek to adopt some of these principles in relation to new digital media – videogames in particular (Squire, 2002), and while these are of interest we would be sceptical about the idea of a temporal 'coming true' – of the idea that such interactive and immersive media experiences as games allow for situated learning in ways that were somehow obstructed in the linear media and learning contexts. That said, a pedagogy equipped to enable situated media learning will draw upon both 'communities of practice' and activity theory, and it may be that new digital media have acted as a catalyst for this, but not the determinant. Cole and Engerstrom (1993) argue that the dialectical interplay between subjects (students) and objects is mediated by tools – this is what Gauntlett refers to when he writes about 'Media 2.0' and 'making and connecting'. Activity theory seeks to draw a more detailed model than the communities of practice idea can extend to, since the progression from apprenticeship to 'mastery' in Lave and Wengers's conception is, activity theorists will argue, lacking the devil of the detail – the tools for situated learning and most importantly the problems with the system, the tensions within the context that students must comprehend in the dialogic encounter. Squire, in application of a range of learning theories to videogames, makes two observations in relation to these two educational models, intended as a more informed alternative to the orthodoxy of effects research around gaming:

> The educational value of the game-playing experience comes not from just the game itself, but from the creative coupling of educational media with effective pedagogy to engage students in meaningful practices. Indeed, research on teachers' adoption and adaptation of materials suggests teachers will adapt the learning materials we create to maximize their potential to support learning regardless of designers' intentions. As such, the pedagogical value of a medium like gaming cannot be realized without understanding how it is being enacted through classroom use.
>
> *(Squire, 2002: 13)*

> Activity theory provides a theoretical framework with strong intuitive appeal for researchers examining educational games. Activity theory provides a theoretical language for looking at how an educational game or resource mediates players' understandings of other phenomena while acknowledging the social and cultural contexts in which game play is situated. Learning is conceptualized not as a function of the player and game; rather, learning is seen as transformations that occur through the dynamic relations between subjects, artifacts, and mediating social structures.
>
> *(Squire, 2002: 15)*

But why is the 'educational game' singled out as the transgressive or transformative tool? Why can we not conceive of the whole of education in this way, and for our ends media education in particular? Are we not always dealing with, and harnessing, the dynamic relations between these subjects, objects and structures when we ask students to work in the 'in between' spaces around our teaching, their media culture and broader areas of reflexive enquiry? Are we not always 'just gaming' in this sense?

Brookfield (2005) provides a compelling set of strategies for a pedagogy both informed by and applying the model of critical theory that seeks to empower by resistance to power structures and dynamics in education as a microcosm of the broader systemworld. By working through this agenda in relation to media education we are able to return to 'the heart of the problem' – the philanthropic nature of the emancipatory discourse. By contrast with, or as a dialogic playing out against the 'communities of practice' thesis, can we try to develop a political agenda without recourse to modernist constructions of truth and distortion?

According to Brookfield, the key learning tasks of a critical theory-informed pedagogy are resistance to ideology, hegemony and power (through revelation and unmasking) in order to learn liberation, reclaim reason and practise democracy. The ways in which Habermas deals with the contradictions of the grand narrative of democracy offer, in his model of the 'ideal speech situation', a process for learners to explore their own and others' lives in relation to democracy. The interplay of reproduction and opposition – echoing the work of Paul Willis – is at the heart of how Brookfield challenges us to teach.

Critical theory is normatively grounded in a vision of a society in which people live collectively in ways that encourage the free exercise of their creativity without foreclosing that of others. In such a society people see their individual well-being as integrally bound up with that of the collective. They act toward each other with generosity and compassion and are ever alert to the presence of injustice, inequity and oppression. Creating such a society can be understood as entailing a series of learning tasks: learning to recognise and challenge ideology that attempts to portray the exploitation of the many by the few as a natural state of affairs, learning to overcome alienation and thereby accept freedom, learning to pursue liberation, learning to reclaim reason and learning to practice democracy.

(Brookfield, 2005: 39)

Nobody is going to argue against any of that, nor that there are many examples of media contributing to oppression and exploitation. But the conjuring trick we want to 'pull off' is to explore the idea of practising democracy in the other way – from Lyotard's argument with Habermas (itself a differend) we take the view that Brookfield's adoption of the binaries between 'Big Ideology' and freedom have been appropriated fully by *subject media* which, unlike English, does not in itself have to be part of the reproductive technology. It is, sadly, hard to reconcile Brookfield's manifesto with our desire for a 'pedagogy of the inexpert' which we will account for fully in our final chapter. The media student, in Lyotard's and Foucault's terms, has been constructed without any way of phrasing her resistance to such a gaze. She sits in between the idea of 'the media' and the project of her liberal educator with only marginal space with which to be fully participative in culture. Suspending the political project is essential. Pedagogy of the inexpert, in which students are given voice to be textual agents on their own terms, will surely lead to a more political praxis in the fullness of time? Caught between the protectionist and innoculatory constraints of the academic modality with its latest incarnation in 'media literacy' – echoing, despite appearances, Newman's truth – and the performativity of the vocational modality, the student in *subject media* is trapped in the traverse between the regulatory principles of education and 'audience' – subjects and objects, a traverse between two constructions which she cannot live in at the same time – a differend. This is the wrong that cannot be presented.

In this chapter we have dealt with the obstructive separation of audience, student and 'the media'. Consistently with other chapters, we arrive at the more awkward but rich (for learning) in between space. As always, we leave the concept (of audience) standing, but challenged – under erasure. In our final interrogation, we suggest that the status of narrative may be more precarious.

8

NARRATIVE AFTER THE MEDIA: FROM NARRATIVE TO READING

> Texts don't stand on their own as bearers of their own self-defining meanings. Any text is always read from a particular point of view, by a subject (or subjects) positioned at a particular point ... the 'true' text – is never more than an abstraction, an idea distinct from particularly positioned readings of aspects of the textual object.
>
> *(Peim, 1993: 73)*

Peim's idea of the textual object as always-already an abstraction has long resonated for those of us with an interest in post-structuralist accounts of reading practices, but in the context of the new sorts of textual relations that Media 2.0 (Gauntlett, 2002; McDougall, 2010) emphasises, Peim's account of the primacy of the 'true text' fallacy to schooled literacy is ever more relevant. In this chapter we re-read the configurations of 'narrative' that *subject media* (McDougall, 2010) puts to work through the lens of current debates in literacy and cultural studies, and consider the extent to which they invest in, and are born of, the idea of the 'true text'. We contend that contemporary ideas in these fields about the nature of 'text', 'author', 'reader' and 'reading' throw up important questions about the usefulness and validity of narrative as a resource in the making and taking of meaning(s). Crucially, we want to argue that the theorisation of reading practices at work in literacies research is fundamental to the study of how people attribute meaning to media, but that this domain has been largely ignored by *subject media* in favour of reductive models of both narrative and media literacy.

We begin our discussion with an account of 'narrative' as it surfaces through the discourses of the curriculum specifications of *subject media* and draw out its central tenets. We consider how ideas about narrative in *subject media* compare with those that dominate other text-conscious subjects like English, and suggest that a cross-disciplinary idea of narrative, what Bernstein (2000) might call a 'horizontal discourse', operates to understand text, reader, author and reading bound concepts, fixed and stable and contributing to meaning making and taking in obvious and predictable ways. At the heart of this paradigm, we argue, is the notion of the true text: bounded, affective, self-sufficient and somehow agentive as it draws together a set of strategies that act dynamically upon readers. We suggest that this configuration reproduces a typically structuralist conception of textual experience characterised by transmission models of reading that encourage us:

> to learn to read ... in specialised ways in order to 'get to what is really there' ... to some extent this implies the ability to identify strategies and techniques being used to produce particular kinds of effects on what we think, believe, or desire.
>
> *(Lankshear and Knobel, 2008: 21)*

We interrogate the certainties of this paradigm with findings from two case study research projects we have undertaken with young people that seek to bear witness to young people's reported experience of reading and gaming, and argue that this evidence exposes the inadequacy of structuralism to describe those experiences. We put to work alternative ideas from literacy studies that draw attention to the social practice dimensions of textual experience (Barton and Hamilton, 1998; Street, 1999; Marsh, 2004), the identity work of reading and ideas about performativity, and which recast literacy as ways of being (with others) in the world. In so doing we emphasise a poetics of meaning making and taking that moves away from what texts do to readers and audiences towards what readers and audiences do with texts. We draw on ideas from cultural studies to push these ideas further still by problematising the centred or bound notion of the objects of textual experience, for example texts and authors. Towards a conclusion we reflect on the implications for the futures of *subject media* in terms of both its identity and distinctiveness, and the kind of learning places and spaces it might make available for young people.

The work of narrative in the schooled context

> The essential purpose of narrative is to tell a story, but the detailed purpose may vary according to genre. For example, the purpose of a myth is often to explain a natural phenomenon and a legend is often intended to pass on cultural traditions or beliefs.
>
> *(QCDA, 2010)*

Peim's (1993) proposed strategy for 'opening discourse' about reading offers a useful starting point for exploring narrative in the curriculum. Peim (1993: 71) suggests that we focus on how the object under scrutiny is learned, what it is, what it is for, what different forms it takes and what sorts of indicators signify 'expertise' in relation to it. We will use these questions to structure an analysis of the framing of narrative within the elaborated code (Bernstein, 2000) of the schooled curriculum as represented by a range of official curriculum documents produced by UK exam boards – GCSE (14–16) and A level (16–19) specifications for English and Media Studies, and the National Primary Curriculum (an inclusive document to frame the entire learning experience of 4 to 11 year olds).

These documents are intended to be read by teachers and lecturers and function to shape curriculum experience through prescription of mandatory aims, objectives and outcomes which are determined, disseminated and audited by a central regulatory body of the UK government – the Ofqual. We have argued elsewhere that the hierarchical relationship between educational policy and teachers is articulated both explicitly and implicitly through these documents (Kendall, 2005; McDougall et al, 2006), and the overt and sustained use of prohibitive modals throughout the documents might be seen as constitutive of this dynamic.

Through these documents narrative is discursively constructed as one of a range of explicitly named codes and conventions (OCR, 2010a :15) of *subject media* that function as 'clues' (OCR, 2010a: 15) towards isolation and identification of textual meaning so that 'candidates understand how meanings and responses are created in media products' (OCR, 2010b: 7). As such narrative is constituting of a grammar that enables the translation of textual experience through appropriation and application of a 'media language' (OCR, 2010b: 7) to reveal the essence of 'form', and bring 'the true text', into view. Coming to know form becomes a way of coming to 'understand how meanings and responses are created in media' products (OCR, 2010a: 7). The prepositional choice here locates 'meaning' as constituted within/by the media object, which has an outcome or effect such as 'passing on traditional knowledge or sharing cultural beliefs' (QCDA, 2010: 1).

In this sense narrative functions as an investigative 'tool' in the workbox of the learner who must labour to detect, unravel, reveal, isolate and dissect meaning.

> Semiotics, narrative structures, reception theories and ideas and information relevant to the study of media texts and media platforms should be taught insofar as they serve to help candidates understand how meanings and responses are created in media products.
>
> *(AQA, 2010b: 7)*

> Candidates should be able to recognise the conventions of the genre in the extract they are analysing, in terms of media language and, where relevant, narrative, and explain how these features are shared with other texts.
>
> *(OCR, 2010b: 8)*

As such narrative might be seen as performing a technological function in the mythology of the 'true text', obscuring what is abstract with something more concretely possessed. So much so that even textual experience that has the potential to expose the insulating processes, in Bernstein's (2000) terms, that create and sustain narrative as a category, for example 'objects that cannot be understood easily through applying conventional narrative theory' (OCR, 2010a: 37), is understood to be indexed to and as such constituting of that same convention.

The discourse of narrative as played out through *subject media* finds equal expression through *subject English* (Peim, 1993), where 'narrative methods' (OCRc, 2010:7) prove functional 'as a tool to help [children] organise their ideas and to explore new ideas and experiences' (QCDA, 2010). This apparent focus on event that might frame or influence textual experience is subsumed by emphasis on how it is that children might need to know narrative. As with *subject media*, successful engagement with narrative in English is predicated on a capacity to recognise and reproduce an essentially typological landscape where,

> children write many different types of narrative through Key Stages 1 and 2. Although most types share a common purpose (to tell a story in some way) there is specific knowledge children need in order to write particular narrative text types. While there is often a lot of overlap (for example, between myths and legends) it is helpful to group types of narrative to support planning for range and progression.
>
> *(QCDA, 2010)*

And in which different topological features effect readers in ways that are likely to be stable and predictable as exemplified here with the primary curriculum's summary of 'traditional tales':

Features of traditional tales

> Traditional or 'folk' tales include myths, legends, fables and fairy tales. Often originating in the oral tradition, examples exist in most cultures, providing a rich, culturally diverse resource for children's reading and writing. Many of these stories served an original purpose of passing on traditional knowledge or sharing cultural beliefs.
>
> They tend to have themes that deal with life's important issues and their narrative structures are often based on a quest, a journey or a series of trials and forfeits. Characters usually represent the archetypical opposites of good and evil, hero and villain, strong and weak or wise and foolish.
>
> *(QCDA, 2010)*

In the schooled context narrative is one of a number of strategies put to work by the skilled 'reader' in the project of making sense. The reading settlement evoked is transactional, with meaning encoded entirely by a notion of author intention: reader meets texts meets meaning provided by author. This idea, of which narrative is part, transcends the subject boundary between media and English, providing a discoursal orthodoxy of reading that is, as Bernstein would have it, horizontal in influence. This is important because it hints at a commonality across text-conscious subjects that is masked by the subject distinctiveness, the vertical discourses, that the discrete assessment cultures of 'media' and 'English' promote. As such it may well be the case that development in one subject area, which might be unorthodox, may not permeate the other.

At this point it is worth dwelling for a moment on Bernstein's idea of the pedagogic code as a way of making sense of how the apparatus of assessment (explicit technologies such as Ofqual, exam boards and their subject specifications alongside the more tacit impulses of teacher identity, for example) might contribute productively towards a dislocation between subjects.

'Power' for Bernstein is the power relations which 'create boundaries, legitimise boundaries, reproduce boundaries, between different categories of groups, gender, class, race, different categories of discourse, different categories of agents' (2000: 5). Power is seen to 'punctuate' social space, always operating to 'produce dislocations' and to establish 'legitimate relations of order' (Bernstein, 2000: 5); power enables and enacts separateness and distinction. Where power creates categories, 'control' relations function to establish different forms of communication within categories. Power in this case might be seen as exercised by QCDA as an expression of a set of much more culturally embedded ideas of what constitutes 'the subject'. These ideas are perhaps bound to the high cultural capital, heritage traditions of *subject English* (against the 'popular culture' orientation of media studies).

For Bernstein relations between categories are examined through the concept of 'classification'. Classification is the concept through which power is translated and accounts for the spaces between categories rather than the qualities or attributes which define or characterise a category. Bernstein argues that:

> The crucial space which creates the specialisation of the category ... is not internal to that discourse but is the space between that discourse and another. In other words, A can only be A if it can effectively insulate itself from B. In this sense there is no A if there is no relationship between A and something else.
>
> *(Bernstein, 2000: 6)*

Within this set of understandings it is the disjunction, the disruption, which 'insulates' categories: in other words it is the 'silence which carries the message of power' (Bernstein, 2000: 6). The degree of 'insulation' between categories, Bernstein argues, determines the degree of classification, weak or strong, and precipitates thereby less or more specialised 'discourses', 'identities' and 'voices' (Bernstein, 2000: 7):

> We can say, then, that the insulation which creates the principle of classification has two functions: one external to the individual, which regulates the relations between individuals, and another function which regulates relations within the individual. So insulation faces outward to the social order and inwards to the order within the individual.
>
> *(Bernstein, 2000: 7)*

Thus the act of positively defining a category is always already an act of suppression of the other 'unthinkable, the yet to be voiced' (Bernstein, 2000: 7). Categories are, and must, be sustained through a process of constant creation:

> although classification translates power into the voice to be reproduced ... the contradictions, cleavages and dilemmas which inhere in the principles of classification are never entirely suppressed, either at the social or individual level.
>
> *(Bernstein, 2000: 15)*

For Bernstein this instability is crucial to the dynamics of his pedagogic code, the ever present possibility, the trace, of the 'unthinkable' central to a notion of change. It is the possibility of deviation that enable the 'elaboration' or 'change' that is at the heart of Bernstein's understanding of the pedagogic code and additionally what makes Bernstein's ideas interesting to the post-structuralist reader and thus purposeful to our discussion.

What we are arguing here is that the analysis of narrative above suggests that the work of insulation between *subject media* and *subject English* has focused on the orientation of each towards different types of text – moving image, commercial and 3D texts in the former, and the more print-based, language-focused 2D texts in the latter – rather than anything more conceptual or paradigmatic. As such the tools of textual analysis, and the inferences they make about the qualities of the textual object and the nature of the textual experience, remain relatively constant. Our contention is that this offers a useful and productive opportunity for working the 'cleavages' between the subjects towards new ways of thinking about textuality.

The two case studies below illustrate how paying closer attention to young people's experience of being with text might signal new possibilities for thinking through curriculum and pedagogy that offer more reflexive meta-narratives about the work of text-conscious subjects and redraw the conceptual arrangements of textual study.

Young people as readers

This section draws on excerpts of data from a study of the reading habits and identities of 16 to 19 year olds studying in further education contexts in the Black Country in the West Midlands of England (Kendall, 2005). Data collected for the study included a large-scale reading habits questionnaire, focus group discussions and auto-ethnographic reading histories of individuals. It is from the focus group discussions that the extracts cited here are drawn.

These groups comprised of between three and five participants, twenty-three participants in total, following programmes of study at Qualifications and Credit Framework levels one, two or three in the context of English further education (16–19 year olds). Participation was voluntary, and participants and groups were self-selecting. The gender make-up of groups was varied: some were all male, some all female and some mixed. However, no groups were mixed by level of study. The discussions took place in informal, quiet spaces away from the classroom setting and were semi-structured. Participants were asked to respond to twenty-one stimulus questions or statements, related to the findings of the region-wide reading habits survey, which they turned over at their own pace 'pack of cards' style. The discussions were led by the researcher, who had previously been a teacher at the college attended by these students, but was not known personally to the participants. The 'cards' invited them to respond to the statistical findings of the reading habits survey, to discuss the national press responses to them (see Kendall, 2007), and to articulate their own ideas and views about their reading practices and identities.

Reading newspapers: more than 'technical'

The participants' discussions of their newspaper reading, their most popular, 'everyday' reading choice (Kendall, 2005), offers a useful route into their discussions of their experience of 'out of classroom' text. Here we see reading 'choice' contextualised by a range of complex social factors which seem to challenge more technicist accounts of reading interactions.

Most participants agreed that newspapers were a popular reading choice although typically they did not make particularly proactive choices about the newspaper title they read, 'whenever you're on the bus there's a newspaper there to read and every morning I read the *Daily Star* before I go out'. Rather they reported a 'convenience' approach, reading what was readily available so that picking up a near-to-hand newspaper seemed to be almost a default position for 'in-between' times. They saw newspaper reading as fulfilling a variety of purposes: information and opinion about the world around them, 'I look at what's going on around the country': to follow interests, particularly sport and especially football; and for entertainment:

> A: the *Sun*'s funny
> B: … it's full of gossip'
> AK: you know it's not true?
> A: Yeah it's more fun to read
> B: Because it's more outrageous and you're wondering whether it's true or not
>
> *(Group 4)*

This latter function of newspaper reading was notably marked among the female students, who found the horoscopes in particular an interesting focus for individual reflection or collective entertainment and/or discussion about a variety of issues in their lives.

Superficially size and physical unmanageability were seen to be obstacles to broadsheet reading:

Like the *Guardian* that's a big paper that is, you can't sit on a train with alike a big paper what if a girl just like walked past and you just wanna see her? You've got the *Sun* that's all right. (Group 1)

I think it's because they look too formal, because they're really big and everyone expects there just to be facts and figures in them. (Group 4)

However, their discussions of broadsheet readers are perhaps more revelatory:

They're aimed at people company people who are rich and that. (Group 1)

Who're brainy. (Group 1)

Old people, businessmen. (Group 4)

More like for rich people. (Group 6)

Business people, old people, snobs. (Group 1)

Although the students were put off by the perception that broadsheets are 'more complicated to read' (Group 2), more often it seemed not to be a perception of the technical reading demands broadsheets might make of them that turned them off, but a failure to recognise or find spaces for their own sense of themselves within the identities they felt broadsheets made available to readers. Those who do read broadsheets are clearly established as the 'other', more 'sophisticated', against the students' own senses of their 'regular', 'ordinary', 'down to earth' selves:

And the language which doesn't really communicate with us. (Group 5)

… they're so sophisticated the broadsheets. (Group 5)

The tabloids are just for regular people just to read because it's just straight in front of them. (Group 6)

Because they [business people/old people] probably think that tabloids exaggerate everything and they think that broadsheets could be like the proper story. (Group 4)

At times here the distinction between a perception of technical difficulty and identity is fused, connecting the ability to 'decode' efficiently and effectively – competence – directly to particular social identities. Importantly these 'competent' social identities are distinct from the 'regular'ness that the students claim for themselves. It is in these terms that broadsheets might be seen to be rejected as 'irrelevant'. Furthermore notions of 'being a reader' are at times bound up with the identity of the broadsheet consumer:

> If there's a really long article and you haven't got time and you're not a reader you just … [tapers out]. (Group 7)

This speaker couples the broadsheet reader identity with 'being a reader', which by default puts her in the opposite category.

The notional non-'reader', where the negative is meant to express motivation and agency rather than inability or incapacity to read in the technical sense, is more attracted to ways of reading that contrast markedly to the preferences of their 'reader' counterparts:

> The tabloids just give you what's going on, what you need to know, condensed so you don't have to think about it you're just told and it gives you an opinion, whereas the broadsheets tell you what's happened so you can make your own opinion. (Group 2)

Equally there is a perhaps a perception about the perceived broadsheet reader's confidence with meaning-making and taking, to which the 'non-reader' is contrasted, as this exchange with a female student in Group 5 might suggest:

> AK: You say that they [tabloids] might exaggerate but it doesn't stop you reading them?
> No.
> AK: Are you, do you think you are influenced by the exaggeration? Can you see through that?
> Not really, I tend to believe what I read in there because you think it's right but then some of the things that come out you think well that can't be right.
> AK: Is that confusing?
> Well yes it is really because you read stuff in the newspaper that says one thing and then you watch the news and it says something else.

Other students perceived that it was specifically the content rather than the 'values' of broadsheets that they were rejecting. Here for example is a male student in Group 6:

> I'm just not into politics at all I just think it's pointless and some of these people just don't know what they're doing.

The 'othering' these students engaged in raises some interesting questions about the kinds of metaphors we use to think through 'non-participation' in reading in particular and education more generally. Often a 'barrier' metaphor has been invoked to describe learners being 'locked out' of educational practice, the rationale being that should the barrier be removed participation will be both possible and desirable for the 'non-traditional' or hard to reach' learners. However, these discussions hint at the limitations of this metaphor as a satisfactory account of non-participation. Rather than 'shut out' (subject to), perhaps a different kind of story, one of resistance and rejection (agency) might be begin to be imagined.

Only two participants, both male, reported reading a broadsheet. One of these was an Asian newspaper and the other the *Guardian,* and discussants drew upon a set of shared ideas about both the signification of broadsheet reading and the demographic of the broadsheet reader, which permeated all the discussions and perhaps made it difficult to express enjoyment of a broadsheet in this peer-regulated context. The student who read the *Guardian* for example quickly added a qualifying codicil to his 'admission': 'Well I read the sport on the back of the *Guardian,* 'cos my dad gets the *Guardian* but it's only because there ain't any other paper to read', which underplayed any intent or agency in his action.

Reading for pleasure

The majority of students did not feel that they spent much time reading for pleasure. Some expressed this confidently:

> If I have some spare time I'd probably just have a cigarette. (Group 3)

> Sometimes when there's nothing else to do. (Group 4)

Meanwhile the majority deferred direct rejection of leisure reading by suggesting they were too busy or that reading was too time-consuming.

> AK: Why do some people never read for pleasure?

> Time too busy with work. (Group 2)

> Time or families or something. (Group 2)

> AK: Do you read for pleasure?

> I can't keep it up for long …. I don't know it's just one of those things that don't seem necessary and it just gets in the way sort of thing. (Group 4)

> Yeah I do when I have time, but sometimes I don't have time and like I'll start a book and whether I think it's good or not doesn't matter 'cos sometimes I just don't have time to carry it on and by the time I pick it up again I've forgot. (Group 5)

This is interesting as it perhaps shows the reluctance on the part of some participants to outright reject what they *recognise* to be the preferred identities and behaviours of their 'schooled' experience (see Kendall, 2007), even though they may be choosing not to *realise* them, in Bernstein's (2000) terms.

Those students who were more candid about their rejection of book reading offered more developed justifications. Here male students in Group 3 talk about their preference for computer games:

> A: It [a game] can challenge you, yeah, it's not boring, sometimes you get bored of newspaper reading and reading like, and computer games you've got like more games to do they don't get boring.

> B: You've got control over it; whereas the book it just takes you in a straight line from start to finish, whereas a game you can take it your own way.

> C: You can choose your own path in a game.

This short exchange offers a glimmer of the dislocation these students feel between the textual experiences they encounter in different domains (home/ college in this case) of practice. The restrictions and limitations they associated with reading books were unlike the freedom they enjoyed in gaming. As readers of books they seemed to feel 'subject to' particular ways of being that encouraged an organised, linear response and deprived them of agency and choice; as players of games they felt licensed to be creative and innovative. As gamers they are perhaps more enabled to 'accept risks, and choose possible future actions by anticipating outcomes' (Gauntlett, 2002: 98), behaviours that Gauntlett associates with Giddens' (1991) notion of late modernity. As such it is interesting to conjecture whether the practice of gaming offers these students a more tentative, provisional reality within which the relationship between reader and text (player/ game) is differently mediated, so that the 'player as reader' of the 'game as text' is positioned as an agent in knowledge-making practice rather than a recipient of 'knowledge'. This resonates with evidence found elsewhere in the data on young women's reading of magazines (Gauntlett, 2002; Kendall, 2008).

Such a notion of 'risk' and 'play' is crucial, argues Gee (2003), to both active and critical learning. Gee asserts that gaming potentially offers the conditions for learning that is both, and identifies three key things that are 'at stake' when we learn actively:

1. We learn to experience (see, feel and operate on) the world in new ways.
2. Since domains are usually shared by groups of people who carry them on as distinctive social practices, we gain the potential to join this group, to become affiliated with such kinds of people (even though we may never see all of them, or any of them face to face).

3. We gain resources that prepare us for future learning and problem solving in the domain and, perhaps, more important, in related domains.

(Gee, 2003: 23)

However, active learning does not necessarily manifest critical learning. For critical learning to occur, Gee proposes that an additional feature is needed:

> For learning to be critical as well as active, one additional feature is needed. The learner needs to learn not only how to understand and produce meanings in a particular semiotic domain, but, in addition, how to think about the domain at a 'meta' level as a complex system of interrelated parts. The learner also needs to learn how to innovate in the domain – how to produce meanings that, while recognizable, are seen as somehow novel or unpredictable.

(Gee, 2003: 23)

The conditions of criticality, Gee further argues, are made possible through gaming, as the player is 'licensed' within the domain, or social practice of gaming to take up a position as 'expert' and play at the margins of what is already possible or knowable to produce new meanings. The meaning of the game as 'text' becomes shape-able as well as knowable and the reader is re-situated to learn:

> how to think about semiotic domains as design spaces that engage and manipulate people in certain ways and, in turn, help create certain relationships in society among people and groups of people, some of which have important implications for social justice.

(Gee, 2003: 46)

Gee's ideas offer possibilities for readers that resonate with Peim's contention of the ways that post-structuralism re-situates the traditional reader to 'accept that all knowledge is provisional, and may be proved wrong in the future ... accept risks, and choose possible future actions by anticipating outcomes' (Gauntlett, 2002: 98).

However, these are rarely the terms on which educational curricula open spaces for reading or readers. The curriculum does not always imagine the conditions within which it is possible to recognise the kinds of reading behaviours, attitudes and identities that readers report as enjoyable, desirable or those that enable the exercising of power in relation to the rule-making of reading and the making and taking of meaning. Thus while the curriculum may be understood as promoting active (in Gee's definition) learning, it falls short of *critical* learning. This is illustrated through the discussants' reflections on the question 'What happens when you read?'

Making and taking meaning – 'What happens when you read?'

When tackling this question all groups were less forthcoming with responses than they had been with previous questions. Typical initial responses were:

Err you open a book, you start reading. (Group 1)

I think it's just processing the words so that you know, I don't know it's really hard because it just happens straightaway, you just can't slow it down you just understand it straightaway. (Group 2)

You start from the top and work your way down! (Group 7)

Although we acknowledge that this is a difficult, challenging and very open question, it is also possible that this was the first time that some participants had been invited to address such a question, which would perhaps account for the uncharacteristic degree of reticence displayed by most participants at this point in the discussions. We argue elsewhere (Kendall, 2005) that syllabus documents specifying the English or literacy curriculum for 16–19 year olds rarely encourage a reflexive exploration of reading practices and processes, tending to prefer mastery of content, personal response and taken-for-granted ways of knowing about texts, readers and reading. The participants therefore seemed to have no 'learned' discursive resources on which to draw to make sense of this question, and they turned instead to the 'common sense' of authoring, mobilising very quickly the ideologically constructed notion of the author identified by Foucault (1991).

The degree of interaction between the participants and researcher shifts notably in the majority of the transcripts at this point, and we felt conscious of the need to continually rephrase and reshape the question and to offer additional prompts or sub-questions.

The initial confusion this question caused tended to be followed by a 'pictures in the head' explanation of the reading process:

A: You're getting pictures from the words.

AK: How does that work?

A: Erm well like, they describe something, the book will say 'big green overgrown monster' and you just have to get that image in your head of a big green monster, pretty tall … (trails off). (Group 1)

You get a picture in your head what's happening. (Group 4)

It's like it's a film someone starts speaking and you imagine someone speaking. They describe a character and you've got that. (Group 5) in a book, depending on what kind it is whether it's fiction or science fiction or fantasy when you're reading the book as soon as you open it up, well what some people say is that you're entering another world, when you're reading you're using your imagination to put yourself in that book, in that position so you can see what is going on exactly. (Group 6)

You kind of see them in your head like pictures of what's happening. (Group 7)

The 'pictures in the head' notion identifies a reader ('you'), an author ('they') and an experience, 'the text' which is shared between the two, generally with the 'author' or creator of text *acting on* and *directing* 'the reader' to achieve particular responses.

They want you to put yourself in a certain situation like the September 11th bombings: they wanted you to be there; they wanted you to feel the pain of the people who were there. I don't think they're pushing you but they're trying to help you to understand the situation because you could actually take it as it is, they want to help you. (Group 5)

This constructs the reader (passive) as one who must come to know what it is that the writer (active) knows already. Reading in these terms is an acquisitive experience through which the reader might come to know more, from darkness to enlightenment. In the comment below the inclusion of 'just' serves to minimise the function and purpose of the reader within the processes of making and taking meaning:

You're just scanning for questions of why the writer's written it and what's it all about and what's the story about. (Group 3)

The author's, in particular the published author's, 'claim' to textual meaning is rarely contested, and discussants consistently claimed for themselves a passive role in their own narratives about how reading 'works', understanding themselves to be 'in receipt' of a 'message' which needed to be understood in order to better understand its originator – the originator's right to be understood remained unquestioned. One is minded of Foucault's notion of the author functioning as an ideological product:

the functional principle by which in our culture one limits, excludes, and chooses; in short, by which one impedes the free circulation, the free manipulation, the free composition, decomposition, and recomposition of fiction. If fact, we are accustomed to presenting the author as a genius, as a perpetual sign of invention

(Foucault, 1991: 119)

Issues relating to, sometimes expressed as concern about, 'understanding' and or 'misunderstanding' the 'message' permeate the transcripts, suggesting perhaps an acquiescence in this discursive construction of 'an author'.

Answers to this question tended to be characterised by more frequent use of fillers, 'erm, er', 'like', and were less fluent and coherent than at other points in the transcripts, suggesting a hesitancy and tentativeness that is not so noticeable in their answers to other questions. Gee's notion of how reading is learned in schools perhaps offers a way of interrogating and interpreting this. Gee argues that the teaching of reading fixates on 'reading as silently saying the sounds of letters and words and being able to answer general, factual and dictionary like questions about written texts' (Gee, 2003: 16). This, he contends, engenders readers who can decode but not really read:

> You do have to silently say the sounds of letters and words when you read (or, at least, this greatly speeds up reading). You do have to be able to answer general, factual, and dictionary like questions about what you read: This means you know the 'literal' meaning of the text. But what so many people – unfortunately so many educators and policymakers – fail to see is that if this is all you can do, then you can't really read. You will fail to be able to read well and appropriately in contexts associated with specific types of texts and specific types of social practice.
>
> *(Gee, 2003:16)*

While readers may then feel comfortable with literal meanings they may be less sure about the other ways in which texts mediate the meaning of social situations: that is to say, the practices of reading as manifest in the language or literacy *classroom.*

Unlike with other questions a high degree of hegemony was evident across the groups in their answers to this question. This was often explored through comparing 'reading' books with 'watching' films or television:

> If it's on TV there's only one way you can take it because there's only one way to portray it unless it's like a documentary or something. If it's like … a soap then they're telling you a story so it can be told one way. (Group 2)

> You can picture in your head what's happening [when you read a book] but that's only if you get into it though, if you don't get into it the words start to slip out of your mind, they just go in one side and out the other (Group 4)

> Because when you're reading you can picture it how you wanna picture it but if you're watching a film the pictures are already there for you. (Group 4)

With both kinds of text, 'meaning' is seen to inhabit a space 'outside' the reader. But unlike making sense of television or film the meaning of books is seen as less easy to pin down, in the sense that the author's meaning is sometimes difficult to 'grasp'. The possibility of multiple meanings was often explained as a straightforward 'getting it wrong':

> It [a film] actually shows you what happens instead of describing it to you, because some people might misinterpret the writing and get the wrong picture, they might not get the picture the writer was trying to put forward. (Group 1)

And respondents were often ready to take responsibility for 'misinterpretations', which they understood to be a product of their own inexperience, immaturity or naivety. Or as the effect of individual subjects encountering sensations, textual experience, to which they might have different responses:

> Everyone has a different imagination, a different view of everything (Group 1)

> AK: What is it about us that makes us see different things?
> A: Good question. (laughs)
> B: We are all insane.
> C: I guess it's just the imagination. (Group 6)

Different interpretations are anecdotal and infinite, dependent upon 'imagination'. Imagination is understood as being shaped by:

> experiences, your surroundings, it could just be your college or the people around you so if you had like let's say an area just full of erm one type of race then you might just picture that sort of but if you're in a multi-culture [environment] you might picture things differently. (Group 7)

Although this comment seems to pick up on what might be described as structural differences between the positioning of individuals to texts, the differences listed are given equal weighting, suggesting a randomness of impact or effect. Here the individual is at the centre of their naturalistic environment rather than in dialogic relation to the structures within which they (always, already) situate and are situated. The curriculum, and the roles and definitions it embraces and constructs for students as readers (and writers), are by contrast asocial absolutes floating freely beyond the structures within which individuals are seen to be placed. Thus while the meaning-making of individuals is contingent, the curriculum contexts within which meaning-making (must) occur are seen as neutral.

Participants did express an awareness of different reading practices:

> [What happens when you read?] It probably depends on like what subject you've taken at college sometimes you're just taught to skim read and pick

out the important things but in history I'm told you've got to read everything because everything's important. So it depends what you're reading like if you're reading a book you don't skim read it because you've got to pick out the details but if you're reading something like for English for analysis you skim read it to pick out the big words. (Group 2)

However, they did not attach a 'politics' to these different choices or demands, nor did they see them as social practices organising power relations between different subject identities within disciplinary groups. Rather they saw and accepted them as a simple 'commonsense' of varying subject disciplines. Furthermore different reading practices were not understood to impact on possibilities for meaning taking and making.

'Giving up' reading – raising further questions

The accounts explored here illustrate the complexities of attempting to make sense of the meaning making and taking of reading, and raise some interesting and important questions about the ways readers construct, represent, manage and value their own reading identities and practices. What also emerges is that these young adult readers have little experience of the range of theoretical ideas and frameworks they might draw upon to think through their experience of text, or perhaps more significantly, little awareness that this is a contested field. As a result they may be over-reliant on the 'commonsense' of rather orthodox methodologies that draw heavily on structuralist orientations which, we argue, serve to situate them as deficient readers: inexperienced, naive detectives seeking out, but too often 'failing' to locate, the neutral 'truth' of the texts they encounter. As some of the discussions above signal, the effect of this might be to draw unhelpful lines in the sand between 'schooled' and 'non-schooled' literacy practices, which create disorientating dislocations for students as they encounter texts in the academic or 'learning' context. The short accounts from the 'gamers' above hint at the pleasures participants associate with new media technologies, illustrating something of the identities, values and behaviours – ways of being – that new and emergent technologies may make available to readers. Our next case study takes up this contention in more detail.

Young people as gamers

This next case study explores finding from the 'Just Gaming' project (Kendall and McDougall, 2009). This study worked closely with eight 16–17 year olds from two further (tertiary) education colleges in England, one in the West Midlands and one in the South East. The colleges were chosen entirely contingently and the project did not aim to look at geographical or contextual issues – although this might have yielded further interesting data it was beyond the scope of the project – but focused on the young male players' interactions with games.

The participants, all male and following academic programmes in media studies that include the exploration and analysis of a broad range of 'textual products' including video game, were self-identifying as keen players of computer games and had already been playing our chosen game, *Grand Theft Auto IV (GTA IV)*. We chose this game for a number of reasons. First, we felt that it would be good to agree some common territory for our players to discuss, Second, *GTA IV*, which is part of a series of very popular *GTA* games, had recently been released in a wave of media hype, and we felt it would be relatively easy to find young people who were already playing it. Third, the *GTA* series is seen as groundbreaking amongst many gamers, and while online elements increasingly come as standard for videogames, *GTA IV* represents the most significant example to date of a mass market narrative-based game with a detailed, complex and open-ended location to explore online alongside or outside of the mission-based storyline. Our interest in the game lies explicitly in this interrelationship of progression through (and thus determination by) a textual experience and agency – 'being with others' in a virtual space and in the dynamics of this duality in relation to the attribution of meaning in literacy practices. Finally *GTA IV* is the kind of game that is the focus of 'moral panic' in the United Kingdom (see for example Greenhill and Koster, 2008), and so it was felt it would offer an additional opportunity to say something about the ideas that inform protectionist accounts of media literacy.

Talking to 17–19 year olds about the game called for careful consideration of ethical issues, as in the United Kingdom *GTA IV* is classified as unsuitable for players under 18. However, huge numbers of 16 and 17 year olds were playing the game. A key priority was not to introduce players to the game but to work with those who were already playing it. As a condition of participation, participants were required to return signed parental consent proformas to confirm that they had already purchased and were permitted to play *GTA IV*. Participants then joined a Facebook group established exclusively for the project, and were asked to submit regular playblog accounts as they moved through the game over a two-week period. The Facebook group enabled a space for the gaming talk to occur, but we recognise that it also frames the interactions in particular ways of which we are careful to take account.

Participants were given plenty of guidance on 'how' to participate: that is, the technicalities (how to join the group, how often to contribute and when and so on). However, the only guidance about the 'what' to contribute was that they should write about their playing experiences in each case. They were free to respond to each other's postings, or to ignore them as they preferred. On several occasions reminder messages were sent to the whole group but these reminders did not include any prompts for content or structure. Individual participants were never contacted by us and we did not comment on any postings.

The second stage of the project involved a semi-structured interview with each player, following a standard pattern of questioning but also referred to postings as prompts – either directly with regard to the participant – for example, 'I noticed you gave an example of …', or more general – 'towards the end of the two weeks the postings became more …'. The rationale for the use of the Facebook group was threefold. First, using a web 2.0 context with which all the participants were already familiar would avoid some of the potentially awkward dynamics of this kind of research. Second, it would allow the participants to take responsibility for the nature of their own literacy practices, and third, it would offer a 'transliteracy' bridge from playing to talking.

The range of stories that emerged from the data about playing and telling have been reported elsewhere (Kendall and McDougall, 2009). Here we want to focus on two areas for further discussion. These relate particularly to the weblog 'talk' about being in the game and the 'talk about the weblog talk' captured in the interviews.

Ways of telling …

> Last night I began the story of Nico Bellic … (Bill)

Like many of our bloggers, Bill quickly settled into the role of 'story-teller', recounting dramatic tales of his adventures in Liberty City. Often postings were weaved together through the imposition of a loose, traditional, narrative thread, which is typical, Crawford and Gosling (2009) argue, of game story-telling, with an 'opener':

> A long night in liberty city, it seems for Nico Bellic and his cousin Roman. After the mass bloodbath, which we created last night's wild antics at the splitsides comedy club in central liberty city, before the face off with police. (Justin)

A 'grand' finale' was clearly gestured:

> So this is my last post, so i thought therefore i should go on a truely world class killing rampage … this is how I got on (Justin)

> I decided to go out with a bang. (Ben)

> OK, its here. The fifth and final hour, the big one … oh yes, you know what I'm talking about … (Sunny)

In the last of these examples Sunny feels the proximity of his onlookers and addresses 'us' directly. Similarly self-conscious of audience, Andy, perhaps our most accomplished story-teller, rejects the past-simple tense in favour of grammar that invites the reader very much into his 'present' and encourages us to experience his journey through Liberty City more immediately;

> I hit the gas and aim my car at there wreckage, when i hit full speed i leap out the vehicle and watch it carrear into the mess. With the remaining

bullets i have i pump the gas tank full of lead and gaze at the explosions as one the flaming carcases of my enemies falls to my feet. (Andy)

The 'in-between' action was for Ben and Justin and their fellow bloggers a fast-paced pastiche on the 'action-movie' genre, a melodrama of 'mass bloodbaths' (Justin), 'killing sprees' (Justin and Dean), 'guns blazing' (Andy) and 'mini riots' (Ben), the writers taking up – and savouring – the position of the excessive action hero 'posturing' at the centre of the narrative – unnerved, amoral, fearless and bloodthirsty:

> i decided to do the impossible spawn a bike on the top of the building and try the craziest jump i have ever performed on the game … (Justin)

> I convinently snatch a women out of her car and when the male passenger challeges my antics i make him run by pointing a gun at him and then shoot the back of his knees making him slide across the pavement. I then approach him like a stereotypical russian gangster and stand over him whinning and put him out of his misery with a single head shot (oh so delightful!!). (Dean)

And there were moments of mock-chilling detail resonant of the Tarantino oeuvre:

> i thort i would change my clothes for a killing spree a nice new suit. black with a red tie. (Simon)

There is something of the cartoonish 'baroque showman' about these descriptions. They are self-conscious, outrageous, carnivalesque 'performances' to the wider blog community, an overlay of friends, college peers and Facebook contact trails:

> before I posted my first blog I did read what everyone else had written and I tried to write in my own style, I did kind of stick to the same structure as other people. (Ben)

> I tried to stick to my own sort of style of writing an keep it sort of close to that but I noticed a few of the blogs were out there. (Dean)

And of course they are performing to 'us' – the researchers (outsiders?) – not blogging but palpably listening to these wild adventures played out vicariously. Telling the story of playing for these participants is an act of 'playful artistry', as Dean summarises in his interview:

> I think to a certain extent there was a kind of competition because everybody wants their blog to be read and everyone wants people to laugh at their blog and they just want a chance to shine.

This is at its most explicit when the gamers tell of 'performing' against others in the multi-player online modes. Here are Dean and Bill pitted against a group of American gamers:

> However, I was subjected to being in a team of 4 with 3 Americans who were useless at the game but talked like they were professors of super bowl. This resulted on us arguing about what's better rugby and American football after them saying rugby is a girl's sport in which I jumped out the car and sent 4 single bullets into the windscreen and windows hoping they change their thoughts on rugby. (Dean)

> After shooting a few people down and evading various 1/2 wanted star levels, I get an invite to play online, fun. With the invite accepted I found myself in a lobby full of rowdy americans wanting to kill me (in the game of course), the game mode is GTA Race meaning you race but can get out of your car at any point, picking up weapons along your way. Just as the game started I heard an overly-enthused american shout the words, 'Holy shit, here we go! (Bill)

This more immediate, 'live' audience offers both Bill and Dean the opportunity to perform their 'gaming-selves'.

'Gaming selves'

This version of the 'macho' male protagonist the bloggers 'play' out for us, themselves and each other in the game and in their telling of the game, is, they suggested in their interviews, remote from their everyday sense and expression of self, agency and the 'real'. Rather than the projection of any deeper aspiration, they described *GTA IV* as:

> a fun thing to play with no restrictions. It's just like a different world really which makes it fun and interesting to play. (Andy)

> a sick and twisted fantasy really and it's down to the human psychic really. People wouldn't actually go out and, get in a car and run over thirty people and jump out and it on the body and do things like that. (Sunny)

This is contrasted with their sense of 'real life' where:

> running away from the police often ends with you getting caught in real life. Somehow you can end up like having a helicopter following you and just magically happen to have a grenade launcher which can blow up the helicopter so that things are great. I could never imagine doing that in real life. At least I hope not! (Dean)

And this playing at the 'other' within the 'unreal' provides a source of enjoyment and pleasure:

> What appeals to me about it? I think its just real light hearted fun and you can get a good laugh out of it even though its crime and its probably not morally correct, you know there's not really that much of a consequence you know? You just get to have a little bit of fun and have a little joke with your mates when you're playing it (Dean)

This playfulness is observable throughout the blogs which show a constant fracturing of the 'in-game' narrative with 'out of game' observations and critiques prompted, for example, by moments of intertextual signification, 'moral' compromise or technical novelty. So although some of our players described themselves as immersed in Nico's 'time'/'reality', for example Justin says:

> I just put myself in the character. You are Nico. (Justin)

and

> I do get pretty involved when I play games and when I do get into the cover thing I dont actually notice myself kind of ducking into cover when I'm actually playing the game yes so you can get really involved and think that you are Nico. (Sunny)

The blog entries offer less 'resolved' narratives. Peppered by moments of internal, meta-aware commentary, they play out instead a more complex plurality. At times meta-awareness is prompted by a sense of 'wonder' at what's new. Here for example Justin describes his first encounter with an in-game 'sensation':

> After collecting him, I then took my eastern uropean cousin for a drink in Blarneys irish pub, before a game of darts, where I participated in a sensation, which I have never discovered before on a video game, my character being drunk. Whilst walking around the beer garden of the pub I found another feature which makes GTA a favourite of mine , not just due to the reveloutionary aspects of gameplay, but the humour, as I chuckled to myself while reading a umbrella on one of the tables with a sign for a mock german beer, Pißwasser, GTA never ceases to amaze me, or to make me laugh. (Justin)

This intertextual moment adds a further fracturing layer. Luke shares a similar moment of surprise, enjoyment and reflection as he marvels at the incidental but closely observed, and to him fascinating detail of the animated cup:

> One particluar sad thing to do is knock a cup out of someones hand on a hill and watch the cup gain momentum and speed down the hill, a tribute to the physics engine. (Luke)

Dean does the same when he contemplates the introduction of 'consequences' which he seems to appreciate as a sort of 'maturation' of the GTA series:

> Finally they have built in the concept of consequences into GTA. I had to step out and face the music. (Dean)

At other times it is an emotional – even moral – challenge that prompts critique, as Ben's tendency to acknowledge the innocence of his victims to a perhaps judgemental audience might suggest:

> Despite being briefly distracted by the lure of slaughtering innocent bystanders. (Ben)

> I passed the time by climbing onto a high surface and taking pot shots at innocent civilians. (Ben)

Equally Justin's revoke in the codicil below – which seems to begin with a silent 'don't worry' to his audience – perhaps indicates a gentle slippage from his otherwise bravado-fuelled narrative:

> I decide to leave him to his watery grave, (he will be fine next time i get wasted or busted, I hope!). (Justin)

However, the moments of disruption are most apparent when the 'in game' male characters interact with female characters. It is at these moments that many of the bloggers express either comedy bravado, like Justin, that plays to the blog audience:

> After this i was distracted by my in game relationship with the character Michelle, like a real girlfriend she clearly only wanted to drain my patience aswell as my wallet. (Justin)

A more self-conscious tentativeness, like Ben here, may be more 'out of game':

> The date looked to be ending in disaster when the taxi drivers erratic driving upset her stomach, but she seemed to enjoy the burgers and I managed to get invited inside. (Ben)

> A hectic nights drinking led to me surprisngly leading Michelle back to her flat unscathed, although after my embarassing behaviour I didn't even ask to go inside. (Ben)

Ben is surprised by his success with 'in game' girlfriend Michelle as he 'manages' to get invited inside while his embarrassment at his behaviour in front of her would seem to play against the direction of the 'moral framework' of the game. What we do see here is that for these young men, as for the young children in Marsh's book *Popular Culture*, in this case 'gaming' does not provide a 'parallel reality but, rather, interact[s] with daily individual and social practices in complex and significant ways' (Marsh, 2004: 45).

Reclaiming 'play'

Play here becomes a very 'grown up' pursuit. Rather than merely ludic, play is concerned with the brokering of particular ways of being in different modalities of practice. Participants play with the game, against and through the game for multiple audiences (us, each other, the online community), performing and re-performing versions of their (male) selves. In relation to young children's lives Marsh pays attention to ritual practices as processes of assimilation and accommodation of new learning and goes on to suggest that:

> This kind of performance is not just about re-telling the narrative as a multi-modal form of reader-response ... it is also about performing a particular kind of ritual that can be used to establish social practices and identities.
>
> *(Marsh, 2004: 42)*

To rethink young men's participation in online cultures as ritualised performance opens up new possibilities for rereading gaming (and indeed the social networking spaces which frame such pursuits) as performing useful functions – what Bean (1999) calls 'functionality', in young people's lives.

Drawing on post-structuralist understandings of self, Gauntlett reminds us that 'we do not face a choice of *whether* to give a performance. The self is always being made and re-made in daily interactions' (2002: 141), and it this performativity, argues Butler, that is central to constructions of gender. What becomes interesting here is that our participants, although on the surface interacting with a text that has been described in the *Daily Mail* and the *Sun* as 'morally dubious', are contemporaneously playing with identities in ways that might be described in MacLure's terms as 'frivolous'. MacLure understands frivolity as 'to be whatever threatens the serious business of establishing foundations, frames, boundaries, generalities or principles. Frivolity is what interferes with the disciplining of the world' (2006: 1). It is precisely this kind of posturing that Butler advocates in her incitement to make 'gender trouble':

> Through the possibility of subverting and displacing those naturalized and reified notions of gender that support masculine hegemony and heterosexist power, to make gender trouble, not through the strategies that figure a utopian beyond, but through the mobilization, subversive

confusion, and proliferation of precisely those constitutive categories that seek to keep gender in its place by posturing as the foundational illusions of identity.

(Butler, 1990: 33–4)

Perhaps unexpectedly then, it is possible to understand our participants as engaged in radical moves that threaten the stability of the binaries around which 'moral panic' discourses converge.

The participants shared an explicit and 'knowing' meta-awareness of how to play against, with or despite the narrative, which resonates with Gauntlett's (2002) idea of the postmodern 'pick and mix' reader of magazines. In Gauntlett's study female readers did not read magazines as 'blueprints' for authoring identity. Rather, magazines seemed to offer possibilities for 'being' that 'might' be engaged with dialogically, and the (female?) reader is invited to 'play with different types of imagery' (Gauntlett, 2002: 206). Such clearly understood 'paralogy' (Lyotard, 1985) – new moves in the game that disrupt orthodox analyses of 'effects' and of reading itself – is perhaps our most compelling evidence that there is no singular 'way of being' in a game.

Such playfulness around identity resonates strongly with those calling for a rereading of masculinities as a way of repositioning young men in relation to literacy practices. Rejecting the kinds of 'school effectiveness discourses' that position boys as 'victims' and 'losers' in terms of achievement in literacy, critics like Jackson (1998) and Kehler and Greig call for 'acknowledgment and unpacking [of] the overlapping and competing ways that boys enact or perform what it means to be a man'. This, they argue, will 'evolve much more complex and messier understandings of masculinities underscored by competing sets of understandings' (Kehler and Greig, 2005: 360). Drawing on the outcomes of small-scale ethnographic research into young men's literacy practices, Kehler and Greig argue for much more 'nuanced readings of boys who themselves are sophisticated readers of particular texts, namely the most authorial and widely read text they know and understand, that of their bodies' (2005: 366).

A further reading of the data might see the 'baroque showman' as an act of resistance against becoming the 'object' of study, with the 'truth' of identity eluded and eclipsed by the 'camp' humour of the interplay. MacLure urges that research methods must find:

more nuanced and less forensic attitude[s] to humour [that] might allow us to recognise its productive role in maintaining solidarity and identity, and to respect its value for marginalised groups as a form of resistance to power and inequality – even where this resistance manifests itself uncomfortably in the research/intervention situation as also a resistance to analysis. This would not mean endorsing or overlooking the misogyny and prejudice that is often coded into such humour. But it would mean also considering the positive qualities that humour involves – such as skill, timing, collaboration and quick-wittedness. Humour also relies on a kind of 'double vision? – the ability to see the absurdity, irony or double meanings in social situations.

(MacLure, 2006: 8)

Drawing on the findings of a study of young men's attitudes and practices around health, MacLure further notes that:

> Much of the joking that circulates in young men's talk shows an astute, if often jaundiced, understanding of their own and others social roles and status. It is not surprising that humour, silence and the ambivalent respect of mimicry have been identified as the strategies of subaltern subjects faced with disciplinary power (cf Bhabha, 1994). Lies, secrets, silences and deflections of all sorts are routes taken by voices or messages not granted full legitimacy in order not to be altogether lost.

(MacLure, 2006: 9)

This kind of posturing 'queers', in Butler's sense what it is possible to 'know', in the sense of 'grasp', about young people's engagement with popular textualities. And MacLure would have us know such shortcomings as intrinsic to, indeed of, the very fabric of social interaction.

In conclusion: toward 'textual agency'

So where does this take our discussion of narrative? We have suggested that narrative as a discourse of sense-making works as a horizontal discourse across English and Media Studies as they are understood in the schooled context. We have further suggested that this account of narrative draws on a particular conceptual framework that is broadly cognisant with structuralist theoretical perspectives. We have presented evidence of young people's own accounts of their textual experience which challenge the usefulness or validity of this sort of approach to an understanding of meaning making and taking. We posit thus that English and media studies share a common discourse about the function and purpose of narrative and that this kind of analysis draws on a particular – and questionable – conceptual framework. We have looked more closely at young people's engagement with texts and can, on this evidence, suggest that the realities of reading are more complex and messy than structuralism can bear witness to, and that students need new theoretical tools to take to their practices. We contend, like Hills, that this is the more meaningful work of English and media. This new kind of work calls for a new kind of pedagogical practice, and this is what we explore in our final chapter.

As the affordances of web 2.0 technologies might draw teachers' attention to the way young people are, and might be, as readers (and writers), we wonder how much more experimental, creative and risky our teaching of reading – in its broadest sense – might need to be if we are to better bridge the gap between 'in school' and 'out of school' literacies, and offer more fruitful (and honest?) learning experiences. These might then offer genuine opportunities for engagement in the kind of active, critical learning discussed above – the kinds that subject media already (and complacently) thinks it is enabling. But it is only through rethinking the theories that underpin our practice that we can truly 'give up' reading to our students. By 'give up' we mean to surrender to them their right and entitlement to see themselves as both agents (active and situating) and subjects (situated) in the making and taking of meaning.

If, then, the 'coming of age' of the internet (as the cliché goes, the point at which it became what Tim Berners-Lee had imagined) is the catalyst for a new learning and teaching paradigm, we must next deal with technology more explicitly.

9

TECHNOLOGY AFTER THE MEDIA

Communication renders social life possible.

(Colin Cherry, 1996: 10)

Part of the problematic here is that explored by Lister and his co-authors in the fifth part of their introduction to *New Media: A Critical Introduction* . Entitled 'Cyberculture: technology, nature and culture', its stated aim is to explore 'the central dilemma facing any study of technology' which they express as 'how to understand the part played by technology's sheer physical form and its influence on how a culture is lived and experienced' (Lister et al, 2003: 7). If technology is to operate as a key concept in understanding media communication 'after the media', we had better be sure what we mean by it, including its physicality: 'technology is something real. Real in the obvious, material sense; we can touch it, it does things' (Lister et al, 2003: 289).

For an idea that media studies is wary of, some might say blind to, technology seems to hold a secure place in a number of key media studies narratives. While practitioners want largely to ignore the history, philosophy and influence of technology, work in many areas is predicated on notions of technological difference, convergence and change. With little justification or argument, descriptions, often historicised, are set up to explain rapid alterations in the way we do things which are 'knowing' to the point of being misleading. These are often tales of technologically induced revolutions, of substantial change wrought by and in the name of 'technology'. And yet the technologies themselves are rarely addressed.

In these circumstances it is not surprising that we are to some extent caught in the crossfire of profoundly divergent accounts which in almost all cases seem a little too keen to convince us either that the revolution is here or that nothing very much has happened. It seems clear to us that neither of these positions is particularly useful, but also that both are privileging 'technology' in unhelpful ways, either by venerating or fetishising it, or by pointedly and unfeasibly ignoring it. When Postman wrote that 'technology is ideology' (1987), he perhaps got closer to the truth than he intended. His was a world, conceptually, where the television's all-seeing blindness was potentially amusing us to all manner of deaths, where 'You have to watch TV to be American' (Postman, 1987).

Postman remains an engaging thinker in a particular kind of humanist tradition, strong on rhetoric but rather shorter on evidence: plausible rather than convincing. In the determinist camp (and one can imagine them out of doors in search of the lost chord) his essential pessimism provides a balance to McLuhan's Pentecostal techno-evangelism. In 'Technopoly: the surrender of culture to technology' he expresses all of our fears, fears that have been bubbling through our art and cultural products since artificially made tools were first used. The fact that this is partly the stuff of science fiction, as we shall see later, is partly the point. Both Postman's high-register analysis and the dark fictions of a writer like Philip K. Dick or filmmakers such as the Wachowski Brothers (*The Matrix* and sequels) are part of a discourse about technology which is open and unresolved:

> Technopoly is a state of culture. It is also a state of mind. It consists in the deification of technology, which means that the culture seeks its authorization in technology, finds its satisfactions in technology, and takes its orders from technology. This requires the development of a new kind of social order, and of necessity leads to the rapid dissolution of much that is associated with traditional beliefs.
>
> *(Postman, 1985)*

Here is the strongest articulation of the determinist creed. Postman is proposing a world which needs technology to understand itself. This, he argues, leads inevitably to a reconstitution of social life.

> Those who feel most comfortable in Technopoly are those who are convinced that technical progress is humanity's superhuman achievement and the instrument by which our most profound dilemmas may be solved. They also believe that information is an unmixed blessing, which through its continued and uncontrolled production and dissemination offers increased freedom, creativity, and peace of mind. The fact that information does none of these things -- but quite the opposite – seems to change few opinions, for unwavering beliefs are an inevitable product of the structure of Technopoly. In particular, Technopoly flourishes when the defenses against information break down.
>
> *(Postman, 1995: 71)*

Despite writing fifteen years ago, Postman foresees the potentials of an 'information society', though he himself is sceptical of the notion of 'benefit':

The relationship between information and the mechanisms for its control is fairly simple to describe: Technology increases the available supply of information. As the supply is increased, control mechanisms are strained. Additional control mechanisms are needed to cope with new information. When additional control mechanisms are themselves technical, they in turn further increase the supply of information. When the supply of information is no longer controllable, a general breakdown in psychic tranquillity and social purpose occurs. Without defences, people have no way of finding meaning in their experiences, lose their capacity to remember, and have difficulty imagining reasonable futures.

(Postman, 1995: 71–2)

In rejecting these arguments we are not questioning their sincerity or power, but we are seeking to problematise the way in which technology features as if a unitary, organised social phenomenon with predictable outcomes and effects. If we think we can ignore technology as a concept, even for the best reason – that 'technology' is not really the issue – then we are missing the point. In order to move to a position where 'the bewildering array of object technologies' provide local colour rather than substance to our examination of abiding social and cultural relationships, we need to know where technology fits in to a media studies which, whether it likes it or not, is being sub-consciously and sometimes consciously defined by the idea of 'technological change'.

This is an imperative for us all at all levels from the elementary school to the academy. Being in the longer view 'new', contains an expectation that we will need at some point to be 'newer'. Equally purporting to study 'media' that are changing (everyone knows this), the imperative becomes almost categorical. How we respond will define what happens next. In a young discipline whose *bons mots* come largely from the visionary McLuhan, whom Debord called 'the spectacle's first apologist' and the 'most confirmed imbecile of the century', it is inevitable that the 'scriptures' will be interpreted in different ways (Debord, 2005, sec. XII). For subject media, the key is content: if 'the medium is the message' we just add 'them' to the content, these 'new' mediums. Incidentally McLuhan also wrote that 'in all media the user is the content' (quoted in E. McLuhan, 2008) but this is less compatible with the project.

As often, the medium turns out to be not so much the 'message' as the 'metaphor', and without too much effort 'the cliché' or 'stereotype'. But more importantly the broader contexts are lost in the desire to characterise mediums as possessing (ready-made) their own aesthetics and social qualities which distance them from their antecedents (Winston, 1998). When Gilder makes the case for a brave new world of individualism and creativity to replace a mass media structured on a 'master–slave' architecture, he is falling into the same trap on the basis of a misreading of McLuhan's dictum. Holmes quotes Carey: 'Media of communication ... are vast social metaphors that not only transmit information but determine what is knowledge: that not only orient us to the world but tell us what kind of world exists' (in Holmes, 2005: 15).

Notice here that we are not talking about 'the media' but rather the means we have of communicating about the world. That these function as 'social metaphors' is hardly surprising since 'being social' is our primary reason for communicating at all. For, as Colin Cherry famously wrote: 'Communication is essentially a social affair. Man has evolved a host of different systems of communication which render his social life possible' (1996: 10).

This takes us back to Aristotle's designation of man as a 'zoon politikon', a social/ political/cultural animal and therefore unlike any other animal. It also returns us to the fact that, in Raymond Williams's memorable phrase, 'communication begins in the struggle to learn and to describe', and moreover 'this struggle is not begun at second hand, after reality has occurred. It is , in itself a major way in which reality is continually formed and changed' (Williams, 1966: 12–13). The part played by our ingenuities and technologies in these transformations is our proper study, since all dismembered accounts of their histories and aesthetics will do no more than shadow these endeavours.

Even Barber's enterprising overview, 'Three scenarios for the future of technology and strong democracy', reads ultimately like a primer on the possibilities and fallibilities of human societies in any age. Barber offers three futures:

- Pangloss: a future of optimistic complacency which does nothing to address the growing inequalities between variously rich and variously poor. With a reliance on market forces we end up in *Bladerunner* (Scott, 1982) or *Super-Cannes* (Ballard, 2000), or saving that another collapse of international capital.
- Pandora: we leave the box open to totalitarian forces who would seek to 'control' us: Holmes speaks of the 'expanded commodification and rationalization of cultural life'. A continuation of the secret and surveillance society leads to despotism and dystopia
- 'Jeffersonia': By enhancing education and participation technology saves the world and replaces it with one that genuinely commits to tolerance and diversity.

(Barber, in Hassan and Thomas, 2006: 188–202)

These are options which have little essentially to do with technology and much to do with politics. They ask vexed questions about what kind of world we want and how are we going to achieve it.

New media and why we don't 'buy' the term

> Because something is happening here but you don't know what it is. Do you, Mr Jones?
> *(Bob Dylan, 'Ballad of a thin man', from the album Highway 61 Revisited, 1965)*

Lister et al argue that since 'for some fifty years the word "media", the plural of "medium", has been used as a singular collective term, as in "the media"', then 'we can surely speak of "the new media"'. Though they acknowledge that this implies 'a kind of social agency and coherence to "new media" that they do not yet possess', the danger is that the 'currency' of terms far exceeds their stock (2003: 9). It is a premise of our argument anyway that 'the media' not only is a term under erasure but also a problematic notion that a young discipline, which if unchecked will soon be 'new media studies', has struggled to outgrow.

While we are not embracing Gauntlett's 'Media 2.0' agenda – or at least the version of it that has been circulated and attacked – he surely has a point when he quips 'Media Studies is often too much about the media'. Conceiving of 'the new media' even tentatively runs the risk that the sins of the father be visited on the son, and this is a consciously gendered metaphor: despite the theoretical invisibility of technology, at the visible heart of new media is kit: gadgetry and 'poke'. Also, as we have repeatedly argued the unitary nature of these terms allows them to function as what Gauntlett describes as 'an independently fascinating set of texts and technologies' to be studied in and for themselves (2006). Add to this the predominance of semiotic accounts and you run the risk of ironically downplaying the techno-social dimensions.

Like David Holmes we would prefer to avoid the dangers of a fetishised 'new' with an exploration of contingencies rather than causes: to offer genealogies rather than epochal histories as suugested in Chapter 5. Holmes writes, more modestly, about 'charting how the emergence of new post-broadcast and interactive forms of communication has provided additional domains of study for communication theory, renovated the older domain of broadcast, and suggested fresh ways of studying these older media' (2005: x). Here 'new' merely describes those that are 'later' and 'latest' without making claims beyond the unavoidability of the fact that 'new' is a loaded term, the most often used term in advertising.

Holmes is, like us, suspicious of the spectacular and epochal: his particular bugbear is the idea of a 'second media age' as in a technological revolution, 'that a second media age of new media, exemplified by the Internet, has overtaken or converged with an older age of broadcast media' (2005: x). This is not to deny the benefits of considering the differing architectures of broadcast and interactive networks, but it is to demand a consideration of 'medium or network form rather than simply content or "text"' (Holmes, 2005: xi). Let us not put aside these non-textual distinctions on account of a widening orthodoxy. Rather let us recognise that our interpretative perspectives are also subject to changes in how media are experienced. Holmes makes this a clear agenda item:

> However, in so far as this book is sociological, sociology is not being opposed to communication and media studies; on the contrary, a central argument of the book is that the emergence of new communication environments has more or less forced traditional media and communication studies to be sociological.
>
> *(Holmes, 2005: xi)*

At the heart of the divide between the work of the academy and an otherwise ubiquitous and dominant *subject media* is the presence (and/or absence) of this interdisciplinary approach. The monologic nature of *subject media* is brought into sharp focus by its assimilation of 'new media', defined crudely by its potential to offer dialogic communication. In *subject media* terms though it becomes just another 'platform' or subsumed into a model of 'industry'. Consider here some of the requirements for Media Studies at A level in the United Kingdom:

Candidates will investigate the processes of meaning making in media production and reception:

- at the micro level within individual products (also termed *texts*)
- and at a macro level in terms of technologies (also termed *platforms*).

In this specification the media platforms are referred to as broadcasting, e-media and print, to include linear broadcasting (audio-visual) and cinema, print media, digital/web-based and emerging media. Candidates will firstly investigate a wide range of media texts to familiarise themselves with media language and media codes and conventions and then embark upon a cross-media study.

The media platforms
Candidates will undertake a study of *one or more* of the cross-media topic areas (see below) across *at least three* different media taken from the following media platforms:

Broadcasting – suggested texts: television and radio programmes both factual and fictional; films; advertisements; trailers and other audio/visual promotional material. It is advised that at least one from each type of text should be studied.

E-media – suggested texts: websites; blogs/wikis; podcasts; advertising and promotional materials; radio; television; music or film downloads; games and emerging forms. It is advised that at least one from each type of text should be studied.

Print – suggested texts: newspapers; magazines; advertising and marketing texts including promotional materials. It is advised that at least one from each type of text should be studied.

Consider how 'technologies' is used here as synonymous with 'platforms' with inevitable consequences. Games become classified as e-media though they are most frequently accessed through a television, and potentially the same radio programme is given different designations according to how it is accessed. This leaves the 'cross-media' designation understandable but equally problematic since there is now some confusion between 'cross-media' and 'cross-platform'. This is not a cheap shot at a workable specification but rather an indication where insisting on 'technology as content' can get you. Here the simple dualism of the old and the new is a built-in implication of the schedule: you must 'do' something technologically new (even if it is a download of something technologically old).

Content
Centres will be required to select *three different media industries* from the list below to study with their candidates.

- Television
- Radio
- Film
- Music
- Newspaper
- Magazine (including comics)
- Advertising
- Computer Games

For each industry, *three main texts* should provide the focus for candidates' study. At least *two* of the chosen texts must be contemporary and *one* must be British. Centres are advised to select contrasting texts so that candidates acquire as wide an understanding of the media industry as possible. What constitutes a 'text' will vary depending on the industry.

For each *text* selected, candidates should consider the following as appropriate:

Text
- genre
- narrative
- representation

Industry
- production
- distribution (and exhibition where relevant)
- marketing and promotion
- regulation issues
- global implications
- relevant historical background

Audience
- audience/user targeting
- audience/user positioning
- audience responses and user interaction
- debates about the relationship between audiences/users and text.

Here technology operates more usefully as a context or implication of some or all of the specified issues. However, the model remains a traditional one, with mass media industries that now include computer games (and comics) continuing to represent the world within classifiable genres and through familiar narratives. This list might have lasted the life of the discipline were it not for a couple of minor modifications, namely 'global implications' and 'user interaction'. In both specifications text remains king but its primary function is to cover bases not to explore issues. Here three texts are 'required' (two contemporary, one British[!]) to provide as wide an understanding of the chosen media industry as possible (and to address issues of narrative, representation and genre). Here is a job for teachers, not a starting point for students: an insistence that learning is to a large extent 'pre-designated' (if not guaranteed), that 'preferred readings, if not fixed, are at least framed. This is at least interesting in a subject where 'user interaction' is a 'contemporary' consideration.

Head out on the (super) highway: continuities and convergences

In May 1869, the railheads of the Union Pacific and Central Pacific railroads finally met at Promontory Summit (Utah) and the first transcontinental railroad was completed. This model of 'communication' is not an irrelevant one since it informs much thinking about communication technologies and their long-term goal to overcome obstacles to non-specific global communication. While we may not, in the future be famous for 15 minutes we might expect an increasing integration of converging technologies via tablets or perhaps even cybernetic implants. Futurist thinkers like Ray Kurzweil are predicting blood cell sized technology and 'enhanced intelligence' by 2029 (Kurzweil, 2005). 'Convergence' has become a buzz word of the new discourses about technology and is often addressed as if it too was a given good, like joining coast to coast. Moreover it is often discussed as a singularity, a long-term project whose success is inevitable and has predictable results.

Actually we need to see 'convergence' in a range of contexts, or else 'convergences' in context. As early as 2001 the irrepressible Henry Jenkins was disagreeing with this central sell of the 'new' *subject media*: 'What's all this talk about "media convergence," this dumb industry idea that all media will meld into one, and we'll get all of our news and entertainment through one box? Few contemporary terms generate more buzz-and less honey' (2001).

In this outspoken critique, Jenkins (2001) underlines many of the issues surrounding technologies that media studies needs, and is only partially managing, to address. We are expected to sit up and listen: 'Consider this column a primer on the real media convergence, because it's on the verge of transforming our culture as profoundly as the Renaissance did.'

Note that this project is ongoing, 'transforming' , a work in progress rather than a techno-utopian end of the road: 'Media convergence is an ongoing process, occurring at various intersections of media technologies, industries, content and audiences; it's not an end state' (Jenkins, 2001).

Jenkins finally points out that the profoundest problem is simply that media convergence has become a singularity when it is in fact multi-dimensional. He lists 'at least five processes':

- *Technological convergence*: Jenkins privileges 'the digitization of all media content'. The old become subsumed into the new (not replaced by them). McLuhan interestingly described this process as translation: 'prior forms of technological extension will not be allowed to exist except by being translated into information systems' (1967: 68).
- *Economic convergence*: Jenkins identifies 'the horizontal integration of the entertainment industry' and the opportunities that transmedia ownership offers to producers and advertisers alike.
- *Social or organic convergence*: Jenkins is interested in 'multitasking strategies' we necessarily develop to cope with what Meynowitz describes as 'communication technologies as types of social environments' (quoted in Holmes, 2005: 1). For Jenkins, 'It may occur inside or outside the box, but ultimately, it occurs within the user's cranium.'
- *Cultural convergence*: Where Jenkins's real interest lies: 'The explosion of new forms of creativity at the intersections of various media technologies, industries and consumers.' Jenkins looks forward to the development of 'a new participatory folk culture' and ' transmedia storytelling, which ... will use each channel to communicate different kinds and levels of narrative information, using each medium to do what it does best'.
- *Global convergence*: the altogether more contested arguments about globalisation and the global village. Jenkins writes benignly of 'The cultural hybridity that results from the international circulation of media content', and suggests that 'these new forms reflect the experience of being a citizen of the "global village"' (2001). Others may see this a classic meta-narrative of late capitalism. Holmes writes of 'The ethnocentric ideology of the global village' (2005: 74), and quotes Hawisher and Selfe's cynical take on this:

According to this utopian and ethnocentric narrative, sophisticated computer networks- manufactured by far-sighted scientists and engineers educated within democratic and highly technological cultures- will serve to connect the world's peoples in a vast global community that transcends current geopolitical borders.

(Holmes, 2005: 74)

Get your motor running: urbanisation and telecommunities

Dependence on technical communicative systems facilitates expanded commodification and rationalization of cultural life.

(Holmes, 2005: xi)

Holmes offers a number of further connections: he talks about 'continuities', though they might also be examples of social and cultural convergence. He stresses the continuities between information and communication technologies and urbanisation, suggesting that contemporary communication happens in 'architectural, urban technically and socially shaped ways' (Holmes, 2005: 3).

When he writes of the 'urban and micro-urban realities' of everyday life he is reinforcing the continuities between the old world and new technologies, or conversely the new world with old technologies. While he accepts that our lives are increasingly 'enframed' by ICT and that 'animated' technologies and interfaces have changed our attitudes to these 'objects' (and perhaps 'things' in general), he suspects that the social relationships constituted by these relationships are nothing new. For the determinist McLuhan, famously, 'We shape our tools and thereafter our tools shape us' (1967: 68). For Holmes this is subtly but decisively altered to 'They (technologies) are not so much tools as environments' (2005).

Here the elephant in the room, determinism, is addressed by thinking of influence rather than impact and contexts rather than contraptions. It is Holmes's expressed desire that these relationships should be studied beyond 'the bewildering array of object technologies' (Holmes, 2005: 3). Clay Shirky, a reluctant internet guru and social media theorist, also made this important point in an interview in July 2010:

> Techies were making the syllogism, if you put new technology into an existing situation, and new behaviour happens, then that technology caused the behaviour. But I'm saying if the new technology creates a new behaviour, it's because it was allowing motivations that were previously locked out. These tools we now have allow for new behaviours – but they don't cause them.
>
> *(quoted in Aikenhead, 2010)*

In this way questions about the correlations between the increasing use of technology and the increased instances in the United States, Australia and the United Kingdom of people living alone are multifaceted rather than causal. Similarly the degree of attachment people appear to have to their communication devices is part of a broader social and cultural picture, not merely a symbol of mental infection or commodity fetishism. Holmes is keen to explore the convergence he sees between 'ICT' and the technologies of urban life, with the internet as both a model of and a metaphor for cyberspace relations which occur both on and off line. These are the virtual realities of the modern city explored both electronically and 'in the flesh'.

As the thrill of 'interaction' matures into more substantial and reliable modes of 'integration', so new possibilities genuinely emerge. This is the progress of the computer gamer from a singular interaction with the computer to an integrated network of varied online relationships. At the same time, however, it is about the privatisation of public space giving an increasing importance to broadcast and interactive networks, though not in a new way: the dog may be new, the tricks we need to teach him are older. McLuhan suggested that technological advances, or rather our frantic adoption of them, often result in the amputation of the technologies that preceded them, allowing no way back. However, though some may bemoan the absence of some mythical family life focused around the piano and the harvest, it was industrialisation and urbanisation rather than televisions and computers that led to this.

In a neglected piece on 'The culture of nations' in his 1983 publication *Towards 2000,* Raymond Williams explained much of this argument with his concept of 'mobile privatization' (in Du Gay et al, 1997: 128–9). Williams describes the processes which, in late capitalism, have led to society being increasingly unitised as individuals and small family units while at the very same time people have greater mobility than ever before (and therefore theoretical access to the wider world).

The Williams piece begins with the telling line: 'Most human beings adjust … to altered … conditions.' Williams is no determinist but he is interested in the conditions created by both the materialities and ideologies of capitalism, as it both prizes the 'sovereign consumer' and moves swiftly on to new markets leaving local peoples to 'pay the bill'. The focus of his critique is an 'old' technology, the motor car, which he sees as both symbol and 'vehicle' of the social order and private, but broadband will fit just as well. While our potential is to have access to widened vistas, to 'head out on the highway, looking for adventure' (source), the reality is what Williams darkly labels 'mobile privatization':

> Looked at from right outside, the traffic flows and their regularities are clearly a social order of a determined kind, yet what is experienced inside them – in the conditioned atmosphere and internal music of the windowed shell – is movement, choice of direction, the pursuit of self-determined private purposes. All the other shells are moving in comparable ways but for their own different private ends. They are not so much other people, in any full sense, but other units which signal and are signalled to, so that private mobilities can proceed safely and relatively unhindered. And if all this is seen from outside as in deep ways determined, or in some sweeping glance as dehumanised, that is not at all how it feels like inside the shell, with people you want to be with, going where you want to go.
>
> *(Williams, in Hall et al, 1997: 129)*

Holmes is keen to work this far-sighted observation to its natural conclusion, insisting that 'both the physical and the electronic urban architectures converge around the principle of continuous subdivision' (2005: 68). The world that is emerging is offered in a mixture of excitement and dread, as the metaphors and descriptions, narratives and theories dissolve into one another. Here the freeway and information superhighway occupy the same metaphorical and functional space as potentially headily liberating but dehumanising places, since both were built to both connect us and disconnect us from a fellow citizens. So it is with 'ever-expanding forms of urbanization – cities on ever greater scales' (Holmes, 2005: 68): as once they were enabled by the connectivity of the freeways, now they are increasingly dependent on electronic connectivities and the atomisation that these allow.

At the heart of this is a typically post-modern paradox, or if you prefer a dialectic: the more we individuals can be integrated into electronic networks the less we will depend on proximal interactions with others, which will in turn make us ever more dependent on the electronic networks. The irony is not lost on Holmes, who says that 'when our social world becomes geographically fragmented, we privately come to rely on the agents of separation that have aggregately produced this condition' (2005: 69). And of course our increasing path-dependence on telecommunication, like our path-dependence on motorised transport, all too easily leaves us more isolated and fearful, and prone (at least imaginatively) to the 'great catastrophe'. The *Mad Max* films which launched the career of Hollywood A-lister Mel Gibson addressed this in the form of an acute shortage of oil, in the same way that the contemporary vogue for disaster movies project the horror of a breakdown in telecommunications.

And if this all seems to read a little like science fiction, then perhaps this is not surprising since as Lister and his co-authors so rightly point out, we are inhabiting 'a sphere in which distinctions between science fiction, sociology and philosophy can become hard to maintain' (2003: 288). They quote Kellner's claim that 'cyberpunk can ... be read as a new form of social theory that maps the consequences of a rapidly developing media society in the era of techno-capitalism' (Lister et al, 2003: 288) alongside his recommendation that we read pessimistic commentators like Baudrillard as 'dystopic science fiction'.

This leaves us with the ever ebullient Jenkins: not on the verge of some vast revolution but very much living and dreaming, hoping and despairing:

> These contradictory forces are pushing both toward cultural diversity and toward homogenization, toward commercialization and toward grassroots cultural production. The digital renaissance will be the best of times and the worst of times, but a new cultural order will emerge from it. Stay tuned.
>
> *(Jenkins, 2001)*

After the individual in society', putting the science back into technology:

> the Euro-American distinction between the individual and the collective – current since at least the Enlightenment, though no doubt preceding this by many centuries – is unsatisfactory.
>
> *(Callon and Law, 1997: 1)*

Divisions between human and non-human, subject and object, and agent and structure – all of the dichotomies generally mobilized to explain the collective have disappeared.

(Callon and Law, 1997: 2)

We certainly get our fair share of utopian and dystopian accounts of technology, which serve to extend the pattern of dichotomies which architecture the whole area: 'old and new', broadcast and interactive, determinist and humanist. And our unwillingness to deal in any meaningful way with the technology itself or the science behind it leaves us further exposed to the potential limitations of a humanist and structuralist approach. As Lister et al admit:

We routinely discuss signs apart from what they are signs of, representations apart from what they represent, meanings apart from matter, and ideologies that mask realities, so that the world we inhabit now seems to be composed exclusively of linguistic, textual or interpretative acts.

(Lister et al, 2003: 296)

This is part of a section that introduces 'actor network theory', the work of anthropologist of science Bruno Latour and his colleague Michael Callon. Latour's critique is partly a critique of the humanism that he sees at the heart of all work on technology, and which he considers a reductive force since it reduces all to rational explanations (meanings) to the detriment of any discussion about the material reality of technological and scientific 'phenomena'. The genuine debate about meaning for Latour should be situated 'in the network of other things, texts, discourses and institutions of which it is part' (Lister et al, 2003: 296).

The result is a collective approach which does not play across easy binaries, which rejects the dualism of individual and collective in order to arrive at a fuller, and more mature, take on the complexity of human and non-human interactions.

Instead of thinking about things in isolation from meanings or of meanings in isolation from things, reality is composed of networks in which human things (meanings, texts, discourses, institutions, signs) interact constantly with non-human things (viruses, biochemistry, immune systems).

(Lister et al, 2003: 297)

Michael Callon offers 'lessons on collectivity from science' in his aptly titled 'After the individual in society'. With his co-author John Law, Callon explores the limitations of our dualist tendencies with regard to the social integration of technology. They argue that the idea that society is a set of relationships between human actors is a misunderstanding. Instead they suggest that it is better understood as a collective association of human and non-human entities. In this context 'The distinction between individual and society is unnecessary.' 'The whole endeavour is a collective act, not merely the actions of individuals within a collective' (Callon and Law, 1997: 7).

Eschewing dualism leads us to a more sophisticated model, which recognises the plurality and multiplicity of interactions between humans, technologies and their shared contexts. Here focus on a 'fixed' point, be that human, object or text, is to immediately access 'the networks of entities which lie behind them' (Callon and Law, 1997: 7). In doing so doubt is cast on Western notions of the strongly independent individual (*homo clausus*) which Callon describes as 'a (temporarily workable) fiction created at the time of the Enlightenment'(Callon and Law, 1997: 7).

Thus the meanings of cultural practices and media practices can be seen within their real relationships with the reality of technologies and society since: 'Actors are both networks and points. They are both individuals and collectives.'

'McLuhan is unavoidable'

> Man, he understood the Internet. He was the Internet in the sixties.
>
> *(Robert Logan, quoted in Horrocks, 2003)*

> McLuhan is unavoidable.
>
> *(Gary Genesco, 1999)*

It has been claimed that McLuhan is enjoying a renaissance. By the time of his death, on the eve of the new 'extensions of man' in 1980, his ideas were very much out of fashion, lacking as they do a political dimension. However, despite Robert Logan's claims that McLuhan is a pre-internet thinker, increasingly used to theorise the post-broadcast landscape, livinginternet.com includes him in its condensed (one-page) summary of internet history, and *Wired* magazine made him its patron saint!.

Some consider this McLuhan revival almost coincidental, that the network 'Marshall McLuhan, visionary thinker' is structurally seductive, combining as it does a blissful naivety, a paratactic style (which allows contradictory elements to flourish in the same 'bed') and admittedly 'pentecostal' flashes of genius. McLuhan says the things we have thought and felt, but unlike us he never goes back to unpack them and discover their limitations. Take his unconscious manifesto statement for a new kind of analysis of 'Communication, media and culture' in 1967: 'If we understand the revolutionary transformations caused by new media, we can anticipate and control them' (McLuhan and Fiore, 1967).

Like almost everything in McLuhan, this deck is fixed, and even in miniature it is clearly a matter of causes rather than contingencies, of explanations rather than explorations. McLuhan's impositions are epochal in their scope but also strangely unhistorical, since 'revolutionary' and 'new' are used unproblematically. McLuhan has a classic 'fall from grace' narrative to impose on us with technology as determining context, and in the Todorovian sense the agency of disruption. Though McLuhan does not conceive of this progression as entirely linear, *The Gutenberg Galaxy* (1962) is written in 107 'pieces' which he hopes will create a mosaic on which patterns might emerge, it plots a progress and considers consequences:

1. Oral tribe culture (tribal).
2. Manuscript culture (scribal).
3. Gutenberg galaxy (mechanical).
4. Electronic age (electronic).

The problematic, though, is in McLuhan's contrary notion that this 'journey' is a return. McLuhan's is a triple narrative of unity followed by fragmentation followed by reunification, predicated on the notion of pre-literate and post-literate cultures (Horrocks, 2003: 218). What excites McLuhan about the electronic age is a potential return to an acoustic world from a literate one, since 'print also isolated the reader and silenced her voice and discussion'. His own writing, stirring even in its rank naivety, hardly strengthens his hand, as Derrida has pointed out. When McLuhan claims, with rhetorical flourish, that 'A goose quill put an end to talk', he is doing so with a resonance that he otherwise claims that literacy deprives language of: 'this multi-dimensional resonance: every word is poetic unto itself' (McLuhan and Fiore, 1967: 14). The global village then is a place to recover our sensorial wholeness, a place where time has ceased and space has vanished. Unlikeliest of all, this transformation is be achieved not by a chemical or spiritual cleansing of the doors of perception, but through technologies, those tools that McLuhan ultimately believes will shape us.

If in this context McLuhan is 'unavoidable', it is merely because his views are unavoidably eccentric, unavoidably inconsistent and in many cases unavoidably mistaken. This is significant only because in a broader sense he is also one of those key twentieth-century thinkers who gave us parts of a vocabulary for talking about that century. Though hardly responsible for the preference in *subject media* of 'the media' as the message, McLuhan nevertheless marked out the area, and it often took others years to redesign it. While narratives of technological revolution still have popular and academic appeal (see Monovich, 2002, or Kelly, 1997 on 'the computational metaphor') there has been a growing scepticism about the dawn of the Second Media Age.

And this scepticism about the current revolution is often founded on profound scepticism about the first. It has become as fashionable to compare the impact of broadband internet to the invention of sliding type as it is to say that if Shakespeare was alive today he would be writing *The Wire / Dr Who / Glee* (delete as applicable). As we have seen, printing as the apotheosis of writing marks a significant moment for McLuhan. In short, 'The mechanisation of printing … turned history into classified data.' This deduction is of a similar order to the one made by Levi-Strauss when he observed tribal leaders imitating his annotation of their behaviour (in other words pretending to write). He too saw this as both a significant act and a significant loss of innocence, as something to do with power and the 'cost' of writing. Derrida read both in a very different way, just as he cast a deeply ironic eye on Plato's dismissal of metaphor since it was conducted in deeply metaphorical language (Horrocks, 2003: 207–8).

More widely it has been recognised that the fetishisation of both technology and 'the new' has led to massive overstatements about the changes that have been wrought, and these overstatements start with what Cook labels 'the Gutenberg Myth' (1997). Printing no more changes the world than the fact that we no longer sit at the centre of the universe or the fact that our existences are determined by genetic permutations. These 'events' have contexts, are percolated through cultural and social products and practices. In practical terms even work on the more dramatic claims about 'time–space convergence' (McLuhan's 'Time has ceased') stresses the continuities rather than dislocations, and the enduring significance of local factors and social practice. Stein, for example, traces ideas about the annihilation of space and time to the end of the nineteenth century, a century whose technologies also added to a sense of a shrinking world. Like Green's work on the impact of the mobile phone on 'social time and space', Stein is keen to stress a series of progressive instrumental changes (Green talks of the understated manner in which control of time and mobility is shaped). Both find contemporary accounts of revolutionary change 'overstated' (Stein, 1999; Green, 2002). Where does this leave McLuhan's act of faith?

> After three thousand years of explosion, by means of fragmentary and mechanical technologies, the Western world is imploding. During the mechanical ages we had extended our bodies in space. Today, after more than a century of electric technology, we have extended our central nervous system itself in a global embrace, abolishing both space and time as far as our planet is concerned. Rapidly, we approach the final phase of the extensions of man – the technological simulation of consciousness, when the creative process of knowing will be collectively and corporately extended to the whole of human society, much as we have already extended our senses and our nerves by the various media.
>
> *(Bennett, Beck and Wall, 2004: 281)*

Yet paradoxically, in the meantime virtuality has brought a set of landscapes much closer to those he described, and much better tuned to the technological humanism and techno-romanticism that he espoused. What was once described by De Mott as 'McLuhancy' was once again provoking debate. And McLuhan certainly still has things to say to us, even if his own work does not always heed his own warnings. Here are two starting points for further work.

The rear-view mirror. Paul Bendetti and Nancy DeHart called their 1996 tribute to McLuhan *Forward through the Rearview Mirror,* and in their introduction claimed that 'his notion of the "rearview mirror" is one of the most important insights McLuhan left us with to understand our own age' (Bendetti and DeHart, 1996: 33). What McLuhan wrote was 'We look at the present through a rear-view mirror. We march backwards into the future.' Thus he went on, to general bafflement, 'The future of the future is the present' (1969). McLuhan's point is that our inability to address the way things are now without significant reference to how they used to be has significant implications for what they will become. Technologically speaking this means a fondness for translation and adaptation rather than collaboration and cooperation.

Figuratively living in the past is a comfortable state, and the past is a place where that stability makes judgements easy and change more difficult. Like Foucault, McLuhan was suspicious of such judgements. As Liss Jeffrey, a McLuhan associate, points out, 'He repeated insistently that we should stop saying "Is this a good thing or a bad thing?" and start saying "What's going on?"' (Bendetti and DeHart, 1996: 11). In terms of a contemporary landscape festooned with gadgetry and subsumed with arguments about 'new media', this seems a real fine place to start.

The extension of our senses: though at times bizarrely woven into his 'return to Eden' narrative (where the stated aim is 'sensorial wholeness' or 'allatonceness'), McLuhan's projection of all media as extensions of the senses remains interesting. For McLuhan, 'media are artificial extensions of sensory experience', which is a useful way of reminding us (and McLuhan himself at times) that they are essentially human, 'natural' implications of our desire to 'see and say'. The following is a side of McLuhan we rarely see: 'All media – or extension of man – are natural resources that exist by virtue of the shared knowledge and skill of a community' (McLuhan, 1994: 132).

At the same time McLuhan is aware, at least in theory, that media communication is primarily sensory communication: to our ears, eyes, fingertips. This is a useful starting point in a world where 'media' and 'medium' are used with no great precision, where ways of communicating are sometimes wilfully confused with technological methods of delivery. In simple terms this means that mediums do not 'die', they are too primitive for such 'affectations'. Jenkins makes the point firmly:

> History teaches us that old media never die. And before you say, 'What about the eight-track,' let's distinguish among media, genres and delivery technologies. Recorded sound is a medium. Radio drama is a genre. CDs, MP3 files and eight-track cassettes are delivery technologies. Genres and delivery technologies come and go, but media persist as layers within an ever more complicated information and entertainment system. A medium's content may shift, its audience may change and its social status may rise or fall, but once a medium establishes itself it continues to be part of the media ecosystem. No one medium is going to 'win' the battle for our ears and eyeballs.
>
> *(Jenkins, 2001)*

Writing in summer 2010 about the ultimate futility of Rupert Murdoch's attempts to set up an internet paywall for his UK newspapers, Clay Shirky may have overstepped this mark. However, 'the death of a delivery technology' will never have the resonance that the demise of a medium has:

If you are reading this article on a printed copy of the Guardian, what you have in your hand will, just 15 years from now, look as archaic as a Western Union telegram does today. In less than 50 years, according to *Clay Shirky*, it won't exist at all. The reason, he says, is very simple, and very obvious: if you are 25 or younger, you're probably already reading this on your computer screen. 'And to put it in one bleak sentence, no medium has ever survived the indifference of 25-year-olds.'

(quoted in Aikenhead, 2010)

Though 'medium' is not the word here either it would be interesting to consider the recent history of television in the context of this final prediction: 'The next medium, whatever it is – it may be the extension of consciousness – will include television as its content, not as its environment, and will transform television into an art form' (in Horrocks, 2003: 221).

Enter the prosumer

Clay Shirky would clearly agree with our earlier assertion that to a woman with a broadband connection everything looks like a social network. His first book *Here Comes Everybody: How Change Happens When People Come Together* (2010) offers a positive take on the implications of a system founded on a matrix rather than a medium, on collaboration rather than throughput. The follow up, *Cognitive Surplus; Creativity and Generosity in a Connected Age,* critically examines the changes. Shirky has a take on the prosumer debate, sidestepping concerns over the difference between 'broadcast quality' and 'broadcast acceptable'.

The book argues that the popularity of online social media trumps all our old about the superiority of professional content, and the primacy of financial motivation. It proves, Shirky argues, that people are more creative and generous than we had ever imagined, and would rather use their free time participating in amateur online activities such as Wikipedia – for no financial reward – because they satisfy the primal human urge for creativity and connectedness.

(Shirky, 2010)

McLuhan has no direct input to this debate, but is nevertheless saying something quite far-sighted in his words and actions in this respect. In his idiosyncratic 'event' texts, his famous mosaic format, he adopted a 'writerly' approach, which encouraged reader participation. Moreover he was the first to popularise the term 'user' (rather than 'audience' or 'viewer'), now a standard term to describe internet participation. His observation that 'in all media the user is the content' might prefix this book and a good many others. This is a more profound return than the one prophesied by McLuhan, a return not to a tribal innocence but to the question of identity. All of our communications always do this, since we are works as much as our writings are, and as Todorov pronounced, 'the meaning of a work lies in the telling of itself, its speaking of its own existence' (in Hawkes, 1977: 100).

> Since all media are extensions of ourselves, or translations of some part of us into various materials, any study of one medium helps us to understand all the others.
>
> *(McLuhan, 1994: 139)*

This at least puts media and their attendant technologies in their place. Having concluded that 'poems make nothing happen' in his threnody for W. B. Yeats, the poet W. H. Auden concedes that they (this 'genre' of writing) are (merely?) 'a way of happening, a mouth'. Likewise McLuhan: 'It has now been explained that media, or the extensions of man, are "make happen" agents, but not "make aware" agents' (1994: 59). And the 'guru Shirky?'

> The whole, 'Is the internet a good thing or a bad thing'? We're done with that. It's just a thing. How to maximise its civic value, its public good – that's the really big challenge.
>
> *(quoted in Aikenhead 2010)*

New apps for old: transmedia narratologies

> We are all groping to grasp a significant shift in the underlying logic of commercial entertainment, one which has both commercial and aesthetic potentials we are still trying to understand, one which has to do with the interplay between different media systems and delivery platforms (and of course different media audiences and modes of engagement.)
>
> *(Henry Jenkins, 2009)*

> New technology, far from dumbing us down, is getting us involved in building a more engaged, democratic and creative world.
>
> *(Marcus du Sautoy, mathematician and Simonyi Professor for the Public Understanding of Science)*

Writing with enthusiasm in the summer of 2010, Marcus de Sautoy invited us to consider what 'they' are doing to books:

> Consider two books: Hilary Mantel's *Wolf Hall* and Lewis Carroll's *Alice in Wonderland*. Not the printed books, the apps – software for mobiles and the iPad. The *Wolf Hall* app is a thing of beauty. It contains the text, of course, but readers can also move slickly between the text, family trees of the Tudors and the Yorkists, extra articles by Mantel and a fascinating video discussion between the novelist and historian David Starkey. All of which gives a

deeper and richer understanding of the novel's historical context and its characters.

(du Sautoy, 2010)

The point he goes on to make, apart from the fact that *Alice's Adventures in Wonderland* is even better, is that in the burgeoning world of what were fleetingly called e-books, the key technology is still that part called 'book'. Most of these are simple translations: 'Currently readers are being offered little more than the novelty of a book on an electronic device.' Those that interest and enthuse du Sautoy, however, are not those with more 'technology', but rather those with more imagination: like, appropriately, those whose app for *Alice's Adventures in Wonderland* aims 'to capture, for adults and children alike, the fantastical nature of the story'.

This leads us to du Sautoy's key sentence: 'This is about recreating what a book is and can be.' Du Sautoy sees this as a huge challenge: 'to reconceive their content to provide a visual and interactive experience that the printed book cannot provide'. In fact he is really talking about augmenting and extending traditional understandings of what a book, is in a context where there is a seemingly insatiable appetite for 'extra' content. He is certainly not burying the book: 'And books are a great invention. They are durable, portable. Their batteries don't run out.'

Nor is he agin telling stories. He is rather in favour of extending those stories and the ways they are supported across a variety of 'delivery technologies which are largely the user's own (or at least own choice). 'I'm particularly interested in apps for non-fiction that are not designed to break up a narrative in a radical way, but rather to augment a storyline.'

He compares this with television's attempts to augment content and experience by use of the red button, though in this case he concludes that 'It's a problem TV has not really been able to crack yet.'

What du Sautoy is partly unwittingly addressing here is the phenomenon of transmedia (some say 'crossmedia') storytelling, which is with varying degrees of consciousness and success working across all delivery technologies. In providing extra material in a variety of relationships with the core original, the producers are enhancing the user experience of a range of stories from *Wolf Hall* to *Star Wars*. Jenkins implicitly (and then later explicitly) got the ball running on transmedia storytelling in his widely acclaimed book *Textual Poachers: Television Fans and Participatory Culture (Studies in Culture and Communication)* (1992), which opened many to potential extension of the value of broadcast content by 'bottom up' fan activity. Jenkins as an academic and a fan was able to take fan culture seriously, listen to fans and experience their fan fiction and fanzines. The range of texts addressed was weird and wild: from *Robin of Sherwood* (*Robin Hood*) to *Star Trek* (predictably) but also from *The Professionals* to *Red Dwarf*.

In the meantime there has been, well, the internet and the 'anoraks' have risen like lions after slumber realising that they are many. Here the medium as 'the matrix' did exactly what it said on the tin: only connect! And while the character of fandom was 'same as it ever was', its reach and influence (in all directions) suddenly increased, well, in fact emerged. *The Blair Witch Project* (1999) gave the film industry its wake-up call, building a gross of more than US$150 million on a production budget of US$35,000 by way of a first exploitation of the internet as a multi-layered marketing opportunity and through the intelligent cultivation of hardcore horror fans as a collection of online communities. This potential tension is what Matt Hills has referred to as '"the dialectic of value" of fan culture', which means that in necessarily contradictory ways 'fan cultures both challenge and intensify commodification' (Hills, 2002: 144). Writing in 2000, Jane Roscoe gives us a flavour of both in the pioneering *Blair Witch* 'project':

> What started off as a cheap and easy way of spreading the word about the film became the perfect forum in which to effectively manufacture the hoax story of the Blair Witch and of the missing students. Months before the official release of the film, there were a number of dedicated websites filtering various pieces of information to an Internet audience intrigued by the rumors about the film, the witch and the students.
>
> *(Roscoe, 2000)*

> The internet did much more than merely advertise the film, it created a community of THE BLAIR WITCH PROJECT fans, who used the websites to communicate with each other and participate more broadly in virtual networks. These sites also became forums in which to respond to the film.
>
> *(Roscoe, 2000)*

When the official website was launched, it received 75 million hits in the first week. Things would simply never be the same again. Actually the paraphernalia presented on the official site (documents relating to both the Blair Witch 'legend' and the disappearance of the 'pesky kids') were something of a throwback, being just the kind of authenticating devices that were once used by writers particularly in the eighteenth century to both disguise and extend often satirical works. The most famous of these is *Gulliver's Travels*, which includes letters and charts which are perhaps intended to confirm the veracity of the narrative. These are the first knockings of a transmedia narrative tradition.

Thus Jenkins's current definition speaks of a world in which the possibilities are being actively addressed both top-down and bottom-up. This inevitably means, to some extent, the colonisation and commodification of fandom, but in capitalist economies this is perhaps both inevitable and the surest sign that the discourse has reached the mainstream. This definition is an insistent one:

> Transmedia storytelling represents a process where integral elements of a fiction get dispersed systematically across multiple delivery channels for the purpose of creating a unified and coordinated entertainment experience. Ideally, each medium makes its own unique contribution to the unfolding of the story.
>
> *(Jenkins, 2009)*

Like so much in this section, a principal issue is the balance between a genuinely innovative set of opportunities provided in part by new technologies, and the often age-old roles and functions which are being fulfilled by them. And this applies to audiences and producers alike, since both have always found ways of getting more from their offer. Merchandising on the back of blockbuster films and popular television has regularly offered creative opportunities, as did the cottage industry that was the pre-internet fanzine.

What has exploded over the best part of thirty years is the amount of academic work on transmedia texts, or at least on fandom, which in itself has arguably become part of the broader narrative. Certainly for fans, interpretation, whatever variety, professional and amateur, adds value. Take the feelings of excitement when most of us came to the Jenkins groundbreaker. It gave us to believe that other valued texts might be worthy of examination in their contexts, as cultural products and as subject to cultural practices. Technology may not have been essential to these developments but it has certainly had an appreciable impact on the volume and character of fan responses and responses to fans.

Fan activity has always enabled a limited version of transmedia storytelling to take place, but in the eleven years since *Blair Witch* much else has been mobilised by producers and artists alike. Henry Jenkins remains at the head of the academic response. In his book *Convergence Culture* (2006) he patiently restates the argument that has been central to this chapter, and reconfirms his and our modest agenda for what Jenkins's own programme calls 'Comparative Media Studies', designed to 'enlarge public dialogues about popular culture and contemporary life'. He is still writing about the 'so-called digital revolution' in a modest way while recording significant change: 'My goal here is to document conflicting perspectives on media change rather than to critique them.' He also states that he is 'to describe some of the ways that convergence thinking is reshaping American popular culture and, in particular, the ways in which it is impacting the relationship between media audiences, producers and content'. This is a worthy agenda, which produces an engagingly diverse set of case studies (from *American Idol* to *The Matrix*).

This transmedia narrative on transmedia storytelling is also engaged with on Jenkins's own website, 'Confessions of an Aca-fan!' which includes both video and text of the keynote he gave at the 'Future of Fiction' conference (FOF4) in which he addressed what he formally calls 'Seven principles of transmedia entertainment'. They are certainly worth briefly presenting since they make a very clear statement about where we are now:

1. Spreadability vs. drillability

This is really *Hannah Montana* versus *Lost* in a non-competitive contest. The former managed to get 'spread' everywhere (books, comics, games), even engaging the star identity of Miley Cyrus (and Billy Ray) to add value to the central narrative. *Lost* did the same thing in a very different way, showing what Jason Mittell calls 'drillability'. To the nth degree it 'encourages viewers to dig deeper, probing beneath the surface to understand the complexity of a story and its telling'. These are not of course mutually exclusive terms. Both of these 'directions' are potentially fruitful contexts for extending discussion on the nature of text (and texts) and how we understand them. This is partly because both call into question the conditions of production and reception, and address the negotiation that is at the heart of both. Dan Brown's publishing phenomenon *The Da Vinci Code* serves as a useful reminder that 'complexity' in this case is not 'in' or 'of' the text but within its 'performance', that extended life through which it lives across the various arenas of publication, marketing and fandom. While these may all be seen as variously supporting, responding to and leeching on the 'hub', they are nevertheless all parts of the 'textualisation' of this 'event'.

2. Continuity vs. multiplicity

The integrity of a transmedia franchise rests on a negotiation between producers and users (consumers/prosumers). The implicit and explicit scaffolding on and around something like Tolkien's *The Lord of the Rings* gives a particular steer to how this negotiation is likely to play out. On the other hand Lucasfilm's stewardship of *Star Wars* is both more explicit and potentially more encouraging, with certain dates within the hyperdiegesis made specifically available for fanfiction and online role-playing: think 'guest' rather than 'squatter', 'ally' rather than 'guerrilla', with all the implications and obligations that these entail.

Matt Hills has written about the presence in lots of *Dr Who* fans of an ideal Doctor against which even the mainstream official version is judged and regularly found wanting (Hills, 2010: 5). As a long-running franchise *Dr Who* is almost certainly energised by both of these impulses, a much-logged continuity and significant aberration (*Star Trek* also fits this model) since its master narrative (television episodes across forty-odd years) has always been augmented by novels, comics, radio recordings and films.

Thus without this being a matter of transmedia strategy or design, the television episodes become understood as a selection from an open-ended collection of adventures in each regeneration. This is an attractive meta-narrative for a show about a time-travelling protagonist which has been becoming ever more concerned with such matters (time travel and continuity) since Steven Moffat took control. Having managed perhaps the most complex bit of plotting ever seen on television in the episode 'Blink' (in every sense a masterpiece denied ultimate reference by its existence within the *Dr Who* 'phenomenon), Moffat now has whole seasons within which to weave or leave his productive memes. Jenkins sees multiplicity as paving 'the way for us to think about fan fiction and other forms of grassroots expression as part of the same transmedia logic – unauthorized extensions of the "mother ship" which may nevertheless enhance fan engagement and expand our understanding of the original'. This becomes particularly poignant when as in the case of cult franchises, the 'mothership' has been destroyed.

3. Immersion vs. extractability

Technology is only one of the means that producers have to achieve one of the nirvanas of contemporary entertainment: the totally immersive experience. Having been to some extent let down by the broken promises of virtual reality (opting instead for an unlikely revival of 3D), we are nevertheless being continuity addressed via a promise of increasingly realistic experiences, which often means experience that is louder, faster and more visceral. However, there are many ways in which we can immerse ourselves in the story, and who can explain why they, even after all this time, still find *Twin Peaks* (1990–91) strangely compelling and totally addictive?

What was extractable from that show (lucratively from a local tourist point of view) was the cherry pie which symbolised a certain kind of narrative about a certain kind of America. Other extractables which have become profoundly symbolic cultural objects include the light sabre (and its sound) and the Vulcan ears sported by fans both in and out of the explicit contexts of fandom. Here again is an explicit example of the huge untapped resource which *subject media*, with its cautious preference for 'set' texts, seems unwilling to access. Fandom represents an 'invitation to treat' which is largely ignored by a *subject media* preoccupied by a notion of 'critical distance' derived from elsewhere and wedded to formal theoretical perspectives (but often not their implications).

Interestingly, although our immersion in a classic novel or film may not lead us as readily to a tangible 'extractable', the principle that we do nevertheless take things away from these experiences is certainly worth exploring. One element of our 'acquisition' of artefacts (whether bought in facsimile or acquired in other ways) is a kind of emulation or hero worship, an explicit recognition of influence. For literary 'icons' like Holden Caulfield the extractable elements may be attitudinal, even gestural (Brecht's notion of Gestus, the quotable gesture might help here: see Willett, 1974: 104). Also consider the massive increase in both popularity and symbolic significance of Gauloise cigarettes and gabardine in the wake of the advent of French *Nouvelle Vague* cinema. All of this represents an extended immersion in a textual experience, but a much more acceptable one than attaching Vulcan ears.

4. Worldbuilding

Jenkins refers to 'what Janet Murray has called the "encyclopedic" impulse behind contemporary interactive fictions' (source), which is an inclination not dissimilar to the original explorers: the desire to 'map and master'. It is a feature of all first-person computer games to a lesser and greater degree, and certainly a feature often of playing those games on-line, a feature that immediately and inevitably makes those worlds more pressing if not more real. It is also a principle of *Second Life* and other online environments, while fansites often site themselves symbolically within these environments, virtual or fictional.

This is an impulse of the news as much as it is an impulse of the first (and any subsequent) *Harry Potter* film. Control and authority become an issue in this wiki-ed world, though all that the notion of a wiki does is make this explicit. This spirit of exploration is clearly something that must be itself explored, rather than merely exploited. The danger, as ever, is of stereotyping the implications rather than genuinely addressing them. The way is clear for a consideration of opportunities: possibilities rather than problems.

5. Seriality

Jenkins reads transmedia narratives as an extended version of the serial, with an ideal projecting story 'chunks' across multiple media systems. Neil Perryman provided a very convincing account of this in relation to the relaunched *Dr Who*. Interestingly Perryman's narrative does not present this project as a series of strategic manoeuvres on behalf of a manipulative production team, but rather as a productive combination of faith in creative people, an instinctive blend of ideas and accidents, and the willingness to negotiate with fans (and not to). Despite the long-term continuity issues, Russell Davies was aware of the danger of disappearing up your own back-reference. Therefore he relied on a simple model: of back referencing through familiar monsters and the odd retro companion, and drove everything else forward, concentrating on providing new rewards for those who would stay a series or more (Perryman, 2006: 477).

In this way all of the meta-textual jiggerypokery was directed towards establishing the new teams: Doctors and companions. In fact for (Christopher) Eccleston, (David) Tennant and now Matt Smith, the pattern has been not so much an unfolding text but rather a series of gatherings around the significant companions, Rose Tyler, Donna Noble and now Amy Pond: epicentres each of significant cosmic disruptions from which narrative debris spins off but to which it ultimately coheres.

6. Subjectivity

Jenkins references the bounty hunter Boba Fett in the *Star Wars* multiverse as a classic example of how the extended reach of transmedia elements can reorganise the hierarchies of the 'mothership'. Helped by a striking costume, a strong if brief on-screen appearance and a popular action figure, Fett's importance to the franchise has been massively enhanced by the 'expanded universe' provided by games, novelisations, comics and television.

This ability to home in subjectively on some fairly minor aspect of the master narrative is a major advantage provided by convergence. The British actor Jeremy Bulloch, who spent seven weeks filming Fett's film interventions, has had this time handsomely repaid with an almost unending series of appearances at *Star Wars* conventions.

This can be an extremely problematic area of critical activity since the primary focus of much of the work students do with texts is primed to replace a presumed surfeit of the 'subjective' with a manufactured and robust 'objectivity'. This assumes not only a primacy of the subjective, which might be argued developmentally, but also an oppositional tension between the two predicated on a model of nature and nurture. Subjective responses are surely not implicitly cruder ones, nor are they incapable of development.

7. Performance

As we have seen throughout, transmedia narratives provide opportunities for fans to participate and perform. Some are fairly tightly controlled, others because they are run by and for fans are genuinely open. These performances occur in many forms and with very different modes of address. They may be reflective, interpretive, informative, affective or nostalgic. They may be homages to dead heroes (literally or figuratively) or alternative endings to the previous season. They may be hilarious mash-ups or sensitive re-edits. In doing these turns we fans are taking our place consciously in an imaginative but also commercial context.

Jenkins presents this as a 'story so far' in a typically modest fashion. Much is happening but we need to see it in its relevant contexts, which are historical and cultural as well technological and industrial. Jenkins is up for all of this but cannot contain his abiding faith in 'new spaces for creative experimentation'.

'He became his admirers': what the audience did (next)

> Media constituted communities ... do not so much 'mediate' interaction as facilitate modes or levels of integration to which correspond specific qualities of attachment and association.
>
> *(Holmes, 2005: xi)*

What are we learning about how media studies should be thinking of itself? The receding importance of a large-scale common broadcast experience, which is merely a statement of fact rather than an argument, has not put an end to broadcasting or the study of texts. It has however, altered profoundly the contexts in which these core elements of *subject media* are misunderstood. The importance of texts has become more specific, more about the uses we make of them, the contexts in which we use them, and less generic. This is the way in which key concepts in *subject media* begin their slow journey to partial obsolescence.

Media consumption has changed irreversibly. Technologies have enabled these changes, but 'users', making manifest McLuhan's coining, have enacted them. Rendering The Wedding Present's 1987 debut 'George Best' as an MP3 file, and making it, and the fact you are 'consuming' it, available to your 'Facebook friends', has little or nothing to do with genre, narrative and representation. It has to do with media exchange.

Equally in a more conventional sense the BBC's decision in 2009 to broadcast the whole of the third season of their 'mature' *Dr Who* spin-off *Torchwood* on five consecutive nights of BBC1 prime time was a sophisticated statement about this changing environment. Setting themselves advantageously between the current wisdom (that personal video recorders make all time 'prime') and common sense (that 'prime time' does not dissolve itself that quickly) schedulers were able to offer five hours of flagship family drama and a substantial science fiction narrative in the middle of the schedule, with the almost certain knowledge that its core audience was most unlikely to care (in fact the night to night audiences reached a very respectable 5 to 6 million).

For freedom from the thrall of the schedule has resulted not in the demise of television as a cultural form, but rather in a golden age, almost as McLuhan predicted: television as art form! The BBC, in particular, that emblematic public service provider, has reaped the predictable benefits of not having its diverse quality subject to the vagaries of competition. Where once we were unlikely to pick the documentary on the Roman games over televised soccer, or the Judith Butler interview over *The Benny Hill Show*, now the Reithian dichotomy of entertainment and education is merely represented by categories on your i-player. Had we world enough and time, we could have it all.

Here text is something we give meaning to at a number of levels in a number of different ways, by processes of use and attachment as well as reflective response. The set-piece, often semiotic, interpretation of a text in splendid isolation seems less and less 'connected' because that is what it is: unconnected, uncontextualised. And these patterns of attachment and use, which implicitly interpret, have little time for static taxonomies. These users consume academic (and academics') blogs and professional media content in the same manner that they 'do' Wikipedia and the latest mash-ups and fan tribute videos: partly because they 'do' all these in a similar set of 'different' contexts. Is it then surprising that many school age children list YouTube as their primary search engine. The impact of 'They're taking the Hobbits to Isengard' or Joel Veitch's animated Viking kittens 'miming' Led Zeppelin's 'Immigrant song' cannot be ignored, colonised or marginalised (the *LOTR* mash-up had more than 4 million hits on one version alone, and there are several).

All this lends some credence to Clay Shirky's proposition that the first fruits of a 'connected age' (the culture Jenkins has long called 'participatory') are creativity and generosity. This is not naively to turn a blind eye to Holmes's pertinent warning that 'the internet itself has become a frontier of monopoly capital', or to Facebook tributes to mass murderers ('RIP ROAOL MOAT YOU LEGEND' provoked an angry, but ultimately futile attack on Facebook itself from British Prime Minister David Cameron). Rather it is a sign that we must be aware in all directions of the abundance of creative connected communication which is offering an unprecedented outpouring of generous creativity and comment. This may be the intellectual and academic freeplay of ideas, which may yet render 'publication' in the traditional sense obsolete (though some entrench themselves against even acknowledging the quality of much online work) or the breathtaking inventiveness and technical skill of fan-cuts and fan tributes.

Jenkins suggests all of this has potential implications for our political processes. He says that convergence makes us 'rethink old assumptions'. Addressing the US election of 2004, he concludes that, while it was 'an important transitional moment in the relationship between media and politics', there was ultimately little more than a general agreement that greater participation by citizens was inevitable without ever agreeing what that 'participation' would be like (Jenkins, 2008: 22–3). This tunes in well with Barry (2001), who wisely concludes that despite a desire for an active and empowered electorate, politics is still embodied in relationships and practices. Similarly Simstein writing of 'citizens' concludes that customer satisfaction models of service quality are unlikely to bring either service or quality, since freedom is not the same as freedom of choice (2001).

The British General Election of 2010 perhaps suggests that we are one whole 'parliament' behind the United States in this regard. The creative highlight of the campaign was undoubtedly the battle between each party's head of communication, marketing the campaign and those web-based *agents provocateur* intent on subversion. In one memorable case a Labour poster depicting Tory leader David Cameron as *Ashes to Ashes* star Gene Hunt was so beautifully subverted by the onliners that the opposition Conservatives put out their own version, and credited the Labour party with the words 'Idea kindly donated by the Labour party'.

However, the now Prime Minister, Cameron was himself subject to the best satirical hit of the campaign when a mash-up featuring new words to the massive Pulp hit 'Common people' was posted. Beginning 'I went to Eton, paid a lot for knowledge' the piece built to an incisive chorus:

> I'll need the votes of the common people
> I must pretend to do the things that common people do
> Then I'll shit on the common people
> Then I'll shit on common people like you.

As Jenkins suggests, 'Don't expect the uncertainties surrounding convergence to be resolved any time soon.' Aristotle suggested that the stability and 'standards of accuracy' of an area of study have a direct relationship to the object of that study: 'The minute accuracy of mathematics is not to be demanded in all cases' (*Metaphysics*, II.3, 995a15, quoted in Barnes, 1984). And if that 'object' piece of work is a woman or a man, balancing Shirky's 'primal human urge for creativity and connectedness' with F. Scott Fitzgerald's rightly famous 'boats against the current, borne back ceaselessly into the past'? Well, as ever, we get the accuracies, affinities and contradictions of the World Wide Web, the great library of Alexandria and a rented room.

In this chapter we have expressed surprise (again) at the lack of attention paid by media studies to technology, and more surprise at its failure to turn this deterministic avoidance into attention to cultural exchange. Instead, subject media has been stuck in the middle, failing to adequately shift its central approaches but at the same time annexing change to units on 'new media', having to look both ways. And this completes our journey through the key concepts and interests of media education. But left at this, our critique will join a long list of 'from a distance' observations. For the practitioner – and the student – the question is always 'What then?' For pedagogy, what to do?

CONCLUSION

Pedagogy after the media: towards a 'pedagogy of the inexpert'

Throughout this book we have argued for an approach to learning and teaching about popular culture which returns to the question of the reflexive reader and resists recourse to the idea of 'the media'. Here we conclude our argument with something akin to a deschooled approach to textual agency – that we provocatively refer to as 'a pedagogy of the inexpert'.

> advocates of the New Literacy Studies may have felt that their approach has meant going against the grain, challenging dominant 'ways of knowing' (Baker et al 1996): but it may be that the grain is not simply that of a 'dominant' society with which they can feel romantically in conflict but with that of their own deepest desires and fears. We all have to live with the psychological consequences of new theories.
>
> *(Street, 1999: 51)*

Street's contention that the starting point for new pedagogical moves may be neither the classroom nor policy but teachers' own identity work, reading ourselves against the grain, is an evocative starting point for considering the work of the teacher after the media. If, as we have argued throughout this book, the knowledge regimes of text-conscious disciplines such as Media (and English) constitute ways of knowing about text that are entirely of the classroom, and as such always already fictitious accounts of meaning making and taking, then where does this leave the teacher? As we see it teachers are left with a choice: to either play out the truth games of the structuralist subject (students, teachers, 'disciplines') or to re-know and re-make pedagogies of meaning making and taking in ways that reposition the subject within the alternative kind of post-structuralist paradigm we have sought to explore in the preceding chapters. It is the possibilities for this second kind of choice that we explore in this final chapter.

We have tried to show that media studies in particular and text-conscious subjects in general have rarely foregrounded the social practice aspects of reading, but have tended rather to fetishise the idea of the text. Out of this have grown specialist ways of knowing, disciplinary cultures, about the character of the textual medium and how this functions to generate meanings. The effect of this has been to transform, or in Bourdieu's sense to 'consecrate' (2002: 23), a set of ideological assumptions about where and how meaning begins and ends into an everyday common sense of 'textualisation' (Hills, 2005: 27) through which 'a mediated and symbolically bounded entity is rendered recognisably discrete'. This has meant that:

> all too often respect specific demarcations of the text, where industry-given and institutionally or communally-constituted constructions of bounded and discrete texts (within art worlds) are typically replayed, and where attempts at studying how boundaries between texts might be eroded nevertheless rely on notions of intertextuality that construct sets of bounded and discrete or identifiable texts which can then be said to interact.
>
> *(Hills, 2005: 26)*

Alongside an emphasis on aspects of material reality, philosophical ideas like that of the author help insulate the boundaries between text, ideas which Foucault argues function entirely ideologically to suppress anxiety about 'the proliferation of meaning' (1991: 119) that might otherwise be mobilised. In this sense, Foucault argues, authorship works to:

> reduce the great peril, the great danger with which fiction threatens our world ... the author allows a limitation of the cancerous and dangerous proliferation of significations ... We are accustomed ... to saying that the author is a genial creator of a work in which he deposits, with infinite wealth and generosity, an inexhaustible world of significations. We are used to thinking that the author is so different from all other men, and so transcendent with regard to all languages that, as soon as he speaks, meaning begins to proliferate, to proliferate indefinitely.
>
> *(Foucault, 1991: 118)*

In fact, Foucault conjectures:

> the author is not an indefinite source of significations which fill a work; the author does not precede the works; he is a certain functional principle by which, in our culture, one limits, excludes, and chooses, the free manipulation, the free composition, decomposition and recomposition of fiction.
>
> *(Foucault, 1991: 119)*

Such emphasis has affected a (mis)focus on what and how texts are, how they are produced, by whom and what they might do to readers. The 'continued prevalence, if not dominance, of this taken-for-granted idea of the text – both inside and outside the academy, and inside and outside cultural theory – has led to a lack of focus on how ... forms of knowledge-production textualise the world' (Hartley, 2003: 138). That is, isolating texts requires a form of 'symbolic work' (Willis, 2000: 69, cited in Hills, 2005: 27). It is a hegemony to which even the more progressive commentary is vulnerable, as Lankshear and Knobel demonstrate in their recent account of 'memes'. Amidst an account of the meme radical, 'contagious patterns of cultural information that are passed from mind to mind by means of selection, infection and replication' (Lankshear and Knobel, 2006: 213), emerges a typology of memes that returns us almost to the familiarity of a stable textual object, characterised in this case by purpose, social commentary, absurdist humour, fan or hoax purposes (2006: 232) and success as judged by 'fidelity, fecundity, and longevity' (2006: 214).

This contrasts with the kinds of contingent, playfulness that characterise the life-world experiences of young people (and which Lankshear and Knobel emphasise at length in their extended discussion of memes) for whom reading, which we are defining broadly as the making and taking of meaning and have exemplified here through newspaper reading and gaming, is deeply embedded in the practices of social and cultural life. So that:

> 'literacy bits' do not exist apart from the social practices in which they are embedded and within which they are acquired. If, in some trivial sense they can be said to exist (for example, as code), they do not mean anything. Hence they cannot be meaningfully taught and learned as separate from the rest of the practice (Gee 1996).
>
> *(Lankshear and Knobel, 2006: 13)*

This is a well-established contention in the field of literacy studies, where acts of reading are conceived as contextually bound, as Barton and Hamilton (1998: 7) summarise:

- Literacy is best understood as a set of social practices; these can be inferred from events which are mediated by written texts.
- There are different literacies associated with different domains of life.
- Literacy practices are patterned by social institutions and power relationships, and some literacies become more dominant, visible, influential than others.
- Literacy is historically situated.
- Literacy practices change, and new ones are frequently acquired through processes of informal learning and sense making.

As such the 'reading subject' becomes a dialogic conceit at once both agentive and relationally situated. Although Barton and Hamilton, and many other advocates of the 'New Literacy Studies', do not necessarily explicitly draw upon a post-structuralist discourse, their understandings of literacy sit sympathetically with post-structuralist sensibilities:

> some literacies become more dominant, visible, influential than others ... Literacy is historically situated .... Literacy practices change, and new ones are frequently acquired through processes of informal learning and sense making.
> *(Barton and Hamilton, 1998: 7)*

Here moments of 'literacy', like those of subjectivity, might be understood not as 'reflections of ... pure forms of objects, but rather the result of temporary discursive luminosity; they allow a thing to exist only as a flash, sparkle or shimmer' (Kendall and Wickham, 1999: 40) and, like the 'play' of subject identity, these are always already shifting and in flux. Thus the meanings reading subjects make for reading and readers are contextually bound: 'What ... [the subject] can know and how it knows is always influenced by its temporality and its participation in a community of meanings' (Usher and Edwards, 2000: 35).

Under these conditions old orthodoxies of teacher expertise, grounded as they are in the kinds of vertical (thinking back to Bernstein) subject discourses that emphasise content knowledge, skills and mastery, are problematised.

Expertise as mastery

It is worth pausing at this point to consider how particular discourses of the subject shape and constitute ideas about expertise. The mastery model of expertise is usefully described in relation to literacy by Crowther et al (2001) through their account of the 'literacy ladder' which constructs literacy as a decontextualised 'tool-kit', an autonomous (Street, 1995) set of skills, in reading, writing, speaking and listening, that once acquired enable the holder to effectively 'function' across a range of contexts. Literacy is achieved through a linear process of 'becoming' as the learner moves up the ladder, mono-directionally, from an 'illiterate' identity (illiteracy) toward the promise of 'literacy' which the teacher simultaneously offers, represents and gatekeeps. Central to this idea is that literacy is a 'something', holistic in breadth and universally useful, which can be summarised and accounted for through the kinds of nationally agreed specifications explored in relation to narrative in an earlier chapter.

These sorts of ideas position teachers and learners in particular kinds of way, offering very specific subject identities, as we have explored elsewhere in relation to literacy (Kendall, 2005). The teacher for example must have already demonstrated their expertise in order to claim a positioning at the 'top of the ladder', and as such represents 'the other' to the learner. Within the current English context, expert identities of English and literacy teachers are shaped, exposed and endorsed through teacher training requirements, approved specialist subject qualifications and requirements to evidence 'personal skill'.

In this story the 'literate' teacher must guide the 'less literate' student towards the goal of 'literacy' – the top of the ladder. Zukas and Malcolm define the teacher in this story as the 'psycho-diagnostician and facilitator of learning':

> The educator as psycho-diagnostician and facilitator of learning ... the role of the teacher is firstly to diagnose the learners' needs, for example by identifying or taking into account learning styles or skills, or other individual predispositions, according to a favoured learning theory. Secondly, the teacher must facilitate their learning by using techniques, tools and approaches which meet those needs.
>
> *(Zukas and Malcolm, 1999a: 3)[1]*

Contemporaneously the learner is construed as an 'anonymous, decontextualised, degendered being whose principal distinguishing characteristics are "personality" and "learning style"' (Malcolm and Zukas, 1999a: 4; 1999b). The learners' 'responsibility' is to acquire 'skills' which are atomised and ordered by hierarchical and linear arrangement, while the teacher's job is to assess learners' needs, plan and prepare an appropriate teaching and learning programme with identified learning outcomes, determine a range of suitable teaching and learning techniques, manage the learning process, provide support to ensure the student meets the desired outcomes, and assess the outcomes of learning.

Clearly here 'teacher' and 'learner' are understood to be entirely different entities exhibiting different qualities and identities. Street (see also Barton et al., 2000) has called this the 'great divide theory':

> illiterates are fundamentally different from literates. For individuals this is taken to mean that ways of thinking, cognitive abilities, facility in logic, abstraction and higher mental operations are all related to the achievement of literacy: the corollary is that literates are presumed to lack all these qualities, to be able to think less abstractly, to be more embedded, less critical, less able to reflect upon the nature of the language they use or the sources of their political oppression.
>
> *(Street, 1995: 21)*

Learners are seen as in deficit, as needing 'help' (Pember, 2001), and in short are identified as having problems that professionals have a responsibility to solve; thus effecting a professional 'contract' of 'care' (Avis, Bathmaker and Parsons, 2002).

At the outset of their learning experience the learner's literacy capabilities are screened, diagnosed and tested to enable the effective design of their route through the curriculum. Within this set of constructions reading and writing are implicit to

---

1 It is noted by Zukas and Malcolm that this is a dominant model in UK higher education literature. A fuller discussion/critique of the sychologisation of teaching and learning in Zukas and Malcom (1999).

the range of 'skill' that it is desirable for students to acquire – as 'skills' that are integral to classroom activities and assessment processes. Indeed in the UK context this is explicitly articulated through the language and organisation of the 'skills curricula', *Functional Skills* (QCDA, 2010a) and the *National Curriculum for Adult Literacy* (2001), that now map into and across the full range of Learning and Skills Council-funded post-compulsory provision. Each of these curricula narrativises literacy as a set of 'competencies', whereby a student will climb a 'literacy ladder' (Crowther, Hamilton and Tett, 2001: 2) towards and in pursuit of an ideal of attaining mastery of a preferred, standardised, appropriate set of literacy forms, the higher status and value of which are accepted as uncontroversial givens. Within the academic disciplines, literacy – perhaps practised, honed and perfected elsewhere – becomes the 'means' by which the individual 'accesses' the content of the curriculum, of functional, instrumental value because 'it' enables students to 'perform' successfully. The content of the curriculum, by extension is 'out there', and it is the students' job to 'use' their literacy skills to seek, find and acquire a set of pre-existing meanings and values. Literacy is tangible, known and knowable, fixed, determined. Reading is for enlightenment, to consume increased amounts of the known quantity, and the reader will, as their skills develop, move from 'following narrative ... recognising words' (*Reading Comprehension at Entry Level*, Basic Skills Agency, 2001: 14) through to 'Trace and understand ... recognise and understand ... organisational features ... Identify the main points ... obtain specific information' (2001: 15) at Entry Level 3, to 'read critically to evaluate information ... use different reading strategies to find and obtain information ... read an argument and identify the points of view' (2001: 15).

Here the relationship between reader and text is represented as uncomplicated and straightforward: the reader will use their knowledge of the 'individual words themselves, their structure, spelling and individual character' (2001: 7) in combination with their knowledge and understanding of grammar and sentence structure to access 'the overall meaning of the text' (2001: 7). An acceptance of the authority of text is central to this model of reading, with the reader a decoder of meaning. The student is offered a stake in what is known but not in how it is known, who it is known by, whether it is worth knowing, or that there might be alternative ways of knowing. The student as a reader is positioned as a consumer of pre-given texts in what is explored above as an essentially structuralist model of making and taking meaning.

Many exponents of this variety of literacy link its successful acquisition to enhanced productivity and envisage benefits both for the economy and for individual workers. 'Businesses in the new hyper-competitive global capitalism', argues Gee in his critique of the New Capitalism, 'march to the drumbeat of distributed systems ... there is no centre. There are no individuals. Only ensembles of skills stored in a person, assembled for a specific project, to be reassembled for other projects, and shared' (2000: 46). Thus improving the literacy 'levels' of the worker comes to be seen as an essential aspect of economic advancement and prosperity, and literacy as 'commodity' becomes central to a political agenda that links literacy with economic productivity (Sanguinetti, 2000; Gee, 2000). Certainly the UK government is keen to assert a perceived correlation between an individual's literacy level and the kinds of income they might expect to command (Pember, 2001).[2] Thus literacy and economic 'enlightenment' seem cast in a symbiotic relationship, a straightforward logic within which one's skills portfolio – of which literacy skills are an important aspect – is directly and unproblematically linked to earning capacity. Within this set of understandings the student is cast as the central protagonist in their own drama of social and economic success, an action-hero-like figure whose success or failure with phonemes, connectives, capitalisation, tense and paragraphing at each rung of the literacy ladder determines their battery of weaponry. Literacy acquisition becomes a game in which the student is subject to but never configuring the rules of engagement. Fundamentally this is a top-down model of literacy education that is driven by a notion of 'apparent' need (Castleton, 1999).

The parallels with *subject media* are easily made. We have made the argument elsewhere that the emergence of 'media literacy' has endowed the subject a broader brief and value to effect and deliver social change – in this case safety and wellbeing – beyond the classroom context. We have suggested that this media agenda is 'fraught with confusion' and characterised by a reluctance to adequately 'theorise' media literacy as *literacy* (Kendall and McDougall, 2009: 247) for two reasons. First, the structural arrangement of the agenda by a regulatory body inevitably provides, intentionally or not, a protectionist agenda, and second, this protectionist impulse is amplified by the dialogue with international groups for whom such a 'risk reduction' approach is unproblematic. An assumed connection is made to the recently published Byron report (Byron, 2009) which was a government-commissioned investigation into a 'problem' lacking a precise definition, in which videogames and virtual world experiences were 'lumped together' with cyber-bullying and online paedophile grooming. The voices from research into how 'digital literacies' are developed from early ages – for example Marsh (2004) and Livingstone (2008) – are, we have argued, insufficiently heard in the development of an overly 'pragmatic' agenda.

As the subject is developed purposefully towards politically motivated social transformation, inevitably, we argue, the parameters of the subject will shift accordingly, and the compulsion for students to know media objects in very specific ways will become more accentuated. As we see in the example above, the implications for notions for teacher identity become clear. The more knowable the subject, the more important the idea of mastery becomes to the concept of expertise. Like Bourdieu before him, Hills reminds us that:

---

2 As head of Basic Skills Unit at DfES Susan Pember outlined than an individual might expect their salary to increase as theire basic skills improved – in particular she suggested than an increase of £50,000 over 20 years was a realistic expectation for those improving their numeracy skills.

> Institutional practices can operate culturally by doing things with texts –
> setting limits to the types of texts that are ascribed value or legitimacy,
> nominating or recognising specific textual boundaries but not others, and
> working on texts in distinctive ways (classifying, reading or interpreting).
>
> *(Hills 2005: 28)*

In-expertise – othering content

Having outlined how configurations of the subject might constitute particular
ways of being for teachers and learners, we would like now to explore an alternative
dynamic of classroom relations which we are calling 'a pedagogy of the inexpert'.
This is intended as neither a tidy nor a literal concept, but more as a rhetorical
provocation to the traditional model of the teacher as 'subject expert'. We hope
to sketch alternative possible subject positions for teachers and students engaged in
text-conscious work that are predicated on the kinds of models of post-structuralist
educational practice outlined by Peim (1993), positions that encourage a new kind
of expertise. We draw heavily on Peim's ideas but update these for the contemporary
environment of 'Media 2.0' in which, we suggest, the fluidity, context-bound and
socially embedded nature of textual relations are more ordinarily and routinely
foregrounded.

The apparent paradox of the inexpert teacher is purposeful and intended to
communicate a shift in teacher expertise from orientation towards a mastery model
of specialist content knowledge, represented by the metaphor of the ladder above,
towards a co-constructivist ethnographic model of 'finding out' that takes as its
common sense the post-structuralist tenets we have explored in this book; that the
textual object is a fiction of textualisation to which models of reading are indexed
and from which the traditional tools of textual analysis emerge.

The alternative we are proposing here is predicated on a contrasting model of
reading developed by Peim, which presupposes that:

> the identity and meaning of things shifts radically given different perspectives
> and cultural contexts … [post-structuralism is] … a multi-directional thing,
> a mobile theory of texts, language, the subject, subjectivity.
>
> *(Peim, 1993: 3)*

This model also resists a '(banal) reduction to pure individualism, a position
likely to claim that reading, and all readings, are purely a matter of individual
preferences or personal predictions' (Peim, 1993: 73). Peim argues that a more
valid, in the post-structural sense, approach to working with textuality is to explore
reading as a category. That is to say, rather than elucidating something about
genre, narrative, content or author, one could ask how reading is learned, what
different kinds there are, what it is, who it is for, what sorts of things signify
expertise, and what sorts of reading are done in different kinds of contexts. This
approach asserts as primary the constructedness of reading within the context of

cultural practice, while simultaneously noticing the positioning and rootedness of individual agency within wider social relations.

While Peim's work focuses on the coordinated discourses of schooled practice, Hills (2005) pays attention to the trajectories of individual agents negotiating what Couldry (2000) calls 'textual fields' through the 'total textual environment':

> there will be a great difference between the total textual environment (the field of possible textual interactions for anyone) and the segments of that field with which particular individuals actually intersect. One person's 'textual world' will only partially intersect with another's. Surely, therefore, we should know more about what individuals' 'textual fields' are like – how do people select from the myriad texts around them, what common patterns are there in what they select?
>
> *(Couldry, 2000: 73, cited in Hills, 2005: 26)*

Couldry's notion of textual fields offers a new focus for the type of exploratory work that Peim challenges us to, crucially inverting the dynamics of traditional investigative endeavour of text-conscious subjects from a concentration on text to a focus on audience. This is not the mass demographic, projected idea of audience of orthodox analysis, but what we have referred to in a previous chapter as the 'diffused' audience; real readers in real contexts, readers that Hills recognises as 'textualised agents [who] make certain texts matter in a way that allows new, text-derived, social groupings to emerge' (2005: 29).

We can begin to see that a pedagogy founded on this set of ideas might look very different from the kind of textual analysis models we have been used to, because a pedagogy based on this kind of understanding would of necessity be process rather than content oriented. That is to say, the focus of study would not be 'the text' but the tracing and analysis of textual fields, the choices individuals make as they negotiate 'myriad texts' and the 'common patterns in their selections'. The work of the teacher in this version of textual practice is not to teach about text, but to facilitate ethnographic enquiry that enables young people to read the 'textualized stories of their lives' (Kehler and Greig, 2005: 367).

Enacting this kind of pedagogical practice requires a very different kind of teacher expertise from the model of mastery outlined previously. It requires rather a reading of teacher identity 'against the grain' to accept our awareness of but unfamiliarity with and most importantly *inexpertise* in the particular textual fields of learners and the ways they make texts matter. The role of the teacher in this dynamic is to facilitate and scaffold learners auto-ethnographic story-telling, and to accept and embrace the more uncharted, as yet unknowable learning spaces that emerge: learning spaces that, we assert, are charged with productive possibility. Of course the idea of the teacher as facilitator is not a new one. See for example the influential work of Knowles on 'androgogy' (1975). What is new in the 'inexpert turn' is the objective of facilitation. Rather than describable, learning in this dynamic becomes unpredictable, paralogical in Lyotard's terms, a collection of '"petits recits", little narratives, that resist closure and totality' (Zembylas, 2000: 160). These little narratives are contrastingly less ambitious than the grand old narratives of *subject media*, but stress 'the particularity of events in our lives ... particularity [that] makes impossible the existence of an authority who can speak from a universal perspective without invoking his or her ideology' (2000: 161).

Zembylas's account of a paralogical science education offers a useful reference point for imagining the conditions of a pedagogy of the inexpert. He argues that in science children's natural curiosity is 'subordinated to logical forms' (Zembylas, 2000: 161), and suggests that children can teach us 'in their invitation to free ourselves to speculate about the foundations of the universe as an infinite series of alternate versions of experiences which never cease to amaze us' (2000: 160). Rather than something 'naturalistic', what we understand Zembylas to be acknowledging is the plurality of story-telling as it deviates from "the conventions of a Habermasian consensus. What this means for science education is a rejection of what he calls a 'persistent faith in the "force of the better argument"' (2000: 166), in other words a rejection of the logocentrism of scientific knowledge "which is always marked by the effects of status, power and influence" (2000: 166). The alternative, paralogical science classroom might, in contrast, question 'the very context of argumentation, which is always marked by the effects of status, power, and influence', and ask 'Who has the power in a classroom? Who is seen as the legitimator of knowledge? What is the role of other ways of knowing such as intuition, imagination and emotion?' and how does the 'the very *nature* of science knowledge as taught through our textbooks as well as the *evolution* of modern knowledge that calls for more specialisation exclude the subjective aspects of teachers' and children's knowing' (2000: 165)?

The account of a paralogical science education we see here calls for both an undoing, of the normative mythologies that construct what we might call 'subject science' and an invitation to invent new possibilities that are not:

> pre-sented in our current discourses. Legend, myth, history, science, intuition, and emotion share common boundaries. Their domains oscillate into one another so that the idea of ever distinguishing between them becomes more and more chimerical.
>
> *(Zembylas, 2000: 166)*

Zembylas's ideas here resonate with Maclure's sketch of the baroque, an approach to qualitative enquiry which seems pertinent to the kinds of ethnographic, paralogical pedagogy we are outlining here, which resists the mastery discourses that tend to characterise classroom-based paradigms of educational research. Maclure's baroque methodology favours a fragmented, dislocated undoing characterised by movement over composure, estrangement of the familiar, disorientation and loss of mastery (Maclure, 2006a: 8) towards a 'frivolity' (2006b) that undoes and is undone. And it occurs to us that this type of approach might usefully form the basis of a very different kind of curriculum and pedagogy that seeks to reinscribe teacher/student relations and the subject/object of study towards a seriously 'frivolous' or 'baroque' pedagogy, posturing 'new imaginaries' for the relation of the researcher to the object', the student to the textual field. We can imagine with Maclure a peepshow that:

> brings the viewer into an intimate relation with the object, one into which desire, wonder and Otherness are folded, and out of which something might issue that would never be seen by shining a bright light upon the object in the empty space of reason and looking at it as hard as possible. But the peepshow also calls attention to the compromised, voyeuristic nature of the researcher gaze and the unavoidable absurdity of the research posture. To view the delights of the peepshow you have to bend down, present your backside to public view, put yourself at risk.
>
> *(Maclure, 2006a: 18)*

Back in our text-conscious classroom this would mean rejecting the key structuralist contentions that we have interrogated throughout this book and taking instead the idea of textual field as the starting point for curricula design. Such an emphasis demands a repositioning of teachers and young people as co-investigators of the dynamic and rituals (Marsh, 2004) of being with others through textual practice, and facilitates the exploration and problematisation of the boundaries between the different modalities within which perfomances of self are given. By drawing attention to these rituals this kind of praxis may mobilise more nuanced understandings of the sense of displacement that young people, and indeed notably and importantly also new generations of young teachers (Burnett, 2009), experience as they transgress the often heavily insulated (Bernstein, 2000) domain boundaries between their life-world and schooled experience.

Getting practical

Throughout this book we have offered everyday strategies that seek to undo the normative values of text-conscious subjects and generate, in Lyotard's sense, 'fresh statements and new options for the social condition about which one is concerned' (Kembylas, 2000: 178): in this case, classroom learning. In this section we explore the production of artefacts as a practical expression of the kind of paralogical ethnography we are proposing.

In the example under discussion here, pre-service student teachers were invited to produce artefacts, in any medium, to communicate an auto-ethnographic account of what they felt to be the key moments in their textual histories. Will's 'Cabinet of curiosities' (Figure C.1) and Jodie's 'Literacy wardrobe' (Figure C.2) are examples of the work produced. Will's 'Cabinet of curiosities' drew on the metaphor of the Victorian collector to re-present personal objects symbolising significant moments in his textual experience. The piece draws attention to both the contingent partiality of the narrative that accompanied the sharing of objects,

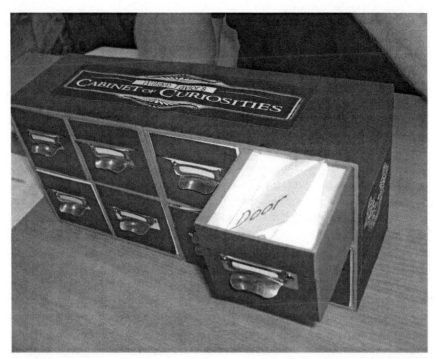

FIGURE C.1 Will's 'Cabinet of curiosities'

FIGURE C.2 Jodie's 'Literacy wardrobe'

and the ephemeral nature of meaning making and taking as subjects move in time through cultural domains. Taking 'getting dressed' as a metaphor, Jodie's wardrobe emphasised the identity work of textual engagement, noticing textualisation as an accroument of self.

A qualification of what we mean by auto-ethnography and how we want it to mean in this context is important here in order to address the criticism of writers like Delamont (2007) about the overly subjective nature of auto-ethnography, namely that it is too experiential, cannot fight familiarity, and that it focuses on the wrong side of the power divide (2007: 3). Auto-ethnography here is an act of personal story-telling through which the student constructs an autobiographical personal narrative – 'a *petit récit*'. This narrative is not understood to be 'truthful' in any totalising sense but is of interest because it represents the teller's projection of a textual identity story *for that moment*. Taking post-structuralist notions of 'self' as a starting point where 'self identity is bound up with a capacity to keep a particular narrative going' (Gauntlett, 1991: 54) these narratives articulate the expressed trajectories of 'individual identities' in relation to the possible textual field. What is important here is not the realities or truth of experience or action but the selection and mobilisation of particular discursive positions to do particular sorts of identity work. In relation to issues of 'power' our rejoinder to Delamont's concern is that undoing the traditional power relations of the classroom is fundamental to the thrust and purpose of our paralogical ethnography.

In producing their artefacts, students made use of a wide range of media and were encouraged to be playful and creative in their response to the assignment brief, which asked for an account of their textual history, prompting them to reflect on early memories, key moments, relationships, education and identity. The use of artefacts builds on the ideas of Awan (2007) and Gauntlett (2009), who have used a 'making is connecting' (Gauntlett, 2011) methodology to explore aspects of young people's media identities. This orientation:

> rejects the passivity of the 'sit back' [and learn] model, and seeks opportunities for creativity, social connections, and personal growth … students are encouraged to work together to ask questions, explore different strategies of investigation, and create their own solutions. This approach is open about the fact that learning is an ongoing process that everyone is engaged in … rather than displaying laminated examples of the 'best answer' on the walls, these classrooms show works in progress, experiments, even things that have gone wrong They encourage a 'hands on' approach to learning, and a spirit of enquiry and questioning.
>
> *(Gauntlett, 2011: 8)*

Fundamental to this approach is the notion that the classroom is a dialogic space to which students *bring* rather than *take* the objects of learning. As such the subject, as discipline, becomes *newly constituted* through the productive process. The narratives to be studied are not the valorised texts of curriculum specifications but the stories (*petits écrits*) students represent through a self-conscious and reflexive act of making. The subject of learning is thus less stable, less predictable, more dynamic and more authentic in the sense that it is an organic, iterative representation of the lived experience of participants. As stories are shared, in this example conference style with participants interacting with each other alternately as story-teller and audience, students compare, revise, review and re-imagine.

Together they collaborate to generate a qualitative data set, a case study of experience and practice, from which to produce readings of textualisation. That is to say they notice and theorise what is remembered, what is absent, what is shared, where value is ascribed and to what, what appears to be culturally or institutionally valorised or consecrated, and the way textuality interplays with relationship building and breaking: the textualisation of being with others. The embeddedness of the narrative in the artefact draws attention to the kinds of multimodality that Kress notices:

> the feel of the plastic container; its texture; the shape of the 'bottle'; the action of pouring or other use suggested by the shape; its imagined and actual fit into the hand; the scent when the lid is undone; all engage more of our body in their materiality than sparser notions of 'representation' might usually suggest. In the engagement with any sign, the materiality of modes ... interacts with the physiology of the body.
>
> *(Kress, 2010: 77)*

As the reading of life history is agentive, so the artefact as metaphor stands in for reading as an act of design rather than simply de-codification; in short the artefact is difficult to know and even more difficult to predict. As such traditional outcome-based models of assessment are troubled as the process becomes expressive of the 'reader's ordering as design' (Kress, 2010: 175), that is to say, the patterning of learning, as articulated through the artefact and the interactions that precede it, follows 'the route of interest, engagement, prompt, framing' (Kress, 2010: 176). The object of learning here is not for the student to come to know a predescribed set of ideas about the nature of the work but to engage in identity work that supports them to engage with the processes of meaning making and taking at a theoretical level. In this context contemporary concerns about plagiarism, authenticity and ownership of assessment objects become erroneous. Indeed the concept of authorship might well become the focus of such ethnographic work towards the kinds of new theorising about authoring that Kress argues are urgently needed (2010: 21).

This sort of approach sketches classroom relations that differently define the work of teachers and students in relation to expertise. Like Foucault's notion of power, 'expertise' in this kind of classroom is not *held* by the teacher but exercised diagrammatically in relation to events and processes. Students are expert participants in the practice of auto-ethnography, each contributing the *petits écrits* of their own 'cabinet of curiosities' to the classroom scenario, while teacher expertise lies not in relation to subject mastery but in a deconstructive impulse to theoretically frame and reframe the patterns and stories of textualised experience.

New times, new questions?

In his 1993 challenge to *subject English* to 'operate a theoretical self-consciousness about its constitution, attitudes and practices' (Peim, 1993: 208), Peim reframed the confident assumptions of English with new questions seeking 'new bearings'. As ideas about textuality and identity have evolved with the new affordances of Web 2.0, so these questions must be newly framed. And so we depart with questions that might be posed by a revaluation of text conscious subjects towards new forms of pedagogical practice and an engagement with the event:

What is a text? What is the difference between a text and an event?

How would you describe your textual experience? What does it look and sound and/or feel like?

What different kinds of spaces and places are there for consuming and producing textual meaning?

What does it mean to be a producer or consumer in these spaces and places?

What different kinds of associations and affiliations do you make? With whom? For what?

How do you understand the idea of authoring? What is being creative?

How do you represent yourself in different spaces and places?

How might we need to think the traditional categories of learning: reading and writing, speaking and listening?

These questions are not to be asked directly, abstracted from the rest of the work we engage with in this book. They are intended to replace the conceptual framework (nouns) with a reflective framework (verbs). In each preceding chapter of this book we have worked through examples of this pedagogy of the inexpert. These include the 'event grid' for a fan remix that would change for every application to every event; the shift from teaching about 'held' power to learning in and about networked space; the re-reading of genre with/by Derrida and with/by *Glee*. They are suggestions for reworking ten cases of 'representation' as networks of discourse, thinking of texts as 'constructed situations', tactics for ethnography and research for new kinds of work with textual agency – with 'audience' and with 'reading' – and teaching strategies informed by parody, paratext and the view that transmedia storytelling might be the subject, the object and the praxis.

At one level all our intervention amounts to is starting with the complex, awkward work – making the problematic texts and events that do not fit into categories very easily, and the kind of student work that is tricky to contain in the curriculum, the rule and not the exception. The questions above start that process, by challenging the framing of the study of texts, events and culture from the outset. Prensky (2010) calls for pedagogy to focus on verbs instead of nouns. Nouns are the objects of study and the tools employed – genres, formats, software. Verbs are the kinds of learning we want to support. While the verbs remain the same, the nouns are constantly changing, and the educator need not be expert in and on them. 'The media' is a big and unwieldy noun.

We have theorised these ideas with a journey through our own convergence – whereby we have been and are compelled to put together more or less older and newer ideas about people, media and life – Lacan with Habermas, Foucault with Hall, Habermas with McLuhan, Zizek with Butler and Jenkins with Hills. And with a lot of Lyotard – who offers up the 'after'. We have ended up 'in between' lots of spaces – neither a textbook nor a text, neither just for students or just for teachers, but for both – a dialogic 'mash-up' of gaming – new 'local' rules and microstrategies for learning about our selves and how we might be together, what is important to us. And how media – but not 'the media' – might be part of all that, of our culture and of who we imagine ourselves to be.

REFERENCES

Adorno, T. (1991) *The Culture Industry*. London: Routledge.

Aikenhead, D. (2010) Interview with Clay Shirky. *Guardian* online: www.guardian.co.uk/technology/2010/jul/05/clay-shirky-internet-television-newspapers/print (accessed on 5 January 2011).

Althusser, L. (1977) *Lenin and Philosophy and Other Essays*. London: New Left Books.

Altman, R. (2003) 'A semantic/syntactic approach to film genre', in B. Grant (ed.), *Film Genre Reader III*. Austin: University of Texas Press.

Altman, R. (1999) *Film/Genre*. London: BFI.

Appignanesi, R. (2003) *The End of Everything*. London: Icon Books.

AQA (2008) GCSE Media Studies specification: http://store.aqa.org.uk/qual/newgcse/pdf/AQA-4810-W-SP-10.PDF (accessed on 10 June 2010).

AQA (2010) A/AS level Media Studies: http://store.aqa.org.uk/qual/gce/pdf/AQA-2570-W-SP.PDF(accessed on 1 June 2010).

Auge, M. (2006/8) *Non-Places: An Introduction to Supermodernity*. London: Verso.

Avis, J., Bathmaker, A-M. and Parsons, J. (2002) '"I think a lot of staff are dinosaurs": further education trainee teachers' understandings of pedagogic relations', *Journal of Education and Work*, Volume 15, Number 2, 1 June 2002, pp. 181–200(20).

Bakhtin, M. (1984) *Rabelais and his World*. Bloomington, Ind.: Indiana University Press.

Ball-Rokeach, S. J. (1985) 'The origins of individual media-system dependency: a sociological framework', *Communication Research*, 12(4), pp. 485–510.

Baran, S. and Davis, D. (2009) *Mass Communication Theory: Foundations, Ferment and Future*, 5th edn. London: Routledge.

Barker, M. (2007) Plenary: Transforming Audiences conference, University of Westminster. 6 September.

Barnes, J. (ed.) (1984) *The Complete Works of Aristotle: The Revised Oxford Translation*. Princeton, N.J.: Princeton University Press.

Barry, A. (2001) 'On interactivity', in R. Hassan and J. Thomas (eds), *The New Media Theory Reader*. Milton Keynes: Open University Press.

Barthes, R. (1993) *Camera Lucida*. London: Vintage.

Barthes, R. (1987) 'The death of the author', in *Image-Music-Text*. New York: Noonday Press.

Barthes, R. (1984) *Mythologies*. London: Harper Collins.

Barthes, R. (1977) *Mythologies*. London: Paladin.

Barton, D. and Hamilton, M. (1998) *Local Literacies*. London: Routledge

Barton, D., Hamilton, M. and Ivanic, R. (eds) (2000) *Situated Literacies*. London: Routledge.

Barton, L. (2004) 'It's all gone tits up', *Guardian*, 17 January.

Basic Skills Agency (2001) *Adult Literacy Core Curriculum*. London: Basic Skills Agency.

Baudrillard, J. (2009) 'The precession of the simulacra', pp. 409–15 in J. Storey (ed.), *Cultural Theory and Popular Culture: A Reader*, 4th edn. London: Pearson.

Baudrillard, J. (1998) *Selected Writings*, ed. M. Poster. Cambridge: Polity.

Baudrillard, J. (1987) *Forget Foucault*. New York: Semiotext(e).

Baudrillard, J. (1986) 'Requiem for the media' pp. 124–43 in J. Hanhardt (ed.), *Video Culture*. New York: Visual Studies Workshop.

Bazalgette, C. (1991) *Media Education*, London: Hodder & Stoughton.

Bazalgette, C. (1992) 'The politics of media education', in M Alvarado and O. Boyd-Barrett (eds), *Media Education: An introduction*. London: British Film Institute.

Bean, T. (1999) 'Intergenerational conversations and two adolescents' multiple literacies: implications for redefining content area literacy', *Journal of Adolescent & Adult Literacy*, 42(6), pp. 438–49.

Belsey, C. (2005) *Culture and the Real*. London: Routledge.

Benedetti, P. and DeHart, N. (eds) (1996) *On and By McLuhan: Forward through the rearview mirror*. Toronto: Prentice-Hall Canada,

Benjamin, W. (1997) 'The work of art in the age of mechanical reproduction', in P. du Gay, S. Hall, L. Janes, H. Mackay and K. Negus (eds), *Doing Cultural Studies: The Story of the Sony Walkman*. London: Sage.

Bennett, P., Beck, A and Wall, P. (2004) *Communication Studies: The essential resource*. London: Routledge.

Bennett, P., Hickman, A. and Wall, P. (2007) *Film Studies: The essential resource*. London: Routledge.

Bennington, G. (1988) *Lyotard: Writing the Event*. Manchester: Manchester University Press.

Berger, R and McDougall, J. (2010) 'Media education research in the twenty first century: touching the void', *Media Education Research Journal*, 01/01, pp. 7–17.

Bernstein, B. (1996/2000) *Pedagogy, Symbolic Control and Identity: Theory, Research, Critique*. London: Taylor & Francis (rev. edn. 2000, Rowman & Littlefield).

Bernstein, R. (ed.) (1991) *Habermas and Modernity*. Cambridge: Blackwell.

Bernstein, B. (1990) *The Structuring of Pedagogic Discourse*. London: Routledge.

Bolas, T. (2009) *Screen Education: From Film Appreciation to Media Studies*. London: Intellect Books.

Boserup, R. (2010) 'Heavy rain', blog post to http://www.pixelgameninja.com/2010/02/heavy-rain/ (accessed on 29 March 2010).

Bourdieu, P. (1996) 'Forms of capital', pp. 241–58 in J. G. Richardson (ed.), *Handbook of Theory and Research for the Sociology of Education*. New York: Greenwood Press.

Bourdieu, P. (1984/2002) *Distinction: A social critique of the judgement of taste* (rev. edn 2002). London: Routledge.

Bourdieu, P and Passeron, J. (1990) *Reproduction in Education, Society and Culture*, London: Sage.

Bragg, B. (1983) 'It says here', from *Life's a Riot with Spy vs. Spy*. London: Go Records.

Branston, G. and Stafford, R. (2010) *The Media Student's Book*, 5th edn. London: Routledge.

Braudy, L. (1992) 'Genre: the conventions of connection', in G. Mast and S. Cohen (eds), *Film Theory and Criticism: Introductory readings*. Buckingham: Open University Press.

Brecht, B. (1974) 'Classical status as an inhibiting factor', in J. Willett, *Brecht on Theatre*. London: Methuen.

Brooker, C. Youtube posting – http://www.youtube.com/watch?v=sZ2iGYwdEi8 (accessed on 11 March 2009).

Brookfield, S. (2005) *The Power of Critical Theory for Adult Learning and Teaching*. Maidenhead: Open University Press.

Buckingham, D. (2010a) 'Do we really need Media Education 2.0? Teaching media in the age of participatory culture', in K. Drotner and K. Schroder (eds), *Digital Content Creation: Creativity, Competence, Critique*. New York: Peter Lang.

Buckingham, D. (2010b) 'Creative' visual methods in media research: possibilities, problems and proposals', *Media, Culture, Society*, 31(4), pp. 633–52.

Buckingham, D. (ed.) (2008) *Youth, Identity and Digital Media*. Cambridge, Mass.: MIT Press.

Buckingham, D. (2003) *Media Education: Literacy, Learning and Contemporary Culture*. London: Polity.

Buckingham, D and Sefton-Green, J. (1994) *Cultural Studies Goes to School: Reading and Teaching Popular Media*. London: Taylor & Francis.

Buckingham, D. and Willet, R. (eds) (2010) *Video Cultures: Media Technology and Everyday Creativity*. London: Palgrave Macmillan.

Burnett, C. (2009) 'Personal digital literacies versus classroom literacies: investigating pre-service teachers' digital lives in and beyond the classroom', in V. Carrington and M. Robinson (eds), *Digital Literacies and Classroom Practices*. London: Sage.

Butler, J. (1990) *Gender Trouble: Feminisms and the subversion of identity*. London: Routledge.

Carr, E. H. (1990) *What is History?* London: Penguin.

Carrington, B. (2006) 'Decentering the centre: cultural studies in Britain and its legacy' in T. Miller (ed.), *Blackwell Companion to Cultural Studies*. Oxford: Blackwell.

Castel, R. (1994) 'Problematization' as a mode of reading history', pp. 237–52 in J. Goldstein (ed.), *Foucault and the Writing of History*. Oxford: Blackwell.

Castleton, G. (1999) 'Inspecting the consequences of virtual and virtuous realities of workplace literacy', *RAPAL* Bulletin, no. 39.

Chayefsky, P. (1976) *Network*, film script: http://corky.net/scripts/network.html (accessed on 8 December 2010).

Cherry, C. (1996) *On Human Communication*. Cambridge, Mass.: MIT Press.

Cohen, A. (1985) *The Symbolic Construction of Community*. London: Routledge.

Cole, M. and Engeström, Y. (1993) 'A cultural-historical approach to distributed cognition', in G. Salomon (ed.), *Distributed Cognitions: Psychological and educational considerations*. New York: Cambridge University Press.

Collins, J. (2009) 'Genericity in the nineties', in J. Storey (ed.), *Cultural Theory and Popular Culture: A reader*, 4th edn. London: Pearson.

Conrad, J. (1998) *Heart of Darkness and Other Tales*. Oxford: Oxford University Press.

Cook, S. D. N. (1997) 'Technological revolutions and the Gutenburg myth' in R. Hassan and J. Thomas (eds), *The New Media Theory Reader*, Milton Keynes: Open University Press.

Crawford, G and Gosling, V. (2009) 'More than a game: sports-themed video games and player narratives' *Sociology of Sport Journal*, 26(1), pp. 50–66.

Crockett, C,. (2005) 'Media literacy: a powerful tool for teachers and parents', in G. Schwarz and P. Brown (eds), *Media Literacy: Transforming curriculum and teaching*. Massachusetts: Blackwell.

Crowley, S. (1989) *A Teacher's Guide to Deconstruction*. USA: NCTE.

Crowther, J., Hamilton, M. and Tett, L. (2001) 'Powerful literacies: an introduction', in *Powerful Literacies*. Leicester: NIACE.

De Certeau, M. (1988) *The Practice of Everyday Life*. Berkeley, Calif.: University of California Press.

De Sautoy, M. (2010) 'Liked the book? Try the app', *Guardian*, 3 July, www.guardian.co.uk/books/2010/jul/03/marcus-du-sautoy-apps-books/print (accessed on 14 February 2011).

Debord, G. (2005) *The Society of the Spectacle*. London: Rebel Press.

Debord, G. (1991a) 'Preliminary problems in constructing a situation', in K. Knabb (ed.), *Situationist Anthology*. place: Bureau of Public Secrets.

Debord, G. (1991b) 'Theory of the derive', in K. Knabb (ed.), *Situationist Anthology*. Berkeley, CA: Bureau of Public Secrets.

Debord, G. (1994) *The Society of the Spectacle*. London: Rebel Press.

Debord, G. (1988) 'Comments on *The Society of the Spectacle*', www.notbored.org/commentaires.html (accessed on 14 February 2011).

Delamont, S. (2007) Paper presented at the British Educational Research Association Annual Conferenece, Institute of Education, University of London, 5–8 September 2007.

Deleuze, G. (1999) *Foucault*. London: Continuum.

Derrida, J. (1981) *Writing and Difference*. London: Routledge.

Derrida, J. (1976) *Of Grammatology*. Baltimore, Md.: Johns Hopkins University Press.

Derrida, J. and Ronell, A. (1980) 'The law of genre', *Critical Inquiry*, 7(1) (Autumn), pp. 55–81.

Deutscher, I. (1984) 'The mysticism of cruelty', in R. Williams (ed.), *George Orwell: A collection of critical essays*. Englewood Cliffs, New Jersey: Prentice-Hall.

Dix, A. (2008) *Beginning Film Studies*. London: Palgrave.

Du Gay, P., Hall, S., Janes, L Mackay, H. and Negus, K. (1997) *Doing Cultural Studies: The story of the Sony Walkman*. London: Sage/Open University.

Dyer, R. (1992) 'Entertainment and Utopia', in *Only Entertainment*. New York: Routledge.

Elliot, N. (2000) 'Pedagogic discourse in theory-practice courses in media studies', *Screen*, 41(1), pp. 18–32.

Enzensberger, H. M. (1986) 'Constituents of a theory of the media', pp. 96–123 in J. Hanhardt (ed.), *Video Culture*. New York: Visual Studies Workshop.

Featherstone, M. (1991) *Consumer Culture and Postmodernism*. London: Sage.

FilmEducation.Org. *Triumph of the Will: Brief overview of the film and its place in history*, posterous.com/getfile/files.posterous.../triumph_of_the_will_wiki_PDF.pdf (accessed on 14 February 2011).

Fiske, J. (1990) *Understanding Popular Culture*. London: Routledge.

Foucault, M (1991a) 'Nietzsche, genealogy, history', pp. 76–100 in P. Rabinov (ed.), *The Foucault Reader*. London: Penguin.

Foucault, M. (1991b) 'What is an author?', pp. 101–20 in P. Rabinov (ed.), *The Foucault Reader*. London: Penguin.

Foucault, M. (1988) *Technologies of the Self: A Seminar with Michel Foucault*, ed. L. H. Martin, H. Gutman and P. H. Hutton. Amherst, Mass.: University of Massachusetts Press.

Foucault, M. (1977) *Discipline and Punish*. London: Tavistock.

Foucault, M. (1971) *Madness and Civilisation: A History of Insanity in the Age of Reason*. London: Penguin.

Friel, B. (1989) *Making History*. London: Faber.

Fuller, M. (2007) *Media Ecologies: Materialist Energies in Art and Technoculture*. Boston, Mass.: MIT Press.

Galbraith, J. K. (1969) *The Affluent Society*. London: Hamish Hamilton.

Gallop, J. (1984) 'Beyond the Jouissance principle', in *Representations* 7 (Summer), Berkeley: University of California Press.

Gauntlett, D. (2011) 'Making is connecting', http://www.makingisconnecting.org/gauntlett2011-extract1.pdf (accessed on 1 October 2010).

Gauntlett, D. (2009) 'Media Studies 2.0: a response', *Interactions* 1(1), pp. 147–57.

Gauntlett, D. (2008) Participation, Creativity and Social Change (lecture) http://www.youtube.com/watch?v=MNqgXbI1_o8&feature=channel_page (accessed on 2 June 2010).

Gauntlett, D. (2007a) *Creative Explorations: New Approaches to Identities and Audiences*. London: Routledge.

Gauntlett, D. (2007b) 'Media Studies 2.0', www.theory.org.uk (accessed on 2 June 2010).

Gauntlett, D. (2006) *Creative Explorations*. London: Routledge.

Gauntlett, D. (2002) *Media, Gender and Identity: An Introduction*. London: Routledge.

Gee, J. (2000) 'Discourse and sociocultural studies in reading', in Kamil et al (eds), *Handbook of Reading Research Volume III*. Mahwah, NJ: Lawrence Erlbaum Associates.

Gee, J. P. (2003) *What Video Games Have to Teach about Language and Literacy*. New York: Palgrave Macmillan.

Genesco, G. (1999) *McLuhan and Baudrillard: The masters of implosion*. London: Routledge.

Gerbner, G. (1970) 'Cultural indicators: the case of violence in television drama', *Annals of the American Academy of Political and Social Science*, 388, pp. 69–81.

Gervais, R. and Merchant, S. (2007) *Extras*, except from www.imdb.com/title/tt1104921/ quotes (accessed on 5 January 2011).

Giddens, A. (1999) Democracy (Reith Lecture 5), http://news.bbc.co.uk/hi/english/static/events/reith_99/week5/week5.htm (accessed on 14th February 2011).

Giddens, A. (1991) *Modernity and Self-Identity: Self and Society in the Late Modern Age*. Cambridge: Polity.

Gillmor, D. (2004) *We the Media – Grassroots Journalism by the People, for the People*, eBook licensed under Creative Commons, ©2011, O'Reilly Media, Inc.

Gray, J. (2010) 'On anti-fans and paratexts – interview with Henry Jenkins', http://henryjenkins.org (accessed on 4 April 2010).

Green, N. (2002) 'On the move: technology, mobility and the mediation of time and space' in R. Hassan and J. Thomas (eds), *The New Media Theory Reader*. Milton Keynes: Open University Press.

Greenhill, S. and Koster, O. (2008) 'Man stabbed queueing for midnight launch of ultra-violent video game Grand Theft Auto IV', *Daily Mail*, 13 April: www.dailymail.co.uk/news/article-562729/Man-stabbed-queueing-midnight-launch-ultra-violent-video-game-Grand-Theft-Auto-IV.html#ixzz1AfjkTl2y (accessed on 1 June 2010).

Gregory, C. (1997) *Be Seeing You: Decoding 'The Prisoner'*, Luton: University of Luton Press.

Griffin, E. (2005) 'Living with the media', in G. Schwarz and P. Brown (eds), *Media Literacy: Transforming curriculum and teaching*. Massachusetts: Blackwell.

Grossberg, L., Nelson, C. and Treichler, P. (eds) (1992) *Cultural Studies*. London: Routledge.

Habermas, J. (1993) 'Modernity: an incomplete project', in T. Docherty (ed.), *Postmodernism: A Reader*. London: Wheatsheaf.

Habermas, J. (1990) *The Philosophical Discourse of Modernity*. Cambridge: Polity.

Hale, J. (2000) *Building Ideas*. London: John Wiley.

Hall, S. (2009) 'The rediscovery of ideology', pp. 111–41 in J. Storey (ed.), *Cultural Theory and Popular Culture: A reader*, 4th edn. Harlow: Pearson.

Hall, S. (1996) 'Who needs identity?', in S. Hall (ed.), *Questions of Cultural Identity*. London: Sage.

Hall, S. (1980) 'Encoding/decoding', in S. Hall, D. Hobson, A. Lowe and P. Willis (eds), *Culture, Media, Language*. London: Hutchison.

Harbord, J. (2002) *Film Cultures*. London: Sage.

Hassan, R. and Thomas, J. (eds) (2006) *The New Media Theory Reader*. Milton Keynes: Open University Press.

Hawkes, T. (1977) *Structuralism and Semiotics*. London: Routledge.

Hebdige, D. (1979) *Subculture: The meaning of style*. London: Routledge.

Heidegger, M. (1962) *Being and Time*. London: S.C.M. Press.

Hermes, J. (2009) 'Audience Studies 2.0. On the theory, politics and method of qualitative audience research', *Interactions: Studies in Communication and Culture* 1(1), pp. 111–27.

Hesse, H. (2000) *The Glass Bead Game*. London: Vintage Classics.

Hills, M. (2010) *Triumph of a Time Lord: Regenerating Doctor Who for the Twenty-First Century*. London: I. B. Tauris.

Hills, M (2005) *How to Do Things with Cultural Theory*. London: Hodder Arnold.

Hills, M. (2002) *Fan Cultures*. London: Routledge.

Hoggart, R. (1967) *The Uses of Literacy*. London: Chatto & Windus.

Holmes, D. (2005) *Communication Theory: Media, technology and society*. London: Sage.

Horkheimer, M. and Adorno, T. (2001) 'The culture industry: the enlightenment of mass-deception' in M. Durham and D. Kellner (eds), *Media and Cultural Studies: Keyworks*. Oxford: Blackwell.

Horrocks, C. (2003) 'Marshall McLuhan and virtuality', in R. Appignanesi (ed.), *The End of Everything*. Cambridge: Icon.

Hunter, I. (1988) *Culture and Government: The Emergence of Literary Education*. Basingstoke: Macmillan.

Irigaray, L. (1993) *Je, tu, nous: Toward a culture of difference*. London: Routledge.

Irigaray, L. (1992) 'When our lips speak together', in M. Humm (ed.), *Feminisms: A Reader*. London: Harvester Wheatsheaf.

Iversen, S. (2008) 'Playing the bastard card', paper presented to *Future and Reality of Gaming* conference, University of Vienna, 17–19 October.

Jackson, D. (1998) 'Breaking out of the binary trap: boys' underachievement, schooling and gender relations', pp. 77–95 in D. Epstein, J. Elwood, V. Hey and J. Maw (eds), *Failing Boys? Issues in gender and achievement*. Buckingham: Open University Press.

Jardine, A. (1985) *Gynesis: Configurations of women and modernity*. Ithaca, N.Y.: Cornell University Press.

Jenkins, H. (2003) 'Interactive audiences', in V. Nightingale and K. Ross (eds), *Media and Audiences: New perspectives*. Buckingham: Open University Press.

Jenkins, H. (2010) 'Transmedia education: the 7 principles revisited', http://henryjenkins.org (accessed on 2 February 2010).

Jenkins, H. (2009) *The Revenge of the Origami Unicorn: Seven principles of transmedia storytelling*, http://henryjenkins.org/convergence_culture/ (accessed on 14 February 2011).

Jenkins, H. (2006/2008) *Convergence Culture: Where old and new media collide*. New York: New York University Press.

Jenkins, H. (2001) 'Convergence? I diverge', *Technology Review* (June) http://web.mit.edu/cms/People/henry3/converge.pdf (accessed on 14 February 2011).

Jenkins, H. (1992) *Textual Poachers: Television fans and participatory culture*. London: Routledge.

Joyce, J. (1988) *A Shorter Finnegans Wake*. London: Faber.

Kehler, M. and Greig, C. (YEAR)'Reading masculinities: exploring the socially literate practices of high school young men', *International Journal of Inclusive Education*, 9(4), pp. 351–70.

Kelly, K. (2006) 'The computational metaphor', pp. 39–40 in R. Hassan and J. Thomas (eds), *The New Media Theory Reader*. Milton Keynes: Open University Press

Kendall, A. (2010) 'Being him rather than the puppet master': boys, being, gaming and literacies', Keynote presentation at ESRC seminar on Literacy and Gaming, University of Lancaster, March.

Kendall, A. (2009) 'Telling stories out of school: young men talk about gaming', United Kingdom Literacy Association conference, 10–12 July, University of Greenwich.

Kendall, A. (2008a) 'Giving up reading: re-imagining reading with young adult readers', *Journal of Research and Practice in Adult Literacy*, 65 (Spring/Summer), pp. 14–22.

Kendall, A. (2008b) 'Playing and resisting: rethinking young people's reading cultures', *Literacy*, 42(3), pp. 123–30.

Kendall, A. (2007) 'Reading reader identities: stories about young adults reading', *Journal of Research and Practice in Adult Literacy*, 81 (Spring), pp. 36–43.

Kendall, A. (2005) *Reading Fictions: Reading reader identities in Black Country FE communities*, unpublished Ph.D. thesis, University of Birmingham.

Kendall, A. (2002) 'The reading habits of 16–19 year olds – initial findings', paper presented at the BERA conference, University of Exeter.

Kendall, A. and McDougall, J. (2011) 'Different spaces, same old stories? On being a reader', in H. Cousins and J. Ramone (eds), *The Richard & Judy Book Club Reader*. London: Ashgate.

Kendall, A. and McDougall, J. (2009) 'Just gaming: on being differently literate', *Journal for Computer Game Culture*, 3(2), pp. 245–60.

Kendall, G. and Wickham, G. (1999) *Using Foucault's Methods*. London: Sage.

Kingston University (2010) Media Representations of Identity – undergraduate module description: http://fass.kingston.ac.uk/courses/undergraduate/modules/module-full.php?code=MD1138 (accessed on 6 January 2011).

Klee, P. (1920) 'Creative credo', in H. B. Chipp (ed.), *Theories of Modern Art: A source book by artists and critics*. Berkeley, CA: University of California Press.

Klimmt, C. (2009) 'Key dimensions of contemporary videogame literacy: towards a normative model of the competent digital gamer', *Eludamos*, 3(1), Online Journal.

Knabb, K. (ed.) (2006), *Situationist International Anthology*, Berkeley, Calif.: Bureau of Public Secrets.

Knowles, M. S. (1975) *Self-Directed Learning. A Guide for Learners and Teachers*. Englewood Cliffs, N.J.: Prentice Hall/Cambridge.

Kress, G. (2010) *Multimodality: A Social Semiotic Approach to Contemporary Communication*. London: Routledge.

Kurzweil, R. (2005) *The Singularity is Near: When humans transcend biology*. London: Viking Press.

Lacey, N. (2009) *Image and Representation: Key Concepts in Media Studies*. London: Palgrave Macmillan.

Lankshear, C. and Knobel, M. (2006) *New Literacies: Everyday practices in classroom learning*. Maidenhead: Open University Press.

Laughey, D. (2007) *Key Themes in Media Theory*. Maidenhead: Open University Press.

Lave, J and Wenger, E. (1991) *Situated Learning: Legitimate Peripheral Participation*. Cambridge: Cambridge University Press.

Law, J. and Callon, M. (1997) 'After the individual in society: lessons on collectivity from science, technology and society', *Canadian Journal of Sociology/Cahiers canadiens de sociologie*, 22(2) (Spring), 165–82.

Leavis, F. R. (1952) *The Common Pursuit*. London: Chatto & Windus.

Lefebvre, H. (2003) *Key Writings*. London: Continuum.

Lillis, T. (2003) 'Student writing as "academic literacies": drawing on Bakhtin to move from critique to design', *Language and Education*, 17(3), pp. 192–207.

Lin, Z. (2009) 'Conceptualising media literacy: discourses of media education', *Media Education Research Journal*, 1(1), pp. 29–42.

Lister, M., Dovey, J., Giddings, S., Grant, I. and Kelly, K. (2003/2009) *New Media: A critical introduction* (2nd edn 2009). London: Routledge.

Livingstone, S. (2010) (London School of Economics) 'Keynote from the 2010 Digital Media & Learning Conference (DML)' held at the University of California, San Diego, La Jolla, California.

Lyotard, J. (1992) *The Postmodern Explained to Children*. London: Turnaround Books.

Lyotard, J. (1988) *The Differend: Phrases in dispute*. Manchester: Manchester University Press.

Lyotard, J. and Thebaud, J. (1985) *Just Gaming*. Minnesota: Minnesota University Press.

MacLure, M. (2006a) 'Entertaining doubts: on frivolity as resistance', in J. Satterthwaite, W. Martin and L. Roberts (eds), *Discourse, Resistance and Identity Formation*. London: Trentham.

MacLure, M. (2006b) 'The bone in the throat: some uncertain thoughts on baroque method', *Qualitative Studies in Education* 19(6), pp. 729–45.

MacLure, M. (2005) 'Clarity bordering on stupidity': where's the quality in systematic review?' *Journal of Education Policy*, 20(4), pp. 393–416. Reprinted in B. Somekh and T. Schwandt (eds), *Knowledge Production: Research work in interesting times*. London: Routledge.

Manovich, L. (2006) 'What is new media?' pp 5–10 in R. Hassan and J. Thomas (eds), *The New Media Theory Reader*, Milton Keynes: Open University Press.

Marcuse, H. (2002) *One-Dimensional Man: Studies in the ideology of advanced industrial society*. London: Routledge Classics.

Marsh, J. (ed.) (2004) *Popular Culture, New Media and Digital Literacy in Early Childhood*. London: Routledge.

Marx, K. and Engels, F. (1978) *Collected Works*. New York: International Publishers.

Masterman, L. (1985) *Teaching the Media*. London: Routledge.

McDougall, J. (2010) 'Wiring the audience', *Participations* 7(1), pp. 73–101.

McDougall, J. (2009) 'Media studies argument boring', Radio 4 *Today* programme interview: http://news.bbc.co.uk/today/hi/today/newsid_8204000/8204849.stm (accessed on 6 January 2011).

McDougall, J. (2006) 'Media education and the limits of assessment', *Media International Australia*, 120, pp. 106–16.

McDougall, J. (2004) 'Subject media: the socio-cultural framing of discourse', University of Birmingham: http://etheses.bham.ac.uk/556/ (accessed on 14 May 2010).

McDougall, J. and O'Brien, W. (2009) *Studying Videogames*. Leighton Buzzard: Auteur.

McDougall, J and Peim, N. (2007) 'A Lacanian reading of the study of Big Brother in the English curriculum', *Changing English*, 14(3), pp. 299–312.

McDougall, J. and Potamitis, N. (2010) *The Media Teacher's Book*, 2nd edn. London: Hodder.

McDougall, J., Walker, S. and Kendall, A. (2006) 'Shaping up? Three acts of textual studies as critique', *International Studies in Sociology of Education*, 16, pp. 159–73.

McGuigan, J. (2009) 'Trajectories of cultural populism', pp. 606–17 in J. Storey (ed.), *Cultural Theory and Popular Culture: A reader*, 4th edn. Harlow: Pearson.

McLuhan, E. (1997) *The Use of Thunder in Finnegans Wake*. Toronto, Canada: University of Toronto Press.

McLuhan, E. (1998) 'Marshall McLuhan's theory of communication: the yegg', *Global Media Journal* 1(1), pp. 25–43. http://www.gmj.uottawa.ca/0801/inaugural_mcluhan.pdf (accessed on 14 December 2010).

McLuhan, M. (1994) *Understanding Media: The extensions of man*. Cambridge, Mass.: MIT Press.

McLuhan, M. (1969a) *CounterBlast* (designed by Harley Parker). Toronto, Canada: McClelland & Steward.

McLuhan, M. (1969b) 'The P*layboy* interview: Marshall McLuhan", *Playboy Magazine*, March. http://www.nextnature.net/2009/12/the-playboy-interview-marshall-mcluhan/ (accessed on 14 February 2011).

McLuhan, M. (1962) *The Gutenberg Galaxy: The Making of Typographic Man*; 1st edn. Toronto, Canada: University of Toronto Press; reissued by Routledge & Kegan Paul.

McLuhan, M. and Fiore, Q. (1967) *The Medium is the Message: An Inventory of Effects*. London: Penguin.

McMillan, D. (2007) *International Media Studies*. Oxford: Blackwell.

McRobbie, A. (1982) 'Jackie: an ideology of adolescent femininity', in T. Bennett, G. Martin and B. Waites (eds), *Popular Culture: Past and present*. London: Croom Helm.

Merrin, W. (2008) 'Media Studies 2.0', http://twopointzeroforum.blogspot.com/ (accessed on 22 March 2010).

Milligan, D. (nd) *Raymond Williams: Hope and Defeat in the Struggle for Socialism*, Studies in Anti-Capitalism, www.studiesinanti-capitalism.net/RaymondWilliams.html (accessed on 5 January 2011).

Mittell, J. (2004) *Genre and Television: From Cop Shows to Cartoons in American Culture*. London: Routledge.

Monaco, J. (2010) 'Memory work, autoethnography and the construction of fan-ethnography', *Participations*, 7(1), Online Journal.

Monaco, J. (1977) *How to Read a Film*. Oxford: Oxford University Press.

Moore, A. (1987) *Watchmen*. DC Comics.

Morley, D. (1992) *Television, Audiences and Cultural Studies*. London: Routledge.

Morley, D. (1983) 'Cultural transformations: the politics of resistance', pp. 104–17 in H. Davis and P. Walton (eds), *Language, Image, Media*. Oxford: Basil Blackwell.

Morley, D. (1981) '"The nationwide audience" – a critical postscript', *Screen Education*, 39, pp. 3–14.

Morley, D. (1980) *The 'Nationwide' Audience: Structure and Decoding*. London: BFI.

Müller, E. (1993) 'From "Ideology" to "Knowledge" and "Power"', interview with John Fiske, Madison, 17 September 1991, authorised version April 1992, published in

German in: *Montage/AV*, 2(1) (1993), pp. 52–66, www.hum.uu.nl/medewerkers/e. mueller/publications/interview-fiske.htm (accessed on 12 December 2010).

Muller, J. (ed.) (2003) *Movies of the 70s*. London: Taschen.

Mulvey, L. (2006) *Death 24x a Second: Stillness and the moving image*. London: Reaktion Books.

Myerson, G. (2003) 'Heidegger, Habermas and the mobile phone', in R. Appignanesi (ed.), *The End of Everything*. Cambridge: Icon Books.

Naughton, J. (2010) 'Everything you ever needed to know about the internet', *Observer*, 20 June.

Neale, S. (1999) *Genre and Hollywood*. London: Routledge.

Newman, J. (1996) *The Idea of a University*. New Haven, Conn.: Yale University Press.

Nietzsche, F. (1999) *Beyond Good and Evil: Prelude to a philosophy of the future*, trans. W. Kaufmann. New York: Vintage, www2.cddc.vt.edu/marxists/reference/archive/ nietzsche/1886/beyond-good-evil/ch04.htm (accessed on 14 February 2011).

OCR (2010a) 'GCSE, Media Studies', http://www.ocr.org.uk/ (accessed on 1 June 2010).

OCR (2010b) 'A/AS level Media Studies', http://www.ocr.org.uk/ (accessed on 1 June 2010).

OCR (2010c) 'A/AS level English Literature', http://www.ocr.org.uk/ (accessed on 1 June 2010).

Oliver, L. (2010) 'Media industry on "brink of carnage", says Guardian digital chief', http://www.journalism.co.uk/2/articles/532538.php (accessed on 14 February 2011).

Paterson, M. (2006) *Consumption and Everyday Life*. London: Routledge.

Peim, N. (2000) 'The cultural politics of English teaching', in J. Davison and J. Moss (eds), *Issues in English Teaching*. London: Routledge.

Peim, N. (1993) *Critical Theory and the English Teacher*. London: Routledge.

Pember, S. (2001) Keynote address given to RaPAL conference, University of Nottingham, June.

Perryman, N. (2008) 'Dr Who and the convergence of media', in J. Storey (ed.), *Cultural Theory and Popular Culture: A reader*, 4th edn. Harlow: Pearson.

Postman, N. (1998) 'Five things we need to know about technological change', http://www. mat.upm.es/~jcm/neil-postman--five-things.html (accessed on 14th February 2011).

Postman, N. (1995) *Technopoly: The surrender of culture to technology*. New York: Vintage.

Postman, N. (1985) *Amusing Ourselves to Death: Public discourse in the age of show business*. London: Methuen.

Prensky, M. (2010) 'The future of media education is stranger than you think', Keynote speech to Media Education Summit, Birmingham City University, 9 September.

Pungente, J, Duncan, B. and Anderson, N. (2005) 'The Canadian experience: leading the way', in G. Schwarz and P. Brown (eds), *Media Literacy: Transforming curriculum and teaching*. Massachusetts: Blackwell.

QCDA (2010a) 'Functional Skills Curriculum', http://www.qcda.gov.uk/qualifications/30. aspx (accessed on 27 July 2010).

QCDA (2010b) 'Primary Curriculum', http://curriculum.qcda.gov.uk/key-stages-1- and-2/Values-aims-and-purposes/about-the-primary-curriculum/index.aspx (accessed on 14 July 2010).

Rabinov, P. (ed.) (1984) *The Foucault Reader*. London: Penguin.

Rage Against the Machine (1992) 'Killing in the name'. London: Epic Records.

Researcher, 4 February, pp. 2–4.

Rorty, R. (1991) 'Habermas and Lyotard on postmodernity', in R. Bernstein (ed.), *Habermas and Modernity*. Cambridge, Mass.: MIT Press.

Rorty, R. (1986) 'Foucault and epistemology', in D. Hoy (ed.), *Foucault: A critical reader*. Oxford: Basil Blackwell.

Roscoe, J. (2000) '*The Blair Witch Project*: Mock-documentary goes mainstream', *Jump Cut*, 43 (July), pp. 3–8. www.ejumpcut.org/archive/onlinessays/JC43folder/BlairWitch. html (accessed on 14 February 2011).

Rose, N. (1996) 'Identity, genealogy, history', in S. Hall (ed.), *Questions of Cultural Identity*. London: Sage.

Ross, K. and Nightingale, V. (2003) *Media and Audiences: New Perspectives*. Buckingham: Open University Press.

Ruddock, A. (2007) *Investigating Audiences*. London: Sage.

Ryall, T. (2007) 'The notion of genre' in P. Bennett, A. Hickman and P. Wall (eds), *Film Studies: The essential resource*. London: Routledge.

Sanguinetti, G. (2000) 'An adventure in "postmodern" action research', in J. Garrick and C. Rhodes (eds), *Research, Knowledge and Work*. London: Routledge.

Scannell, P. (2007) *Media/Communication*. London: Sage.

Schudson, M. (1987) 'The new validation of popular culture: sense and sentimentality in academia', pp. 556–63 in J. Storey (ed.), *Cultural Theory and Popular Culture: A reader*, 4th edn. Harlow: Pearson.

Schulman, N. (1993) 'Conditions of their own making: an intellectual history of the Centre for Contemporary Cultural Studies at the University of Birmingham', *Canadian Journal of Communications*, 18(1). www.cjc-online.ca/index.php/journal/issue/view/65/showToc (accessed on 13 March 2010).

Segal, L. (2009) 'Gender trouble by Judith Butler', *Times Higher Education*, 23 April 2009.

Shirky, C. (2010) *Here Comes Everybody: How change happens when people come together*. London: Penguin.

Shields, R. (2004) 'Henri Lefebvre', in P. Hubbard and R. Kitchen (eds), *Key Thinkers on Space and Place*. London: Sage.

Simstein, C. (2001) 'Citizens', in R. Hassan and J. Thomas (eds), *The New Media Theory Reader*. Milton Keynes: Open University Press.

Squire, K. (2002) 'Cultural framing of computer/video games', *GameStudies*, 2(1), Online Journal.

Stald, G. (2008) 'Mobile identity: youth, identity and mobile communication media', in D. Buckingham (ed.), *Youth, Identity and Digital Media*. Cambridge, Mass.: MIT Press.

Stam, R. (2000) *Film Theory: An introduction*. Oxford: Blackwell.

Stein, J. (1999) 'Reflections on time, time-space compression and technology in the nineteenth century' in R. Hassan and J. Thomas (eds), *The New Media Theory Reader*. Milton Keynes: Open University Press.

Stern, S. (2008) 'Producing sites, exploring identities: youth online ownership', in D. Buckingham (ed.), *Youth, Identity and Digital Media*. Cambridge, Mass.: MIT Press.

Storey, J. (ed.) (2009) *Cultural Theory and Popular Culture: A reader*, 4th edn. Harlow: Pearson.

Strange, R. (2008) *John Henry Newman: A mind alive*. London: Darton, Longman and Todd.

Street, B. (1999) 'The implications of the "new literacy studies" for literacy education in English', *Education*, 31(3), pp. 45–59.

Street, B. (1995) *Social Literacies: Critical approaches to literacy development, ethnography, and education*. London: Longman.

Tapscott, D. and Williams, A. (2007) *Wikinomics: How mass collaboration changes everything*. New York: Atlantic Books.

Taylor, P. (2010) *Zizek and the Media*. London: Polity.

Thomson, E. P. (1980) *The Making of the English Working Class*. London: Penguin.

Thompson, P. (2000) *The Voice of the Past: Oral History*. Oxford: Oxford University Press.

Usher, R. and Edwards. R. (1994/2000) *Postmodernism and Education*. London: Routledge.

Volosinov, V. (1973) *Marxism and the Philosophy of Language*. New York Seminar Press.

Wardle, J. (2010) 'A comparative analysis of learner and fan experience: do contemporary drama structures have the potential to model improvements in the learning experience?' Bristol University unpublished doctoral thesis.

Watson, P. (2007) 'Genre theory and Hollywood Cinema', in J. Nelmes (ed.), *Introduction to Film Studies*, 4th edn. London: Routledge.

Wenger, E. (1999) 'Communities of practice: the key to a knowledge strategy', *Knowledge Directions*, 1(2), pp. 48–63.

Wesch, M. (2009) 'The machine is (changing) us: YouTube culture and the politics of authenticity', http://www.youtube.com/user/mwesch (accessed on 15 January 2010).

Willett, J. (trans.) (1974) *Brecht on Theatre*. London: Methuen.

Williams, A. (1984) 'Is a radical genre criticism possible?' *Quarterly Review of Film Studies*, 9(2), pp. 121–5.

Williams, R. (2009) 'The analysis of culture', pp. 32–40 in J. Storey (ed.), *Cultural Theory and Popular Culture: A reader*, 4th edn. Harlow: Pearson.

Williams, R. (1966) *Communications*. London: Penguin.

Williams, R. (1962) *Communications (Britain in the Sixties)*. Harmondsworth: Penguin.

Williams, R. (1961) *The Long Revolution*. London: Chatto & Windus.

Williamson, J. (1986) *Consuming Passions*. London: Marion Boyars.

Willis, P. (1990) *Common Culture*. Milton Keynes: Open University Press.

Willis, P, (1984) 'The new vocationalism', in I. Bates *et al., Schooling for the Dole? The new vocationalism*. London: Macmillan.

Willis, P., Jones, S., Canaan, J. and Hurd, G. (1990) *Common Culture: Symbolic Work at Play in the Everyday Cultures of the Young*. Buckingham: Open University Press.

Wilson, E. (1998) 'Fashion and postmodernism', pp. 444–53 in J. Storey (ed.), *Cultural Theory and Popular Culture: A Reader*, 2nd edn. Harlow: Pearson.

Wimsatt, W. K. with Beardsley, M. (1954), *The Verbal Icon*, Louisville, Ky.: University of Kentucky Press.

Winship, J. (1997) *Inside Women's Magazines*. London: Pandora.

Zembylas, M. (2000) 'Something "paralogical" under the sun', *Lyotard's Postmodern Condition and Science education. Educational Philosophy and Theory*, 32(2), pp.159–184.

Zizek, S. (2010) 'Return of the natives', http://www.newstatesman.com/film/2010/03/avatar-reality-love-couple-sex (accessed on 15 July 2010).

Zizek, S. (1999) 'The spectre of ideology', in E. Wright and E. Wright (eds), *The Zizek Reader*. Oxford: Blackwell.

Zizek, S. (1992) *Looking Awry: An introduction to Jacques Lacan through popular culture*. Cambridge, Mass.: MIT Press.

Zukas, M. and Malcolm, J. (1999) 'Models of the educator in higher education', paper presented at the British Educational Research Association Conference, University of Sussex, Brighton, 2–5 September, http://www.leeds.ac.uk/educol

INDEX